Norman Morgan

BUILD UP

A detailed study of the murders at
10 Rillington Place

Volume I of II

Mereo Books

2nd Floor, 6-8 Dyer Street, Cirencester, Gloucestershire, GL7 2PF
An imprint of Memoirs Books. www.mereobooks.com
and www.memoirsbooks.co.uk

BUILD UP
Volume 1

ISBN: 978-1-86151-583-4

First published in Great Britain in 2023
by Mereo Books, an imprint of Memoirs Books.

The address for Memoirs Books can be
found at www.mereobooks.com

Mereo Books Ltd. Reg. No. 12157152

Typeset in 11/18pt Sabon
by Wiltshire Associates.
Printed and bound in Great Britain

Preface

"Murders from 'lust of killing' when the murderer is fully sane must be rare. John Reginald Christie appears to have pursued a most consistent path of premeditated murder in order to satisfy his sexual desire. Finally, he proved true to type by leaving his house where he alone could preserve his guilty secret. As was inevitable, another occupant of the house commenced to clean up the flat. On stripping the wallpaper, he discovered a cupboard containing the bodies of three women. Later search revealed another body (Christie's wife) beneath the floorboards of the front room and two skeletons in the garden as evidence of his earlier frolics. The fact that a man called Evans was convicted and executed for the murder of his baby daughter in the same house between the first and second periods of Christie's activities, certainly caused more controversy than has been seen for a long time and undoubtedly aided the abolition of the death penalty."

Francis E Camps, 'Camps On Crime', David & Charles, 1973

"But why did Christie not clear up the mystery finally, after his reprieve had been denied and there was no more hope?

I can tell you, I think. He determined to leave a great mystery behind him. A controversy which would rage for years. Christie knew that murderers, even the most horrible murderers, become forgotten. They are remembered only when they leave a mystery. If the problem to be solved is interesting enough, people will go on arguing about it for years.

And Christie knew he was leaving behind him the problem whether an innocent man had been hanged. That would keep the name Christie alive for centuries."

Rupert Furneaux, The Two Stranglers of Rillington Place, Panther Books, 1961

"In every chain of reasoning, the evidence of the last conclusion can be no greater than that of the weakest link of the chain, whatever may be the strength of the rest."

Thomas Reid, Essays on the Powers of the Human Mind (ed. 1812)

Contents

Introduction

Diagram of ground floor and garden of Ten Rillington Place

Timeline

VOLUME ONE

Introduction

Many people grow up developing an interest in fictional crime. They enjoy reading about their favourite detective or sleuth unravelling intriguing cases, invariably bringing the wily murderer to justice or to his/her own end in the final chapter. The readers are usually drip fed a blend of relevant information and 'red herrings' along the way. The modern genre seems to include the extra element of terror as, while the hero homes in on the villain, the villain, with evil intent, homes in on the hero.

While from time to time I read crime fiction, I find it is not a patch on the real thing. Real crime offers a lot more – the background of the people involved, the circumstances leading up to the crime, the crime itself, the cover-up, the detection, the trial and all the post- trial fallout. Victims tend to be partially responsible for their fate, perpetrators tend not to be all bad, the lawyers tend to be biased and not as fair minded as they are supposed to be. Then there are often the motives behind those who sift through the 'ashes' of the crime and try to make out that the verdict was false. The real thing has a lot more to offer than the tortured trail of the novelist.

My own interest in true crime stems from my early teens. I was intrigued by the A6 murder, for which James Hanratty was found guilty. He was hanged for the murder of Michael Gregson. Hanratty changed his defence during the trial, introducing his 'Rhyl alibi'. The jury did not believe it. Later, Louis Alphonse confessed, to a Sunday newspaper, that he had killed Gregson. The latest twist to this case came earlier in 2005 when it was disclosed that DNA evidence placed Hanratty at the scene of the crime. No doubt, though, this is not the last word on the A6 murder.

The other crime that acted as a catalyst was the assassination of President Kennedy in Dallas in November 1963. As soon as the news came through, everyone 'was glued to the TV'. From the Friday when Kennedy was killed to the following Sunday when the supposed assassin, Lee Harvey Oswald, was himself murdered by Jack Ruby, there was a total sense of disbelief in what was happening. It did not fit together even back in 1963, though at the time we did not know why. The Warren Commission was set up to investigate the Kennedy assassination. The Commission though selectively picked through the evidence and used only that which upheld the lone assassin theory. However, too much contradictory evidence remained and the Commission's interpretation of a number of key issues was too fantastic (e.g. the 'magic bullet'). It was not long before books appeared that tore the Warren Commission's arguments apart. Kennedy was not killed by a lone assassin; he was caught in triangular fire. As the famous Zapruder film of the assassination showed, the fatal shot that insured Kennedy's death came from in front – not necessarily from the infamous 'Grassy Knoll'. Different conspiracy theories emerged as to who was responsible – some at least far more plausible than the official version. No fiction writer has ever devised a plot that comes anywhere near the intrigue of the Kennedy assassination and its aftermath.

British and American crime is littered with fascinating and controversial cases and, unfortunately, there is a continuing stream of new ones. At the end of such cases, there were aspects that didn't fit. On the one hand, there were cases where the accused seemingly got away with murder. The prime examples of such cases are Robert Wood, who was acquitted of murdering Emily 'Phyllis' Dimmock in 1907 (the 'Camden Town' case) and William Herbert Wallace, who although found guilty at his trial of murdering his wife in Liverpool in 1931, later had his conviction quashed by the Court of Criminal Appeal. On the other hand, there were men who were convicted and subsequently executed when their guilt was anything but certain. Prime examples are Herbert John Bennett, who was hanged for the murder of his wife in Yarmouth in 1900, and Bruno Richard Hauptmann, who was electrocuted for the kidnapping and murder of Charles A Lindbergh Jnr, the 20-month-old son of the famous aviator.

One of the major British *causes célèbres*, where the pieces really don't fit, surrounds the linked trials of Timothy Evans (1950) and John

Reginald Christie (1953). I am old enough to remember Parliament in 1964 voting to abolish the death penalty. Those advocating the abolition argued strongly that Timothy Evans, who was hanged in 1950, was innocent of the crime he had been convicted of.

I first came across Christie when taken by my mother on a visit to Madame Tussauds. When passing through the exciting 'Chamber of Horrors', I came face-to-face with him. There was a tableau of his kitchen with him standing at the front looking down at me!

Christie – Madam Tussauds Waxworks

The first book I read on the Evans/Christie case was Ludovic Kennedy's *Ten Rillington Place*. After reading the book, it seemed obvious that Christie was most evil and Timothy Evans was as much one of his victims as were all the women and the child he had strangled. But years later, by chance, I picked up a copy of John Eddowes' *The Two Killers of Rillington Place*. Eddowes' arguments, on first reading, were difficult to accept as they cut across Kennedy's version, the latter being the 'standard version' that had moulded my perception of the case. Nevertheless, Eddowes raised doubts in my mind which, at the very least, needed to be resolved by reference to any other reliable sources that might be available. On referring to those other sources, it quickly became apparent that substantial and significant elements of the Kennedy version of the Evans/Christie case were completely untenable. Certainly, if Evans did not kill his wife and/ or daughter, Christie must have done so. But was there really a valid case against Christie?

The more I read on the Evans/Christie case, the more complex it became. The backdrop was:

- two men having confessed to murdering Beryl Evans, but no one ever being tried for her murder;
- extensive writings on the case, but with most authors cherry picking and even twisting the evidence to support their own theories;
- the case having been the subject of two major inquiries;
- Evans' questionable execution having been used by political activists as a lever to change the law on capital punishment in the UK.

I decided to try and return to the essentials of the case to sort out what was fact from what was nothing more than selective interpretation and downright nonsense. I also wanted to consider what motives and logic could possibly have been behind Reg Christie's and Timothy Evans' behaviours at the time of the murders of Beryl Evans and Geraldine Evans and in the aftermath of those killings. Could order be brought to the confusion, and could a clear resolution be found to the question of who killed the mother and her daughter? It was not just the 'what'; it was the 'how' and the 'why' as well. It was not just ignoring what did not fit; it was what did the misfits really mean?

In this book I will endeavour to revisit the key issues, one by one, and try to sift the fact from the fiction.

Diagram of ground floor and garden of 10 Rillington Place

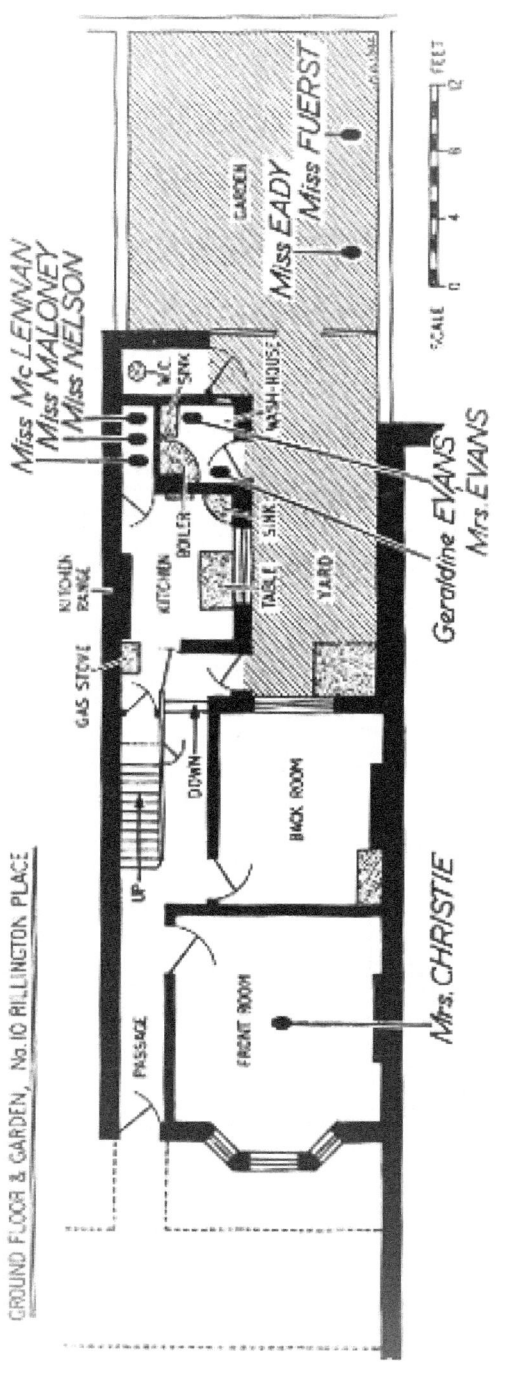

Fig. 2

Plan of the ground floor and garden of No. 10 Rillington Place showing where the various bodies were found

Timeline

Built from timelines in *Trials of Timothy John Evans and John Reginald Halliday Christie*, edited by F Tennyson Jesse, published by William Hodge & Company, 1957 (Notable British Trials Series Vol: 82) and Murder, Myths and Realities of 10 Rillington Place by John L Curnow, (web-book), 2014. Updated for more recent events.

Year	Date Event
1869	Rillington Place is built.
1898	28th March: Ethel Simpson is born in Halifax.
1898	8th April: John Reginald Halliday Christie is born in Halifax.
1906	Christie's maternal grandfather dies and he sees him laid out. Christie goes to Holy Trinity School, Halifax.
1909	Christie gets a scholarship to Halifax Secondary School.
1913	September: Christie leaves school and gets job as Assistant Cinema operator.
1915-16	Christie ridiculed for his failure in initial sexual interactions.
1916	September: Christie enlists for Army service.
1917	April: Christie called up for Army service. 2nd April to 29th July: Christie with BEF in France and Flanders. Gassed and loses voice for 3½ years.
1919	March: Christie invalided out of Army. Later Christie meets Ethel Simpson Waddington.
1920	10th May: May Christie marries Ethel Simpson Waddington in Halifax.
1921	April: Christie' first conviction. Sentenced to imprisonment for 3 months for stealing Postal Orders when a temporary postman.
1921	November: Christie's speech returns.
1922	Christie again loses speech for 6 months.

1923	Christie's father dies aged 76.
1923	January: Christie's second conviction for fraud. Put on probation for 12 months.
	Christie leaves wife in Sheffield and goes to London. He has various jobs including being in the RAF at Uxbridge from December 1923 – August 1924
1924	September: Christie sentenced to 9 months' hard labour for stealing money and goods.
	20th Nov: Timothy John Evans born in Merthyr Tydfil.
Late 1920s	Christie supposedly knocked down by motorcar.
1929	May: Christie sentenced to 6 months' hard labour for malicious wounding of Maud Cole with a cricket bat.
	19th September: Beryl Susanna Thorley born in Lewisham.
1933	1st November: Christie 3 months' hard labour for stealing motorcar. Wife visits him in prison and returns to him in London on his release.
	December: Christie becomes patient of Dr Odess.
1937	Summer: The Christies move into top flat at 10 Rillington Place.
1938	December: The Christies move down to ground-floor flat.
1939	September: Christie becomes Special Constable in War Reserve. Stationed at Harrow Road.
	8th June: Ruth Margarete Christine Fuerst comes to England from Vienna.
1943	August: Ruth Fuerst murdered by Christie at 10 Rillington Place.
	December: Christie released from War Reserve Police.
1944	Christie meets Muriel Eady while working at the Ultra Radio Works in Acton.
	October: Muriel Eady murdered by Christie at 10 Rillington Place.
1946	25th April: Timothy Evans convicted of stealing a car and driving without a licence.
1947	Christie cited as co-respondent in successful divorce suit of serving soldier.

1947	20th September: Evans marries 18-year old Beryl Susanna Thorley, telephonist Grosvenor House.
1948	24th March: Mr and Mrs Evans move from 11 St Mark's Road, renting the top-floor flat at 10 Rillington Place.
	10th October: Geraldine Evans born.
1949	August: Lucy Endecott, 'the blonde girl', comes to stay with the Evanses.
	August: Row over the blonde and Evans leaves with her.
	5th October: Stanley Setty reported missing.
	21st October: The Stanley Setty 'bundle' found in Essex.
	Late October: Mr and Mrs Christie advise Mrs Evans not to take pills to cause an abortion.
	Next day: Christie advises Evans to stop his wife taking pills. Mrs Evans tells Evans that Christie is going to do an abortion.
	End October: Builders begin work at 10 Rillington Place.
	Sat 5th: Nov Beryl Evans last seen alive by her father.
	Tues 8th November: Workmen finish work on wash-house roof. Beryl Evans murdered.
	Joan Vincent claims (1953) to have called on Beryl and found the Evans' kitchen door jammed against her.
	Christie still ill with enteritis and has to see Dr Odess that evening.
	(Evans' 1st statement in Merthyr) Returns home to find wife dead on the bed, poisoned by an abortifacient.
	(Evans' 2nd statement in Merthyr) Returns home to find wife dead from Christie's abortion attempt. Evans helps Christie carry her body to Kitchener's flat and Christie says 'I'll dispose of it down a drain.'
	(Evans' 3rd and 4th statements – the confessions at Notting Hill.) Evans loses his temper and strangles his wife with a rope and puts her body in the wash-house after midnight when the Christies are asleep.
	(Christie and Mrs Christie, 2nd statements 1949) Both hear noises overhead in the night.
	(Christie 1953.) Christie kills Beryl at lunchtime helping her commit suicide, using gas and a stocking but fails to have intercourse.

Wed 9th November: (Mrs Christie, 1st statement 1949.) Mrs Christie puts the hall light on for Evans at around 10.30 p.m. as the floorboards are up. He tells her that his wife and the baby have gone away to stay with friends in Bristol for a month.

Thurs 10th November: Carpenter Robert Anderson working in hallway of 10 Rillington Place in the afternoon.

(Evans' 2nd statement and Defence at trial.) Couple from East Acton to call for Geraldine, as arranged by Christie.

Evans gives up his job.

Evans visits his mother, Mrs Probert.

(Evans' Notting Hill confessions.) Evans strangles his baby and takes her down to wash-house late at night.

Fri 11th November: (Christie, 3rd statement 1949.) Carpenter working in hall.

(Scott Henderson Report.) Plasterer's mate leaves wash-house empty.

Evans sees Mr Hookway of Portobello Road, who values furniture at £40.

Sat 12th November: (Scott Henderson Report.) Carpenter begins replacing boards in hall.

Christie goes to Dr Odess complaining of fibrositis and has his back strapped.

Sun 13th November: Evans goes to see rag-dealer in the afternoon. Evans tears up bedding and wife's clothes.

Mon 14th November: Rag-dealer takes away clothes.

(Scott Henderson Report) Carpenter finishes relaying hall and gives old boards to Christie at mid-day.

Furniture dealer takes away Evans' furniture, leaving Geraldine's pram, chair and suitcase in Christie's front room.

(Christie, 2nd statement, 1949.) Christie says Evans tells him he has £60 for the furniture.

Evans catches 12.55 a.m. Paddington to Cardiff train.

Tue 15th November: Evans arrives Wales, 6.40 a.m., and goes to the home of his aunt. Mrs Lynch, at Merthyr Vale.

Sat 19th November: Christie has an appointment with a registrar at St. Mary's Hospital. 'In agony.'

Mon 21st Nov: Evans leaves Wales for London.

Wed 23rd November: Evans visits 10 Rillington Place. Evans returns to Wales.

Sun 27th November: Evans' sister, Mrs Ashby, calls at 10 Rillington Place.

Mon 28th November: Mrs Lynch writes to Mrs Probert, (her husband's sister, Evans' mother).

Tues 29th November: Mrs Ashby, Evans' sister, telegraphs Beryl's father.

Mrs Westlake, Evans' step-sister, calls at 10 Rillington Place and Christie does not allow her to go upstairs. She tells Christie they will call police if there is no news of Beryl by December 2nd. Mrs Probert writes to Mrs Lynch.

Wed 30th November: Reply arrives from Mrs Probert and Mrs Lynch reads it out to Evans.

3.10 p.m.: Evans reports to police station at Merthyr Tydfil and states that he has put his wife's body down a drain.

Evans' 1st statement to Welsh police.

London police lift manhole in front of No. 10 and telephone back to Wales.

Evans' 2nd statement to Welsh police involving Christie to which Evans reverted at his trial.

Evans sends message via police to his mother asking her to get Geraldine.

Thurs 1st December: 1.00 a.m. Police call on Mrs Probert.

Police search Evans' flat at No. 10 and find Stanley Setty cuttings and a stolen briefcase. They decide to charge Evans with larceny and bring him to London.

Police question Christie, who goes with them to the police station and is there from 11 p.m. to 5 a.m. They interview Mrs Christie separately and leave a constable at No. 10 overnight.

Fri 2nd December: Det. Insp. Black and Det. Sg. Corfield go to Wales to fetch Evans before the bodies are found.

11.50 a.m.: Bodies of Mrs Evans and Geraldine found by police in wash-house.

Afternoon: Dr Donald Teare sent for. Cause of death strangulation. Beryl's father identifies the bodies.

Welsh Police informed and instructed not to tell Evans.

(Christie 1953.) Christie's dog digs up skull in garden.

8.15 p.m. Mrs Christie goes to the police stations and identifies two piles of clothing as belonging to Beryl and Geraldine Evans.

9.30 p.m.: Evans arrives at Paddington from Wales. Met by Chief Insp. Jennings and taken to police station where two piles of clothing are on the floor.

9.45 p.m. Evans' 1st Notting Hill statement – short confession in Jennings' notebook.

9.55 p.m. to 11.15 p.m. Evans' 2nd Notting Hill statement – the full confession to both murders on which the prosecution relied.

Sat 3rd December: 9.40 a.m. Evans charged with the murder of his wife Beryl.

Evans tells DI Black he sold his wife's ring in Merthyr.

Evans appears before the magistrate and is remanded.

While on remand at Brixton Prison, Evans, voluntarily, partially repeats his confession to P.M.O. Dr Matheson.

Sun 4th December: Evans says to Mrs Probert 'I never done it, Mum, Christie done it.'

Mon 5th – Thur 8th December: Police take more key witness statements, especially from the Christies and the Larter workmen.

Wed 7th December: Female skull found in basement of bombed house in St. Mark's Road.

Beryl and Geraldine Evans buried.

Thurs 15th December: Evans charged with the murder of his daughter, Geraldine.

Evans, on legal aid, first sees his solicitor, Mr Freeborough, and retracts his confession.

Evans again before magistrate when depositions of evidence are taken. Mr Freeborough takes statements from Evans and Mrs Probert but does not cross-examine any witness.

1950   4th January: Mr Freeborough delivers brief to Counsel, Mr Malcolm Morris.

8th January (about): Mrs Probert collects the pram and chair from Christie's front room on police instructions.

Wed 11th January: Trial of Timothy John Evans, 1st day.

Fri 13th January: Evans found guilty and condemned to death.

14th January: Christie goes to Sheffield for a holiday.

20th February: Evans' appeal dismissed.

March: Mrs Probert sends final plea to Home Secretary that her son must have had a brainstorm.

The Home Secretary, Mr Chuter Ede, finds no grounds for reprieve.

9th March: Evans hanged at Pentonville.

Mr Kitchener went blind and did not return to 10 Rillington Place.

April: Christie is recommended change of accommodation for reasons of health.

Summer: 10 Rillington Place put up for sale.

August 3: 10 Rillington Place bought by Charles Brown.

1950-51 Christie goes to Poor Man's Lawyer Centre claiming 'sole use of garden.'

1952 A psychiatrist at St Charles' Hospital recommends to Christie that he should go to Springfield Hospital as a voluntary patient.

6th September: Christie certified fit by Dr Odess. This is Christie's last visit to his doctor.

7th September: Christie starts employment as clerk with British Road Services at Hampstead at £8 a week.

6th December: Christie gives up his job 'to better himself.'

10th December: Mrs Christie writes to her sister, Mrs Bartle.

Fri 12th December: Mrs Christie last seen alive delivering laundry.

Sun 14th December: Mrs Christie murdered by Christie.

17th December: Christie sells wedding ring and gold watch for £2 10s.

Pre-Christmas: Christie writes to Mrs Bartle saying Mrs Christie has rheumatism in her fingers.

19th December: Mrs Rosina Swan, 9 Rillington Place, has two conversations with Christie.

End December: Mrs Beresford Brown notices Christie's daily disinfecting.

Mrs Grimes and Mr Stewart, residents of Rillington Place, inquire after Mrs Christie. Christie tells them she is looking after his sick sister in Birmingham.

1953   5th January: Christie pays rent to Charles Brown for last time.

6th January: Mr Hookway of Portobello Road buys all Christie's furniture for £12.

10th January: Rita Nelson last seen alive by Hannah Rees.

17th January: Mrs Bartle writes to Mrs Christie but gets no reply.

26th January: Christie draws £10 15s. 2d. from his wife's Savings Bank.

? January: Christie murders Kathleen Maloney.

? January: Christie murders Rita Nelson.

15th February: Hectorina MacLennan seen by her brother for the last time.

24th February: Charles Brown sees Christie for the last time.

End February: Christie meets Hectorina MacLennan with Baker.

3rd March: 1.30 a.m. Hectorina MacLennan and Baker arrive at 10 Rillington Place and stay nights of Tuesday, Wednesday and Thursday.

Fri 6th March: Christie murders Hectorina MacLennan.

13th March: Christie meets Mrs Reilly and offers his flat.

16th March: Mr and Mrs Reilly agree to take Christie's flat.

20th March: Christie takes his dog out and returns alone.

21st March: Christie receives advance rent for three months.

Christie leaves 10 Rillington Place and the Reillys move in.

Christie books a room at Rowton House for 7 nights.

24th March: Christie hires a locker at Rowton House and walks out.

Charles Brown calls to collect rents and turns Mr and Mrs Reilly out.

Mr Beresford Brown discovers the three bodies in the alcove in the kitchen on the ground floor at 10 Rillington Place.

The police find Mrs Christie's body under the front room floorboards later that night.

Newspapers publish the alcove story.

25th: March The identities of all four women are established and the last post mortem completed by Dr F.E. Camps.

27th-30th: March Bones of the two skeletons collected from garden and assembled minus one skull.

30th: March Inquest opened on first four bodies.

Tue 31st: March a.m. Christie arrested on the Embankment near Putney Bridge.

1st April: Christie appears before the West London Court on charge of murdering his wife Ethel.

Christie received into custody at ``````````.

4th April: Dr Hobson, psychiatrist, interviews Christie.

8th April: Christie again before the West London Court.

15th April: Christie at West London Court charged with the murder of the three women in the alcove as well as his wife.

20th April: Christie has another interview with Dr Hobson.

22nd April: Christie before the Magistrates' Court in Clerkenwell. He learns of discovery of the skeletons and tells Dr Hobson he was responsible.

27th April: Christie tells Dr Hobson and his solicitor, Mr Arthur of Cliftons, that he is also responsible for the death of Mrs Evans, but not of Geraldine.

29th April: Christie again before the Magistrates' Court in Clerkenwell.

6th May: Christie's 6th appearance in Court.

Christie remanded and committed for trial at the Central Criminal Court on all four charges.

18th May: The bodies of Mrs Evans and Geraldine exhumed.

20th May: Dr Curran for the prosecution examines Christie in the presence of Dr Hobson.

24th May: Dr Curran examines Christie alone.

5th June: Christie makes statement to police in prison as to his murder of Fuerst in 1943 and of Eady in 1944.

8th June: Christie makes statement to the police in prison as to his murder of Beryl Evans in 1949 and tells of his disposal of Eady's skull.

22nd-25th June: Trial of John Reginald Halliday Christie at the Old Bailey for the murder of his wife Ethel.

24th June: Christie found guilty of the murder of his wife.

25th June: House of Commons/public concerns and request for an Inquiry into the hanging of Evans.

29th-30th June: Rev. W.G. Morgan, Anglican Chaplain of Pentonville Prison, has conversation with Christie who uses phrase, 'the more the merrier.'

6th July: Mr Scott Henderson Q.C., appointed by the Home Secretary to inquire into the case of Evans.

9th July: Scott Henderson and a deputation see Christie at Pentonville Prison.

13th July: Scott Henderson Inquiry completed and findings published.

14th July: Report of Inquiry presented to Parliament.

15th July: Christie hanged at Pentonville.

24th July: Christie's untameable cat destroyed by the RSPCA.

29th July: Debate on the Scott Henderson Report in the House of Commons.

28th August: Mr Scott Henderson issues Supplementary Report.

5th November: Further Debate in the House of Commons.

1955   10th February: Debate on Capital Punishment (Royal Commission's Report) in the House of Commons quoting the case of Evans.

'The Man on Your Conscience' by Michael Eddowes published

1957   'Trials of Evans and Christie' by F Tennyson Jesse published.

1961   'The Two Stranglers of Rillington Place' by Rupert Furneaux published

'Ten Rillington Place' by Ludovic Kennedy published.

'The Crimes at Rillington Place' by John Newton Chance published

1965	Brabin Enquiry set up by the Home Secretary to 'examine the evidence given in the cases of 'Rex v Evans' and 'Regina v Christie' relating to the deaths of Mrs Beryl Evans and Geraldine Evans.
1966	10th August: Brabin Report. Concluded 'I have come to the conclusion that it is more probable than not that Evans killed Beryl Evans. I have come to the conclusion that it is more probable than not that Evans did not kill Geraldine.'
	As a result of the Brabin Report, Evans granted a posthumous free pardon by the then Home Secretary, Roy Jenkins.
1971	Film *'10 Rillington Place'* released, based on Ludovic Kennedy's book.
1994	*'The Two Killers of Rillington Place'* by John Eddowes published.
2005	Senior Judge dismisses Mrs Westlake's request to refer the Timothy Evans case to the Court

Key persons and outline

There were five persons who came together in 1948-1949. That coming together would lead to them all being murdered or executed by 1953.

A biographical summary of each of the five up to early November 1949 is necessary.

John Reginald Halliday Christie

Reg Christie was born in Halifax on 8th April 1899. His father, Ernest, was a carpet designer. He had married Mary Halliday in 1881. Christie had one elder brother, four elder sisters and one younger sister. They lived in comfortable circumstances.[1]

According to his own account in a 1953 Sunday Pictorial article, his childhood and youth were marked out by a number of unfortunate circumstances and events. Although his mother was deemed kind and protective, his father was authoritarian and he was bossed about by his elder sisters.

When Christie was about 8 years old he visited a room where his grandfather, who had recently died, was laid out in his coffin. This was his first experience of a dead body. Christie stated that he was fascinated and that fascination with corpses remained with him. An early manifestation was his visits to graveyards and his seeking to look on coffins in the vaults.[2]

In his adolescence, his first sexual encounter went badly wrong. He fell in with an experienced mill girl, but he was unable to perform. She told her friends of Christie's failure and word spread. Christie was derided to his face for his sexual incapability and that deeply hurt him. He was forced to obtain sexual gratification from prostitutes. They could not threaten him.[3]

The combination of an austere father, loving mother, bossy elder sisters, fascination with corpses and early sexual disaster, have been deemed to have caused Christie to evolve a perverse attitude towards sexuality that would eventually lead to his interludes of depraved killing of women.

Christie left school at the age of 14. He was of above average intelligence and had shown ability, especially in mathematical subjects.

He worked for a short while as a warehouseman before becoming an operator in a local private picture house. In September 1916 he enlisted in the army, though he was not mobilised until April of the following year when he had reached 18 years of age. He trained as a signaller. In April 1918 he was sent to France as part of the reinforcement of the British Army facing the Germans' final major offensive. Christie saw action from May 1918, but shortly afterwards he was wounded when a mustard gas shell exploded near him. His injuries were gas related – temporary blindness, loss of speech for 3½ years and hysteria. He was taken back through the hospital lines, ending up in a convalescent home back in England. Christie was eventually demobilised in October 1919.[4]

Christie returned to Halifax in the autumn of 1918, to his old job as a cinema projectionist. He met Ethel Simpson at evening classes and they married on 10th May 1920. They set up home together, though, according to Christie in his Sunday Pictorial article, there was difficulty with the sexual relationship.[5]

Police photographs of Christie at the time of his first conviction

Between 1921-1933 Christie led an awkward life. He took a number of jobs and had a number of convictions and prison sentences for petty theft. In April 1921 he was sent to jail for three months, without hard labour, for stealing postal orders when he was working as a temporary postman. In early 1923 he was again in the magistrates' court for fraudulently obtaining hotel accommodation and food. He was put on probation for 12 months.[6] He then left Halifax for London. Ethel remained in Halifax and they were to remain apart for 10 years.

During those 10 years, Christie drifted around in terms of where he lived and where he worked. Sometime in the 1920s, he may have been knocked down and incurred knee and shoulder injuries requiring hospital treatment (Sunday Pictorial article). In 1924 he stole money and confectionery from a cinema after getting himself locked in when the cinema closed for the evening. He also stole a bicycle. Christie was sentenced to a total of nine months in prison, with hard labour, which he served at Wandsworth prison.[7]

In 1928 he was cohabiting with a Mrs Cole at a flat in Battersea. The relationship deteriorated and came to a head when Christie caused her to suffer a head wound by hitting her with a cricket bat. A neighbour heard Mrs Cole screaming and intervened. After the police investigated, Christie was arraigned before a magistrate. He was found guilty and sentenced to six months in jail, with hard labour. Again, he served the sentence at Wandsworth Prison.[8]

Christie continued his drifting around London after his release from jail in 1929. He returned to criminal ways in the autumn of 1933, when he stole a car from the firm he was working for. He was accosted by a police officer while asleep in the stolen car. The officer did not believe his alibi and the car was taken to the local police station. It was identified as stolen and Christie was charged with theft. At Uxbridge Magistrates' Court he was convicted and given three months in prison, with hard labour. Yet again the sentence was served in Wandsworth Prison.[9]

While in Wandsworth he received a visit from his wife, Ethel. They decided to come back together. When Christie was released in January 1934, he and Ethel set up home in Notting Hill. They had a number of addresses in that area before, in 1937, they moved to live in the top floor flat at 10 Rillington Place. The Christies moved from the top floor flat to the ground floor flat in December 1938. This gave them control of the small garden at the back of the premises.[10] Living with Ethel again seemed to have a settling effect on Christie; there were no more incidents of stealing.

At the beginning of the Second World War, Christie responded to the call for 20,000 special police constables. His criminal past should have ruled him out, but it was not checked. He remained in the police until he left voluntarily at the end of 1943. He was deemed competent, if over-officious, and received two commendations.[11]

During the latter stages of this time as a special constable, Christie committed his first murder. When his wife was away visiting her relations in Sheffield in the late summer of 1943, Christie enticed an Austrian woman, Ruth Fuerst, to 10 Rillington Place. Aged about 21, she was in poor financial circumstances and probably got to know Christie while he was on his beat. The only account of how she was killed came from Christie in 1953, and he painted himself in a good, probably fabricated, light. Her death was more of an accident than driven by any sexual motivation. After he murdered Fuerst, he hid her body under the floorboards in the front room as he had received a telegram that his wife was on her way home from Sheffield with her brother. The brother slept in the front room, over the body. When he left and Ethel was away at work,

Christie as a wartime special constable

Christie moved the body to the wash-house in the yard while he dug a 'grave' at the top end of the garden. Christie, under the cover of darkness, transferred Fuerst's body from the wash-house to the shallow grave.[12]

Although Christie must have had a difficult and worrying time disposing of Fuerst's body, he admitted in 1953 that he had found the experience of killing her 'thrilling'.[13]

After leaving the police, Christie commenced work at the Ultra Electric factory at Park Royal. While there he developed a friendship with a 32-year-old woman, Muriel Eady. Ethel and Eady's boyfriend joined Christie and Muriel for tea at 10 Rillington Place and visits to the cinema. But later in 1944 Christie, having won Muriel's confidence, conspired to kill her. On the pretext of having medical knowledge and being able to cure her catarrh, he tricked her into coming to 10 Rillington Place alone, when his wife was away in Sheffield.

The killing of Muriel Eady was the first in which Christie used the technique which would become his hallmark. As part of his fake medical treatment he got Muriel to accept having a mask put over her face. The mask was part of a contraption into which Christie passed coal gas, disguising its distinctive smell by percolating it through a solution containing Friar's balsam. The gas, rich in highly poisonous carbon monoxide, which haemoglobin absorbs 300 times more readily than oxygen,[14] would have quickly rendered Muriel unconscious. Then Christie was able to sexually molest and strangle the helpless woman. Again, Christie found the experience thrilling.[15]

Christie buried Muriel's body in a shallow grave in the back garden, alongside that of Ruth Fuerst. Muriel's disappearance was noted, but it was eventually assumed that she may have been killed in a 'V2' attack – a German rocket had struck a dance hall in Putney that she was known to frequent.

Christie's killing spree stopped. In 1945 he was having an affair with a Gladys Jones when her husband returned from war service. He found out about the affair and ambushed Christie, inflicting blows on Christie with his fists. There was a further repercussion when Jones took out divorce proceeding against his wife. Christie was cited as the third party and had to appear in court in July 1947. He denied involvement, calling Jones a liar. Nevertheless, the divorce was granted.[16]

Christie remained outwardly respectable, if with eccentric mannerisms. He continued working for Ultra Electric until April 1946 before he became a clerk in the Post Office Savings Bank.[17] His wartime killings remained concealed.

Christie, post war

When the Evanses came to the top floor flat around Easter 1948, a neighbourly relationship between the Christies and the Evanses developed.

Ethel Christie

Ethel was born Ethel Simpson in Halifax on 28th March 1898. Her father, William Simpson, was a foreman at an engineering works in the town. He had married Amy Baker around 1890. Ethel had an older brother and sister. Her father died when she was only six years old. Ethel left school at the minimum age; her first employment was as a school milliner's errand girl. She advanced to office clerking positions, having learned shorthand and typing at evening classes. Ethel was an attractive young woman, as seen in her photographs.

Ethel Christie as a young woman

In 1920, aged 22, Ethel met Reg Christie and after a short courtship they married.[18] According to Christie, the couple's sexual relationship was difficult. Ethel, again according to Christie, suffered a miscarriage, which left her unable to bear children.

Despite both Christie and Ethel being in work, Christie turned to petty theft in the early 1920s. After spending three months in prison in 1921 and being placed on a year's probation in 1923,

Christie left Halifax. Ethel, though, remained behind. By 1923, again according to Christie, Ethel had entered into a relationship with her employer – Mr Garside – and this was behind him leaving Halifax and Ethel.[19]

Ethel Christie and Reg Christie post war

Ethel worked at the English Electric company in Bradford for five years between 1923–8. She was then made redundant and moved to Sheffield, where her mother, sister and brother lived. She took up employment as a shorthand typist in a steelworks.

At that time, she entered into a relationship with Vaughan Brindley. Ethel apparently told Brindley that her husband had been gassed in the war and later died of his wounds. The relationship thrived and by 1932 Brindley wanted to marry Ethel. Brindley wanted children, but he was concerned that despite he and Ethel having unprotected sex, she never became pregnant. Brindley stalled. Ethel asked his father to intervene, but this led to Brindley breaking off the relationship completely.[20]

Ethel was back on her own, aged 34. It was then that she went to see Christie in Wandsworth prison and decided to set up home again with him in Notting Hill. She eventually moved to 10 Rillington Place with Christie. She was able to find work, making use of her shorthand and typing skills. Ethel also made regular trips back to Sheffield to see her family.

When the Evans family came, she befriended Beryl and, after Geraldine was born, she would keep an eye out for the baby when Beryl had to go out.

Timothy John Evans

Timothy Evans was born on 20th November 1924 in Merthyr Vale. His mother was Thomasina Evans (née Lynch). His father, Daniel Evans, had deserted Thomasina before Tim was born. There was an earlier daughter in the marriage, Eleanor (Eileen). Thomasina later, in 1933, married Penry Probert. They had a daughter, Mary, who was born in 1929.[21] The Proberts, with Tim, moved from South Wales to London in 1936.

While still living in Merthyr Vale, when Tim was nine years old, he badly cut a toe on a piece of glass while swimming in the river Taff. The toe became tubercular. It meant Tim spent a lot of time over the next ten years in hospitals and sanatoria, severely curtailing his education. Tim did not learn to read or write. His family mentioned that he went into tantrums if he did not get his own way.[22]

Evans left school aged 14. He may have lacked formal learning but he was not mentally defective. He had a patchy employment record during the Second World War but he moved on to capable employment as a van driver. By then he was fit and strong for his height of 5 foot 6 inches. The police would come to describe him as 'quite wordly.'[23]

Timothy Evans, Paddington Station 2nd December 1949

His underlying health issue prevented him from doing National Service. He did, though, serve in the Home Guard and as a civil defence messenger.[24] In 1946 he was fined 60 shillings at West London magistrates' court for stealing a car.[25]

In 1947 Evans met Beryl Thorley. She was only 17 at the time. They were married in September that year and Beryl became pregnant shortly afterwards. The couple, who initially lived with Evans' family, needed accommodation of their own and in Easter 1948 they moved to the top floor flat at 10 Rillington Place.[26]

Evans' went through a series of job changes, but from July 1948 he largely worked as a van driver for Lancaster Road Food Products. After Beryl stopped working, Tim's wages, even supplemented with overtime, were inadequate. He regularly enjoyed drinking at local pubs - the Kensington Park Hotel ('KPH') and the Elgin. He supported Queens Park Rangers.

Tim and Beryl Evans

Beryl Susanna Evans

Beryl Susanna Thorley was born on 19th September 1929 in Lewisham. Her father, William Thorley, worked for a bus company. Her mother was Elizabeth Thorley (née Simmons); she died in 1947. Beryl had a younger brother, Basil.

Beryl was only 5 foot 2 inches tall and weighed just 7½ stone.[27] She was argumentative.

When Beryl met Evans in January 1947 she was working as a

telephonist at the Grosvenor Hotel. She married Evans on the 20th September 1947. As mentioned above, the Evanses moved to 10 Rillington Place at Easter 1948 after Beryl had become pregnant, as the couple needed a home of their own before Geraldine's birth.

Beryl got on well with Mrs Christie, who looked out for the baby, allowing Beryl to go out. But the Christies and other neighbours became more and more aware of the rowing between Tim and Beryl over debt. For a while, in the summer of 1949, the arguing was made even worse when Beryl's friend, Lucy Endecott, came to stay. Evans' mother and Christie intervened to stop the trouble. Lucy was put out and Tim went with her. He was back home next day.

Beryl Evans

Beryl became pregnant again in the summer of 1949, but she wanted rid of the child. She tried pills and other devices to induce a miscarriage. None worked. She talked openly of having an abortion.

A back-street abortionist from the neighbourhood and Christie were mentioned in connection with such a procedure.

As summer turned to autumn, the debts and the rows got worse. The relationship between Beryl and Tim was in deep trouble. She felt her life sinking into one of drudgery. She wasted money and her housekeeping was poor. Tim went off to the pub at every opportunity, oblivious of his wife's need for company.[28]

Beryl Evans was last seen alive on the morning of Tuesday 8th November 1949. Mr and Mrs Christie and one of the workmen doing repair work on the ground floor at 10 Rillington Place attested to seeing her going out with the baby.[29]

Geraldine Evans

Geraldine Evans was born on 10th October 1948 at Queen Charlotte's Hospital. Evans' mother, Mrs Probert, helped Tim and Beryl by buying equipment and clothing for the baby. Geraldine was taken to see her grandmother regularly.

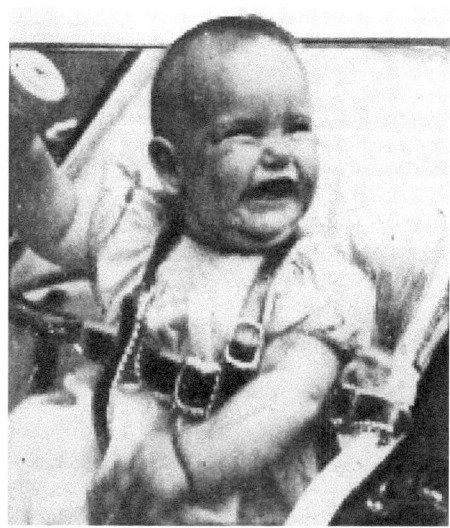

Geraldine Evans

Although most authors state Geraldine was fourteen months old in November 1949, she was actually only thirteen months old.

Geraldine was a healthy child at the time of her death.[30]

Outline

At the beginning of November 1949 there must have been an extremely tense atmosphere in 10 Rillington Place, emanating especially from the top floor flat.

On the ground floor, Mrs Christie was a respectable and decent woman. Ethel was somewhat subservient to her husband. Christie appeared outwardly respectable, albeit with odd mannerisms. But underneath, a psychopathic personality coupled with sexual aberration had led him to murder two women and bury them in the back garden. His secret, though, remained undetected.

On the middle floor, the elderly tenant, Mr Kitchener, was not in residence. He was in hospital suffering from eyesight problems.

On the top floor was the family of Tim Evans, his wife Beryl and their baby daughter, Geraldine. Their financial situation was dire. Beryl had failed to make rent payments and the landlord was about to issue a summons. She had also failed to pay instalments on the hire purchase agreement for the furniture. Beryl accused Tim of not giving her enough money and he accused her of squandering the money he did give her. On top of this, Beryl was pregnant and desperately trying to avoid having a second child. With Beryl argumentative and Tim having a fiery temper, there had to be great tension in the flat.

On the 30th October, workmen arrived at 10 Rillington Place to make repairs to the roof of the wash-house and toilet in the yard and to sort out the problems of damp and rotten floorboards on the ground floor. Their work was not finally completed until Monday 14th November.

Although it was generally accepted that Beryl was strangled on Tuesday 8th November and Geraldine on Thursday 10th, it was only Evans who said so. Dr Teare, in his post mortem, could only state that they had both died around three weeks before, i.e. about the second week in November. However, how they were strangled and by whom (Evans or Christie) remained open to question. There were questions too over who put the bodies in the wash-house and when.

In any event, Evans sold his furniture and left 10 Rillington Place on Monday 14th November. He claimed his wife and the child had gone away on holiday to Bristol or Brighton. On 15th November he arrived at the home of his uncle and aunt, the Lynches, in Merthyr Vale. He was to stay there until Wednesday 30th November on the pretext that his boss' car had broken down and was awaiting repair in Cardiff. He initially told Mrs Lynch that his wife and child were on holiday in Brighton. During that time, he went back to London to see Christie. Christie and Evans gave very different accounts of that meeting. On arriving back in Merthyr Vale, Tim told the Lynches that his wife had walked out of the flat and left the baby, but he had got her taken care of by a couple from Newport.[31]

On the morning of 30th November, Mrs Lynch received a letter from Evans' mother, Mrs Probert, in which she disowned her son. She wrote that Evans had told her Beryl and the baby had gone to Brighton. She mentioned, too, that the furniture had disappeared out of the flat.[32] Tim's excuse for being with the Lynches was unravelling, and he was running out of money.

On the afternoon of 30th November, Evans went to the police at Merthyr Tydfil and told them that he had put his wife's body down a drain. He gave a first statement claiming she had poisoned herself trying to abort the baby. The Merthyr and Metropolitan police followed up on Evans' remarkable admission. While it was proved false, nevertheless, Evans' wife and daughter were missing. Evans changed his story, giving a second statement that implicated Christie in killing his wife through a failed abortion. Further, Christie had arranged for the baby to be cared for.

On 2nd December, during a second search at 10 Rillington Place, the bodies of Beryl and Geraldine Evans were discovered hidden in the wash-house. Evans was brought back to Notting Hill Police Station. In a room, beside piles of clothing taken from the bodies of Beryl (with cord on top) and Geraldine (with a tie on top), Evans confessed to killing his wife and child.

But it was not that simple. Far from it.

These accounts draw on Jonathan Oates' book, John Christie of Rillington Place, *(2012, Wharncliffe True Crime, Barnsley). Oates did excellent biographical work drawing on primary sources including the National Archive.*

References Chapter 1

1. Christie's childhood and siblings – Oates, pp 1-3

2. Christie's early fascination with dead bodies – Oates, pp 4-5

3. Christie's use of prostitutes – Oates, p5

4. Christie's First World War service and wounding – Oates, pp 8-10

5. Christie returns to Halifax after the war and meets Ethel Simpson – Oates, pp 10-2

6. Christie's early convictions in Halifax – Oates, pp 13-5

7. Christie jailed in London for theft in 1924 – Oates, pp 17-8

8. Christie jailed in London for malicious wounding in 1928 – Oates, pp 20-2

9. Christie jailed in London for theft in 1933 – Oates, pp 23-4

10. Christies come back together and settle at 10 Rillington Place – Oates, pp 25-6

11. Christie serves as a Special Constable in the War Reserve – Oates, pp 30-8

12. Christie murders Ruth Fuerst in 1943 – Trial of Christie, Jesse, pp 187-8

13. Christie gets a thrill out of killing Ruth Fuerst – Oates, p36. Referenced back to National Archive EP02–9535

14. Blood 300 times more efficient in absorbing carbon monoxide than oxygen – Camps, p156

15. Christie again thrilled by killing Muriel Eady – Oates, pp 38-40

16. Christie cited in a divorce case – Oates, p41

17. Christie occupations 1944-50 – Oates, pp 41-2

18. Ethel Simpson early life – Oates, pp 10-1

19. Ethel stays in Yorkshire and has an affair with her employer – Oates, pp 15-16

20. Ethel has another serious affair that nearly led to marriage – Oates pp 19-20

21. Timothy Evans' childhood family – Oates p43

22. Evans' tubercular foot seriously hampered his education – Oates, pp 43-4

23. Nevertheless, Evans deemed 'worldly' – Trial of Evans, Jesse, p58

24. Evans served in the Home Guard – Oates, p44

25. Evans' minor conviction – Oates, p45

26. Timothy and Beryl Evans move to 10 Rillington Place – Oates pp 46-7

27. Beryl Evans height and weight – Oates p46

28. Relationship between Beryl and Tim under strain – Oates, pp 48-53

29. Beryl Evans seen alive on the morning of Tuesday 8th November 1949 – witness statements, J Eddowes, p194, p200, p204

30. Geraldine healthy at time of death – Dr Teare post-mortem, Camps, pp 227-8

31. Evans returns to 10 Rillington Place on Wednesday 23rd November – Trial of Evans, Jesse, p45

32. Evans' mother exposed his lies to his aunt – J Eddowes, p43

Chapter 2

Scenarios, Sound Facts and Areas of Contention or Contradiction

Timothy Evans and Reg Christie both knew who killed Beryl Evans and who killed Geraldine Evans. Prima facie, we cannot be certain exactly what each man knew concerning the killings. The position is clouded, as each man gave different accounts of some key events, depending on his motivation at the time. It is hard to decipher when each was being truthful and when each was lying.

Scenarios

There are eight possible scenarios for the killings of Beryl and Geraldine. Each of these needs to be outlined. For parts of the book they act as a framework for considering the sound evidence and the matters that have remained contentious and contradictory.

The eight scenarios are as follows.

Scenario 1: *Evans killed his wife and daughter and disposed of their bodies himself, unbeknown to the Christies (Notting Hill Confession)*

Evans had the means, motive and opportunity to kill his wife. They were living together in a small flat that must have been a 'tinderbox', given the couple's dire financial circumstances and the prospect of things getting even worse with a second baby coming along. Critical debts were going unpaid. Evans effectively stated this in his Notting Hill confession. On top of this, there were indications of other relationships and Evans' readiness to go out drinking. Evans had a temper. Beryl was argumentative. There were numerous witness statements, including Evans' own statements, confirming that the relationship was becoming increasingly bitter. That bitterness had already extended to incidents of physical violence.

Could it have been like this?

Timothy Evans returned home on Tuesday 8th November and had to sustain a barrage of nagging from his wife. He struck out at her, hitting her across the face. After a delay, during which time her face became swollen, she started to nag him again. At this stage he lost all control and responded in the most extreme fashion. He strangled her with a rope. That could explain Dr Teare's findings in Beryl's post mortem.

Technically, if Evans had killed his wife in a fit of rage, a case of manslaughter could have been argued on grounds of provocation. There was, though, the problem of a ligature having been used. The use of such a device would mitigate against the act being sponta-neous. The expectation would be that an act of strangulation in a fit of rage would be committed by using one's hands around the victim's throat.

The following morning, Evans would have gone to work at the normal time. The baby would have been left uncared for and without her mother. That was a big threat to Evans – the baby's crying could have been heard and what he had done to Beryl could have been exposed. Even if Evans came back to care for the baby during the day, how could the baby's cries have gone unnoticed? Again, the baby would have been left in the same circumstances on Thursday 10th November when he went to work, driving to Brighton.

On Thursday evening he unexpectedly got sacked. Was his failure to deliver three packages in Brighton the last straw for Lancaster Foods? Was it because he had used up time in going back to 10 Rillington Place during the day to tend to the baby? Did he then return home, having lost his job that evening, and murder his child out of sheer desperation?

Evans had the means, motive and opportunity to strangle the baby. Strangling his wife in a rage was always possible, but would he have been capable of strangling the child in cold blood?

Evans did tell Sergeant Trevallian that the constant crying of the baby got on his nerves. But there was also the cover-up motive – the crying could be overheard by the Christies or the workmen when he had already told the Christies that Beryl and the baby had gone away on holiday. If it was realised that the baby was still in 10 Rillington Place, questions would have been asked about the whereabouts of her mother. It would then only be a matter of time before her body was found and Evans would be charged with her murder. It would have been easy for Evans to strangle the child and dispose of her body beside her mother's, if he crossed the psychological boundary to doing so.

Edna E Gammon in her book, *A House to Remember, 10 Rillington Place*, (Memoirs Books, Cirencester, 2011) put forward a variant of this scenario. She considered Evans killed both his wife and daughter on the evening of Tuesday 8th November. That removed the problem of the baby's crying attracting attention, thereby leading to the early discovery of Beryl's body.

Dr Teare's post mortem evidence did not rule out this possibility. He could only narrow the time of death to between three to four weeks before his post mortems.[1] It was Evans himself, in his second statement at Notting Hill, who timed his wife's death as Tuesday 8th November and his daughter's death as Thursday 10th November.

Scenario 2: *Evans killed his wife and daughter. Christie found out immediately after and orchestrated the disposal of the bodies and Evans' departure (Newton Chance solution)*

Beryl Evans was murdered by her husband at the culmination of a bitter row. Evans, realising the child could give away what he had done, strangled her as well shortly afterwards. Christie recognised that the rowing on the top floor had been followed by silence and went upstairs to find out what was going on. He walked in on a scene of two dead bodies. Rather than turn Evans in, he decided to help him. He orchestrated the disposal of the bodies and Evans' departure from 10 Rillington Place. This is in line with John Newton Chance's solution in his book The Crimes at Rillington Place (Hodder & Stroughton, London, 1961).

The means, motive and opportunity for Evans to kill his wife were the same as for scenario 1. The actual killing also mirrored scenario 1.

Evans had the means, motive and opportunity to kill his baby. The baby was in the bedroom and defenceless. Her crying would be overheard when he went to work next day and this would lead to the discovery that he had killed Beryl. He strangled the child for self- preservation.

While Evans was dealing with the bodies, Christie came into the flat. Christie took stock of what confronted him. Conscious of the two bodies buried in the back garden and concerned they were not deep enough, his overriding need was to ensure the police came nowhere near 10 Rillington Place. He would help Evans cover up the murders rather than turn him in. Christie gave Evans instructions on what he needed to do. Evans had no choice but to do what Christie wanted. The bodies were moved to Kitchener's flat. It may well be that Evans was supposed to take them away in his van when the opportunity arose. However, on the Thursday evening Evans got unexpectedly sacked. The bodies, pro tem, could not be moved from the house. Christie decided that they should be moved to the wash-house once the workmen had finished using it. He and Evans moved the bodies at the weekend. Christie intended to move the bodies on when any fuss over the disappearance of Beryl and the baby had died down. To draw attention further away from 10 Rillington Place, he instructed Evans to sell up and leave.

Scenario 3: *Evans killed his wife; Christie found out; some form of joint enterprise in getting rid of the child*

The initial stages of this scenario would have been the same as for Scenario 1. Beryl was strangled by her husband following yet another row, this one going too far. But in this scenario, Christie discovered the killing the next morning. Rather than turn Evans in, he decided to help him dispose of Beryl's body and look after the child when Evans was at work. But the child's crying was a threat. Then Evans was sacked and lost his use of the van. Beryl's body could not be removed from 10 Rillington Place. The baby had to be murdered so its crying did not give the mother's murder away. Christie effectively controlled Evans. He orchestrated the killing of the baby, the disposal of the bodies and Evans' departure from 10 Rillington Place.

The means, motive and opportunity for Evans to kill his wife were the same as for scenarios 1 and 2. The actual killing was the same as for scenarios 1 and 2.

The narrative for Scenario 3 diverged from scenarios 1 and 2 for what happened on the evening of Beryl's death. In the late evening Evans wrapped his wife's body and moved it down to Mr Kitchener's flat. The noise of moving the body awoke the Christies in their ground floor bedroom. They heard a thud overhead and noises like furniture being moved.

The next morning, Evans cared for the baby and left her wrapped up in her cot when he went to work. After Evans left, Christie went upstairs to find out what the noise was in the night. He either noticed a silence or heard the baby crying. He would have knocked on the Evanses' kitchen door and called out Beryl's name. On getting no response, he would have gone in to look around the flat. He would have found the baby all alone in her cot. But where was Beryl? His initial thought may have been to go downstairs and tell Mrs Christie. On the way down, he would have recalled that the thud in the night seemed to come from Kitchener's flat. He knew how to get in. He came across Beryl's body.

Christie would have had to decide whether to call the police or whether to start covering up what had happened. Christie was himself a strangler. He had two of his victims buried in the back garden. His murders had remained undetected for some 5 - 6 years. He was loath to draw the police into 10 Rillington Place. In investigating the murder of Beryl Evans, could the police make the link between Rillington Place and the earlier disappearances of Ruth Fuerst and Muriel Eady back in the war years? Christie would have been scared that the police could extend their search to the garden and uncover his earlier murders. He could not be sure that the bodies were deep enough; bones had occasionally resurfaced. In any case, Christie had a 'soft spot' for Evans; why betray him to the police when he himself had covered up two murders? Better for both Christie and Evans if Beryl's body could be disposed of away from 10 Rillington Place.

Christie decided to look after the baby so the crying would die down and to tell his wife nothing. When Evans returned from work on Wednesday 9th, Christie was on hand to meet him. Christie confronted Evans with the knowledge that he knew he had killed his wife. Christie held Tim's life in his hands. Christie would orchestrate what needed to be done.

It may have been originally intended that Evans would take his wife's body away in the van. Then, late on Wednesday evening, Mrs Christie intercepted Evans coming in and asked about Beryl and the baby. Christie was nearby. Evans told her they had gone away to Brighton on holiday. What then if Mrs Christie overheard the baby crying? On the Thursday, Evans again went to work and Christie tended to the baby. On Thursday evening, after work, Evans was unexpectedly sacked. Not only that, he lost access to the van. The chance to hide Beryl's body in some remote location well away from 10 Rillington Place was gone.

When Christie learnt that Evans had lost the use of the van he realised Beryl's body would be remaining inside 10 Rillington Place. With the workmen still on site, it would take time to dispose of it.

The means, motive and opportunity for killing the child stemmed from her crying, which was a danger as it could attract attention. If the baby was discovered without its mother, that would quickly lead to Beryl's disappearance being probed. With her body still in Kitchener's flat, her murder would come to light soon after. It was then that Christie decided the baby had to be got rid of so that its crying would not be heard by Mrs Christie or brought to her attention by the workmen. More likely that Christie committed the deliberate murder of the child, while Evans watched and did nothing, than Evans strangled his child. Either way, though, it was a joint enter- prise and both were equally guilty under the law.

Christie then told Evans the bodies would need to be put in the wash-house after the workmen had finished their work there. He would get rid of the bodies more permanently later on.

When Mrs Christie was out of the house on Saturday 12th November, Christie and Evans took the bodies to the wash house. In the process Christie triggered the severe back pain that caused him to have to go to see his doctor that very day.

Christie had already told Evans he had to sell up and leave so the police would not bother searching 10 Rillington Place if they later followed up on Tim's, Beryl's and Geraldine's disappearance. Evans sold up and left on Monday 14th.

Scenario 4: *Evans killed his wife; Christie found out; Christie tricked Evans over getting the baby cared for; Christie killed the baby*

The initial stages of this scenario would have been the same as for Scenario 3. Beryl was strangled by her husband following yet another row, this one going too far. He strangled Beryl with a piece of rope he had to hand.

The means, motive and opportunity for Evans to kill his wife were the same as for scenarios 1, 2 and 3. The actual killing was the same as for scenarios 1, 2 and 3. It continued following Scenario 3 - Evans took his wife's body down to Mr Kitchener's flat; the Christies were woken up by the noise of the body being moved about; next morning Evans went to work, leaving the baby unattended; Christie went up to investigate the noises in the night and discovered Beryl's body; rather than turn Evans in, and risk the bodies in the back garden being discovered, he decided to help him.

The narrative for Scenario 4 then diverges from Scenario 3. The means, motivation and opportunity to kill the baby all fell to Christie. On Wednesday, he tended to the child and realised her bouts of crying could be easily overheard downstairs. He could tell Evans the child needed to be got away from 10 Rillington Place. But this would be a ruse. Christie had decided to kill the child and satisfy his real psychopathic lust.

When Evans returned from work Wednesday 9th, Christie would have confronted him, making him realise he held his life in his hands. Evans had no choice but to do what Christie wanted.

Christie told Evans that the baby had to go from the flat. There was far too big a risk of Mrs Christie or the workmen hearing its bouts of crying. The discovery of the baby, all alone without her mother, would draw attention to Beryl's disappearance when her dead body was just one floor below the Evanses' flat! Christie, though, could arrange things. He pretended he had already spoken to a young couple in East Acton and they would be happy to take care of Geraldine. Evans was to have Geraldine prepared, ready to be collected next morning. On Thursday morning, when Evans was at work, Christie strangled the child and hid her body elsewhere in Kitchener's flat. Evans never knew.

On the Thursday evening, after work, Evans was unexpectedly sacked. He lost access to the van. The chance to take Beryl's body from 10 Rillington Place to some remote location was gone. When Christie found out, he told Evans he needed to sell up and leave 10 Rillington Place, but not before they could hide Beryl's body temporarily in the wash-house. The body was moved after the workmen had finished using the wash-house and when Mrs Christie was out of the house. Christie and Evans placed the folded and wrapped bundle under the sink and covered it up with pieces of wood that the builders had discarded. This action brought on Christie' s severe fibrositis. After Evans had got rid of the furniture, Beryl's clothes and the bedding, he left 10 Rillington Place on Monday 14th. Christie later moved Geraldine's body into the wash-house. Christie told Evans he would move Beryl's body to a drain, but it would have been physically impossible for him to do so. Perhaps he intended to bury the bodies in the back garden when he knew for sure everything had died down on the Evanses' disappearance. Luckily for Christie he did not move the bodies. Had the police found the garden disturbed they would have found the skeletons of Christie's wartime victims.

Scenario 5: *Evans and Christie conspired to kill Evans's wife. They then had to kill the baby to cover up the mother's murder*

10 Rillington Place having been such a compact house, Christie would have been well aware of the rows going on between Tim and Beryl and that they were due to the couple's mounting debts and Beryl wanting to terminate her pregnancy.

Evans looked up to Christie as being the authority figure in the house. He appeared learned and he had been a police officer. From time to time, Christie would invite Evans into his front room for a chat. Christie was manipulative in those sessions. It was only a matter of time until Evans unburdened his worries, particularly his worsening situation with Beryl. Evans may well have said he would be glad to be rid of her, or something along those lines. Christie, seeing the chance to satisfy his psychopathic lust, ran with that suggestion and stoked it up. In due course they hatched a plot to kill Beryl.

If the motivation for the murder of Beryl was joint, Christie decided the means and opportunity. The weekend of 4th-6th November had seen a series of more acrimonious rows between Beryl and Tim. Christie was fully aware. It was time to unleash the plot. When Evans came home from work on Tuesday 8th November, another row started. Tim struck Beryl hard across the face. After a while, by which time her face was swelling, she turned on Evans again. By now Christie had come upstairs with his strangling rope. Christie, in accordance with the plot, took the initiative and strangled Beryl. Christie and Evans then moved the body downstairs into Mr Kitchener's flat.

The scenario for killing the child and the means, motivation and opportunity were the same as for scenario 3. Christie again satisfying his psychopathic lust, deliberately strangling the child as Evans looked on. The disposal of the bodies in the wash-house and Evans' departure were the same as for Scenario 3.

Scenario 6: *Christie killed Mrs Evans and there was some form of joint enterprise in getting rid of the child*

Beryl was murdered by Reg Christie. He then implicated Evans in her murder to make sure Evans did not go to the police. Christie and Evans, in some form of joint enterprise, were responsible for the death of the baby and for moving the bodies to the wash-house. Evans departed 10 Rillington Place.

The means, motive and opportunity for both murders were all down to Christie.

Christie lusted after Beryl, but the opportunity to sexually abuse her under the pretext of performing an abortion went wrong when she resisted his attempt to make her unconscious using his gas contraption. He knocked her out and, afterwards, strangled her. When Evans returned the same evening after work, Christie met him as soon as he came in and accompanied him upstairs to where Beryl's body lay. Christie put his spin on how Beryl died and convinced him that he would be implicated in the fatal abortion. Beryl's body was doubled up and wrapped in a blanket and green tablecloth and moved to Mr Kitchener's flat. The intention was that Evans would take her body away in his van and dump it where it would not be found.

Christie looked after Geraldine on the Wednesday and Thursday when Evans was at work. Despite his efforts, the baby, missing her mother, cried regularly. Fortunately, either the crying was not heard by the workers or Mrs Christie or they did not deem it out of the ordinary.

On Thursday evening when Evans returned home having lost his job and the van, the chance of getting Beryl's body away from 10 Rillington Place was gone. Christie recognised the danger. He convinced Evans that the baby's crying, and him having to go upstairs so often to tend to her, would soon draw Mrs Christie upstairs to see what was going on. This was especially dangerous after Evans had told Ethel on Wednesday evening that Beryl and the baby had gone away on holiday. If Ethel discovered the baby, she would want it cared for. That would draw in Mrs Probert. Then Beryl's disappearance would be too suspicious and that would draw in the police. Their routine searches would lead to Beryl's body being found in Kitchener's flat. Worse still for Christie – what might be found in the garden?

Christie cold-bloodedly strangled the child with Evans standing by and doing nothing. Both were guilty of the joint enterprise murder.

The rest of this scenario follows scenario 4 – both men taking the bodies to the wash-house at the weekend when Mrs Christie was out and Evans, persuaded by Christie, selling up and leaving 10 Rillington Place on Monday 14th November.

Scenario 7: *Christie killed Mrs Evans. Evans killed the child and disposed of the bodies (Christie's confession)*

Within the context of this scenario, Christie could have killed Beryl Evans in one of two ways.

Firstly, according to his 1953 confession, he could have killed her because she wanted to commit suicide but could not do so. Secondly, and according to Evans, he could have killed her under the guise of performing an abortion. For both ways the motivation for the killing was Christie's sexual/psychopathic lust. The means was Christie's already established strangling technique. The opportunity was given to Christie by Beryl herself. In Christie's version, Beryl attempted to gas herself on Monday 7th November, but Christie intervened to stop her. She was depressed with her husband and pleaded with Christie to help her go through with the suicide. Christie agreed and came up to the Evanses' kitchen around lunchtime on Tuesday 8th to perform the 'mercy killing'. He attempted to make her unconscious using his gassing contraption. When he passed it over her face, she panicked. Christie in turn panicked and struck her hard across the face. He then strangled her. Any attempt to sexually molest her came to nothing. Christie left Beryl lying on the kitchen floor. He went downstairs to await Evans' return from work.

In Evans' version, Christie persuaded Beryl and Tim that he could get rid of the baby Beryl did not want. She willingly submitted herself into Christie's hands on 8th November. He struck her and strangled her. Again, though, he did not interfere with the pregnancy or assault her sexually.

Commentary – Evans' version would effectively be what is covered in Scenario 8.

The scenario then relies on Christie's confession.

When Evans came home in the evening of 8th November, Christie was there to meet him and provide a plausible explanation for Beryl's death. If she committed suicide the police would not see it that way. Everyone knew of the Evanses' rowing and Evans would be deemed to have killed her. If she died in the failed abortion, wasn't Evans a party to that? In either case, Evans would have accepted Christie's explanation that he would be deemed responsible for his wife's death.

Evans then took his wife's body from the kitchen to the bedroom and Christie went downstairs. Christie played no further part in the aftermath of Beryl's death. Evans strangled Geraldine. Certainly, Evans would have had the same motivation, means and opportunity to kill the baby as he did in Scenario 1; the need to stop the baby's crying being overheard. He hid his wife's and the baby's bodies in the wash-house. He then sold up his furniture and departed 10 Rillington Place.

Scenario 8: *Christie killed Mrs Evans and the baby, having misled Evans over the fake abortion and getting the child cared for ('Merthyr 2')*

Beryl was murdered by Reg Christie under the guise of performing an abortion. He then persuaded Evans not to go to the police. Christie tricked Evans into believing he would get the child looked after, but instead he strangled the child and kept that a secret from Evans. Christie moved the bodies to the wash house. Evans departed 10 Rillington Place. This is in line with Evans' second statement to the Police at Merthyr Tydfil ('Merthyr 2') and his defence at his trial.

Christie would have been tempted with young Beryl living in the same house for over a year. He would have been well aware of the Evanses' chronic debt problems, of Beryl's pregnancy and her wanting to get rid of the baby. But at the beginning of November 1949, there was every chance Beryl could be gone if the landlord put the Evanses out for not paying their rent.

While Beryl's desire to end her pregnancy gave Christie the opportunity, he had the psychopathic motive and the means to strangle her.

Christie could have used his supposed medical knowledge to trick Tim and Beryl into believing he could perform an abortion on Beryl. Did Christie only intend to anaesthetise her using his coal gas apparatus, sexually abuse her and tell her the abortion failed? She was still pregnant and would accept any discomfort as the natural consequence of the failed abortion? Or did his psychopathic lust trump that?

But it went wrong. Beryl panicked when Christie tried to put the mask of his contraption over her face. She could have screamed, gone downstairs and denounced Christie. Christie, in turn, panicked and struck her across the face, maybe even knocking her out. Did Mrs Vincent call and he had to stop her getting into the flat? Christie weighed up his options and decided all he could do was to strangle Beryl. He moved her body to the bedroom and arranged it on the bed so the weal around her neck was hidden. He darkened the room and cared for the baby.

Christie had to intercept Evans when he came home and convince him he would be implicated in the death of his wife through the failed abortion. Christie took control of Evans. He told Evans to continue to go to work and he would attend to the baby while he was away.

When Evans took the baby to the kitchen to feed and change her, Christie started taking Beryl's body down to Mr Kitchener's flat. He was struggling and Evans came out and helped him. Evans took the feet, so he did not see the weal on Beryl's neck.

On Wednesday, Christie recognised the baby had to die because it could lead to Beryl's murder being discovered too soon if his wife or the workmen heard her crying. Anyhow, it was another opportunity for Christie to kill, even though Geraldine was only a baby. The motivation was his lust to kill and his ability to strangle was now well established.

On Wednesday evening, Christie fooled Evans by pretending that a young couple in East Acton would take the baby. He told Evans to prepare the baby to be collected next morning. He also told Evans that he should tell anyone who asked about Beryl and the child that they had gone away on holiday – the story he gave to Mrs Christie, his mother, his employer and the Lynches. After Evans had left the baby for collection by the young couple and gone to work on Thursday 10th, Christie strangled the baby and hid the body elsewhere in Mr Kitchener's flat.

When Evans returned home on Thursday evening, he told Christie he had given up his job and lost the van. The chance of getting Beryl's body out of house was gone. Christie decided, in order to draw attention away from 10 Rillington Place and the bodies, that Evans must sell up and leave. Evans set his depart- ure in motion.

Christie moved Beryl's body from Kitchener's flat to the wash-house on Saturday 12th November, after the workmen had stopped using it and when Mrs Christie and Evans were out of the house. He placed the folded and wrapped bundle under the sink and covered it up with pieces of wood the builders had discarded. This action brought on Christie's severe fibrositis. Later, after Evans had sold up and gone from 10 Rillington Place, Christie moved the baby's unwrapped body from Kitchener's flat and hid it behind the wash-house door.

In the course of this book, it will be necessary to consider each scenario in terms of the sound facts that fit and do not fit. Each scenario will also need to be considered against the areas of conten-tion and contradiction. There will still be gaps that will need to be addressed as logically as possible.

Sound Facts

It is necessary to set out what we know about Beryl's and Geraldine's murders with a fair degree of certainty. The 'facts' for the period up to Evans' trial are set out as follows. References are provided, but there are other sources corroborating the sound facts. In some cases, chapter references are provided where the facts are consid-ered further.

10 Rillington Place was a run-down Victorian town-house at the end of a cul-de-sac in the Ladbroke Grove district of West London. It was divided into three flats, one on each floor. Timothy and Beryl Evans and their thirteen-month-old daughter, Geraldine, lived in the top floor flat that comprised only two rooms – a bedroom and

a kitchen. An elderly, retired gentleman, Mr Kitchener, was the tenant in the first floor flat. He was going blind and was in hospital during the whole of the time of the murders and until after Evans had left 10 Rillington Place for good.

10 Rillington Place lit up downstairs

Reg and Ethel Christie lived in the ground floor flat, which comprised three rooms – a front room, a bedroom and a kitchen. There was a hall that led to the passageway that opened into the backyard. On the left side of the yard there was a wash-house that no longer served as such because the copper was broken. Beyond that was the communal toilet. The yard opened onto a small back garden, which was exclusive to the Christies. Mr Kitchener and Mr and Mrs Evans would pass all three of the Christies' rooms when they went along the passageway to use the communal toilet. If Beryl was not going past to use the toilet, the Christies would have noticed. And certainly, each of the Christies would have had a fair idea of what the spouse was doing. *(Reference – diagram of ground floor)*

Repair work was carried out on the ground floor and outbuildings of 10 Rillington Place from 30th October to 14th November 1949. The workmen were there at the time Beryl and Geraldine were murdered. A new concrete roof was put over the outside toilet and wash-house. There was some debate over when the work on the wash-house was completed. Certainly it was completed by the morning of Wednesday 9th November. However, the wash-house continued to be used by the workmen for storing their tools until the afternoon of Friday 11th. There was debate on whether the wash-house was swept out on Friday 11th. Work was done outside and inside the front room including replacing rotten floorboards between Tuesday 8th and Friday 11th. Rotten floorboards were lifted and replaced in the hall and passageway. This work started on Thursday 10th and the floor was not fully back down until Saturday 12th November. *(Detailed consideration – Chapter 8)*

Mrs Evans wanted to get rid of the child she was carrying. Evans and the Christies confirmed this.[2] *(References – Evans 1st Merthyr statement, Mrs Christie's 1st statement, Christie's 1st statement)*

The last time Beryl was seen alive, other than by her killer, was the morning/lunchtime of Tuesday 8th November 1949.[3] *(The Christies and one of the workmen attested to this)*

Evans went to work on Tuesday 8th, Wednesday 9th and Thursday 10th November. He lost his job on the evening of the 10th and lost access to the firm's van.[4] *(This was established in Evans' statements and confirmed by the Christies)*

Christie visited his doctor on Tuesday 8th November as he was still suffering from enteritis and needed to extend his off work certificate.[5] *(Confirmed in his doctor's records)*

Beryl could not have been killed on Monday 7th November. The workmen were not at 10 Rillington Place that day. Mr Jones could not have seen Beryl going out, warning her of a ladder on the stairs, until the morning of Tuesday 8th at the earliest.

Beryl could not have been killed on Wednesday 9th. There would not have been enough time for Evans to have arrived back from work to either find Beryl dead or to kill her and, with or without Christie, to have arranged the cover up. Evans' mother stated, that on Wednesdays, Tim and Beryl would leave Geraldine with her while they went to the pictures. Exceptionally on Wednesday 9th

November, Evans came alone. He was calm and natural and he told Mrs Probert that Beryl and the child had gone to holiday with Beryl's father at his home in Brighton.[6] Later that evening at around 10.30 p.m., Mrs Christie, as she regularly did on Wednesdays, put the hall light on for Beryl and the baby coming home. But Tim was alone. With Christie standing nearby, he told Mrs Christie that Beryl and the baby had gone away to Bristol.[7] Beryl had to have been killed on Tuesday 8th. *(Confirmed by the Brabin Report p31, the Christies in their statements, Mrs Probert to the police and Evans at his trial)*

Evans ripped up his wife's clothing and the bedding and gave them to a rag dealer.[8] *(Confirmed by Evans and DC Evans)*

He did not destroy the baby's clothing or equipment but left them with Christie on the day he departed, Monday 14th November. The baby's things were kept in the Christies' front room until recovered by the police.[9] *(Confirmed by Evans and Christie)*

Evans arranged to sell his furniture to Mr Hookway, who operated from the Portobello Road. Mr Hookway and Christie were acquainted with one another. (Confirmed by Hookway and Christie) The furniture was collected on the afternoon of Monday 14th November.[10] *(Confirmed by Evans and Christie)*

Evans left 10 Rillington Place after the furniture was taken away on Monday 14th November. He caught a late train from Paddington to South Wales, arriving at the home of his uncle and aunt, Mr and Mrs Lynch, in the early morning of Tuesday 15th November. Evans told the Lynches that his boss' car had broken down and was being repaired in Cardiff. He also said that Beryl and Geraldine were staying with her father in Brighton.[11] *(Confirmed by Evans and by the Lynches)*

While staying at Merthyr Vale, Evans sold his wife's ring to a jeweller. Evans disclosed the fact to DI Black on 3rd December.[12] The police recovered the ring from a jeweller in Merthyr Tydfil.

While staying in Merthyr Vale, Evans spoke fondly of Geraldine and at least in the early part of his stay he was relaxed.[13] *(Confirmed by Mrs Lynch)*

Evans left Merthyr on Monday 21st November and returned on Thursday the 24th. He went back to 10 Rillington Place and saw Christie. Each man's account of what happened between them was different. Mrs Christie confirmed Evans called, though she only heard his voice.[14] *(Consideration in Chapter 5)*

When Evans returned to Merthyr Vale, he told the Lynches a new story concerning Beryl and Geraldine. Beryl had left him and Geraldine was being cared for by some people from Newport. Mrs Lynch was suspicious and wrote to her sister-in-law, Evans' mother.[15] *(Confirmed by Mrs Lynch)*

On the morning of the 30th November, Mrs Lynch received a response from Evans' mother. Mrs Probert wrote disparagingly about her son, especially the debts he had left behind and the furniture missing from the flat. She also mentioned that Tim had told her that Beryl and the baby had gone to stay with Beryl's father on holiday in Brighton. This did not tally with the new story Evans had told the Lynches when he returned from London on 24th November. *(The letter was Exhibit 5 at Evans' trial.[16])*

On the afternoon of 30th November, Evans went to the police at Merthyr Tydfil and told them he had put his wife's body down the drain. He then gave his first statement ('Merthyr 1'). He stated that his wife had poisoned herself trying to get rid of her unwanted baby. He had put her body down the drain and arranged for his baby to be cared for.[17]

The Merthyr police notified the Metropolitan police and asked them to check Evans' story. The Metropolitan police reported back that the body was not in the drain outside 10 Rillington Place and, in any case, it took three officers to open it.

When Evans was told there was no body in the drain and he

could not have opened it anyway, he said he would now tell the police the truth. He made his second statement ('Merthyr 2'). This stated that the abortion Christie performed on Beryl resulted in her death; her stomach was 'septic poisoned'. Evans did not know what happened to his wife's body after it was taken down to Mr Kitchener's flat. Christie had arranged for the baby to be cared for by a young couple he knew in East Acton.17 *(Detailed consideration in Chapter 3)*

The police searched 10 Rillington Place on 1st December. They recovered a briefcase from the Evanses' flat and some newspaper cuttings on the Hume/Setty case. (Hume, not long beforehand, had killed Setty, parcelled up his body and dropped it onto the Essex Marshes from a light aircraft he piloted.)

No evidence was found of Christie or his wife being abortionists. The police made only a cursory search of the garden; it had not been disturbed recently. Due to a misunderstanding, the washhouse was not searched.[18] *(Police record)*

Two officers from the Notting Hill police – DI Black and Sergeant Corfield – were sent to Merthyr Tydfil to bring Evans back to London. The pretext was to question Evans over the stolen briefcase. *(Police record)*

Detective Chief Superintendent Barrett and Detective Chief Inspector Jennings carried out a further search at 10 Rillington Place on 2nd December 1949. This time the wash-house was searched. When some timber was moved, a bundle was found under the sink. Mrs Christie was asked to identify it but could not. After the bundle was hauled out and opened, it was found to contain the doubled-up body of Beryl Evans. Further searching of the wash-house led to the discovery of a second body. Geraldine Evans' body was behind the door, which opened inwards, again hidden behind pieces of wood.[19] *(Police record: Evans' trial)*

Dr Donald Teare conducted post mortems on the bodies of

Beryl and Geraldine Evans at Kensington mortuary that same afternoon. Chief Inspector Jennings was in attendance. Death in both cases was by strangulation using a ligature. Beryl was 16 weeks pregnant but there had been no interference with the pregnancy and no obvious signs of sexual interference either.[20] *(Post mortem reports) (Detailed consideration in Chapter 4)*

A message was sent to the Merthyr Police. The Metropolitan officers were to cease interviewing Evans and bring him back to London. The transfer was put into effect. On the journey by train back to London nothing was said to Evans about the bodies that had since been found at 10 Rillington Place.[21] *(Police record)*

On arrival at Paddington station, Evans was met by DCI Jennings and then driven to Notting Hill police station. He could see two piles of clothing on the floor of the office he was taken to. The one for Beryl had the blanket, green tablecloth and sash cord used to wrap her body on top; the one for Geraldine had a striped tie on top. The tie had been cut from the baby's neck to ensure that the knot tied by the murderer was kept.[22] *(Information from DCI Jennings and DI Black)*

Chief Inspector Jennings told Evans that the bodies of his wife and daughter had been found in the wash-house at 10 Rillington Place. Both had been strangled. Jennings also added that he believed Evans was responsible. Evans lifted the tie from the baby's bundle. He affirmed what Jennings said.[22] *(Information from DCI Jennings and DI Black)*

Evans made two statements to Chief Inspector Jennings and Detective Inspector Black on the evening of 2nd December. The first was a short admission to murdering his wife and child. The second was a more detailed confession. In short, he stated how his wife had been allowing debt on rent and furniture to build up while squandering money. There were continuous rows over money and her wanting to end her pregnancy. The rowing had come to a crisis on the evening of Tuesday 8th November 1949. When Evans arrived home from work that evening the rowing started right away. Evans hit her across the face. She retaliated and, in a fit of temper, he strangled her with a piece of rope he had brought home. Evans placed Beryl's body in the bedroom and then moved it to Kitchener's flat. While there, he wrapped it in a blanket and green tablecloth and tied it up. Later in the night, when the Christies had gone to bed, he took Beryl's body down to the wash-house and hid it under the sink. He blocked it up with pieces of wood. He went to work on the following two days, tending to the baby when he was home.

On Thursday 10th, he asked his boss for his wages to send to his wife. The boss gave him the money and sacked him. He went home and strangled the baby with his tie. That same night, after midnight when the house was quiet, he took the baby's body to the wash-house and hid her body behind the door, covered with pieces of wood. Evans then sold his furniture and after it was taken away on the afternoon of Monday 14th November, he left 10 Rillington Place and went to stay with his aunt, Mrs Lynch at Merthyr Vale.[23] *(Evans' 'Notting Hill 2' statement) (Detailed consideration in Chapter 5)*

On the morning of Saturday 3rd December, Evans was charged with the murder of his wife (he would not be charged with the murder of his daughter until later). A formal hearing at the West London Magistrates Court followed. En route, Evans told DI Black that after he had killed his wife, he took the wedding ring off her finger and sold it in Merthyr. At the court hearing, Evans was remanded to Brixton Prison.[24] *(Police record)*

At Brixton he partially repeated his confession to the Prison Medical Officer, Dr Matheson.[25] *(Dr Matheson account)*

In 1953, a reporter, Mr Baker, who was making a case for Evans' innocence, took a statement from Evans' mother. On 4th December she visited her son at Brixton Prison. Evans told her 'I did not touch her, mum, Christie did it. I didn't know the baby was dead until the police brought me to Notting Hill. Christie told me the baby was in East Acton.'[26]

Evans met Donald Hume in the prison hospital. Evans told him he had a policeman for an alibi, and the baby was killed because it would not stop crying. Christie did it while he was in the room. Hume told Evans he was stupid to confess. He should blame everyone but, himself.[27] *(Hume's account obtained by Percy Hoskins, Daily Express crime writer, in a meeting with Hume in 1958)*

Evans withdrew his confession on 15th December and would base his defence in his trial on the second statement - 'Merthyr 2' - he had made to DC Evans at Merthyr Tydfil police station. This effectively placed the responsibility for his wife's and the baby's deaths on Christie.[28] *(Basis of Evans' defence at his trial)*

Evans appeared before magistrates on 15th December when witness evidence was heard. It was not challenged by Evans' solicitor, Mr Freeborough. Evans appeared again on 22nd December when police evidence was given. After the second appearance, he was sent for trial at the Old Bailey.[29] *(Court record)*

The principal witness statements taken by the police were from the Christies, the workmen, Mrs Vincent (a friend of Beryl Evans) and Mrs Lynch. The police made all the statements available to the prosecution service, but the prosecution service did not pass the workmen's statements (and worksheets) or Mrs Vincent's statement to the defence. The police also interviewed Mrs Probert (Evans' mother), Mrs Ashby (his sister), Mrs Westlake (his half-sister) and Mr Basil Thorley (his brother-in-law). [30]

Evans was tried for the murder of his daughter at the Old Bailey on 11th-13th January 1950.[31] *(Trial Transcript)*

Areas of Contention and Contradiction

The points of contention are best listed in terms of whether Christie killed Beryl Evans, whether Evans killed his wife, the killing of the child and other issues. As appropriate, they are discussed through the book and in the evaluation chapter, Chapter 19.

If Evans killed Beryl Evans (Scenarios 1-5)

If Evans strangled his wife in a fit of temper, why did he not throttle her with his bare hands? Why would there have been a length of rope so conveniently at hand?

Evans supposedly strangled his wife with a piece of rope and left the rope around her neck. The rope was not found with the body and the police never recovered it. What happened to the rope?

If Evans killed his wife on the evening of Tuesday 8th November, how could he have left her body in his flat or Kitchener's flat and the baby in her cot and gone to work on the Wednesday? Would he not have stayed with the body and the baby on the Wednesday and later told his employer he was sick?

In his confession, Evans stated that he moved Beryl's body to the wash-house on the night of the 8th/9th November. She weighed 105 pounds and was awkwardly doubled up and wrapped. Surely it would have been impossible not to have made sufficient noise to bring the Christies out of their bedroom to see what was going on?

If Evans had killed Beryl and Christie knew and the baby was still alive early on the evening of Thursday 10th, why did Christie not reconsider his position when Evans told him he had lost his job and access to the van? Why did he not go to the police then?

If Evans did kill Beryl and the baby and did hide the bodies in the wash-house, all on his own, why would he have wanted to leave

10 Rillington Place? He would be losing control of the bodies. He would be found out soon enough. Either Christie would have found the bodies and told the police, or Evans' family or Beryl's family would have got police inquiries instigated.

With Larters' workmen carrying out repairs to the wash-house and on the ground floor of 10 Rillington Place at the time Beryl and Geraldine were killed, what was the earliest date that the bodies could have been hidden in the wash-house and not been noticed? Would Evans have been able to put the bodies there on the nights of 8th/9th and 10th/11th of November? Would it have been possible for him to have moved them on Friday 11th or Saturday 12th?

If Evans strangled his wife and child and placed the bodies in the wash-house, how come the Christies between at least 14th November and 2nd December did not notice them?

Why was the wood hiding the bodies not used as firewood?

How could the Christies' dog not have picked up the scent and drawn the Christies attention to the bodies?

Did the fact that Christie went to see his doctor, Dr Odess, with severe back pain/fibrositis on 12th November, suggest that Evans did not take the bodies to the wash-house or that he and Christie together took Beryl's body there?

Does the fact that Evans left his wife's body behind at 10 Rillington Place suggest he felt it was safe to leave it with Christie for ongoing disposal, perhaps down the drain?

Evans left 10 Rillington Place on 14th November 1949 after he had sold his furniture to Mr Hookway. He took his wife's wedding ring with him and sold it to a jeweller in Wales. When Christie left 10 Rillington Place in March 1953, after his final killing spree, he had already sold his furniture to Mr Hookway. He had already sold his wife's wedding ring to a jeweller. Coincidence, or Christie's hand in both departures?

Christie was nobody's fool. If Evans had murdered his wife,

he would have realised it soon enough. He certainly would have followed up the thud in the night. But if he found the wife's body and the baby unattended, why did he not inform the police straight away? Would he have wanted to go to the police? If the police had started to swarm all over 10 Rillington Place, they might well have uncovered the bodies in the back garden. Those bodies were buried too close to the surface and Christie knew it but could do nothing about it. Was it a lower risk strategy for Christie to steer clear of the police and take control of Timothy Evans?

Evans in his 'Merthyr 2' statement claimed he believed Christie put his wife's body down a drain and passed his daughter to a young couple in East Acton to take care of her. Yet in his confession he stated exactly where his wife's body was placed in the wash- house and that both bodies had been hidden behind pieces of wood. But he also confessed he had struck his wife before he strangled her. Did the police feed the confession, or was Evans speaking from first-hand knowledge?

In his confession, Evans mentioned hitting his wife in the face. There was no suggestion that Chief Inspector Jennings told him she had been hit like this. Jennings, who attended the post mortem earlier that day, would have been aware that Beryl had been struck in the face.

If Christie killed Beryl Evans [Scenarios 6, 7 and 8]

Beryl rose early on Tuesday 8th November and got Evans to tell Christie as he went out to work that 'everything was all right.' According to Evans' 'Merthyr 2' statement, that was the signal for the abortion to go ahead. Presumably the procedure was to be performed by Christie that morning. However, Beryl and the baby were seen outside the house later that morning. Mr Jones in his second statement stated he saw Mrs Evans leaving with the baby in the pram. He also mentioned that there was a companion with them. Mrs Christie stated in her first statement that she thought she saw Beryl and the baby leaving around dinner time. Christie, in his second statement, stated he saw them outside about 1 p.m. when he was in the front room. There is no timing for when Beryl, the baby and the pram returned. So, was Mrs Evans actually out of 10 Rillington Place at the very time Christie was supposed to be upstairs murdering her?

For Christie to have murdered Beryl Evans, under the premeditated pretence of performing an illegal abortion, seemed unusually risky, even for Christie. What about his wife noticing him going up to the Evanses' flat and being up there for long periods? What about the workmen going in and out of the building? What about visitors calling to see Beryl? What about Evans' reaction when he found his wife dead – would he go straight to the police or to his family? What about disposing of Beryl's body? What about the two bodies Christie had already buried in the back garden?

If Christie was suffering from enteritis on Tuesday 8th November, why would he have wanted to try and molest Beryl Evans?

At around the time Christie was supposed to have been murdering Beryl, he was apparently disturbed by Mrs Vincent. She tried to get into the Evanses' kitchen but considered the door handle was held against her. But Mrs Vincent originally stated that that visit to the Evanses' flat occurred on the previous day, Monday 7th November. Furthermore, she claimed to have come back on the next day (Wednesday 9th or Tuesday 8th) only to have been stopped from going upstairs by Christie. Christie told her Beryl had gone away. At that time, she also claimed to have seen the baby's pram in the Christies' front room. But Evans did not ask the Christies to look after the baby's equipment and clothes until just before he left 10 Rillington Place on 14th November. Why would any credence have been given to Mrs Vincent's seemingly confused statements?

Christie had a routine of going to see his doctor on Tuesday evenings. He did see Dr Odess on Tuesday 8th November. He needed a certificate to remain off work. That he visited that day was confirmed in the doctor's patient records. Further, if Christie had broken his routine and gone to see the doctor at an earlier surgery, would not Ethel or Dr Odess have mentioned such an exception?

So, if Christie was away when Evans returned from work, Evans would have walked in alone and found his wife's body. He could have gone to the police or his family and Christie would have been exposed straightaway as her killer. How could Christie possibly have allowed that to happen?

All Christie's undisputed killings were 'one transaction' murders. Yet if he killed Mrs Evans he did so in a 'double transaction'. She was struck violently in the face and that caused swelling and bruising. For such features to have formed she must have been struck at least 20 minutes before she was strangled. How could Christie have allowed such a delay?

Dr Teare's original autopsy in 1949 on Beryl Evans and the subsequent examination in 1953 (attended by the three top pathologists of that time, Dr Teare, Professor Simpson and Dr Camps) only identified one of the hallmarks of Christie's system. There was no evidence of coal gas having been administered. There was no evidence of sexual interference. There was no evidence of a tuft of pubic hair having been cut off. The only hallmark of a Christie killing was that Beryl had been strangled. Dr Teare was of the opinion that a rope had been used as the ligature. So, if Christie did it, why did the killing not have more of the Christie hallmarks?

And, furthermore, there had been no attempt to interfere with the pregnancy. Dr Teare only saw an old scar that could have come from syringing.

Christie's modus operandi was to entice his victims to come to his flat, most likely on the pretext of being able to alleviate some medical condition. This, though, would only occur when Christie had 'free run' of his flat – on account of his wife being away visiting relations in Yorkshire or because he had killed her. Beryl Evans was not a visitor enticed to Rillington Place. She was a resident who lived with her husband in the house and she talked regularly to Christie and his wife. Why would Christie have taken the risk of killing such a victim?

Having won his victim's confidence, he would then have the opportunity to inflict his ' treatment'. He would get his victims to 'relax' by making them breathe through a contraption that bubbled London coal gas through a solution of Friars' Balsam. On rendering them semi-conscious on account of the high volume of highly toxic carbon monoxide in the gas, Christie would strangle them using his 'strangling rope'. At the same time he would have sexual intercourse with them. The gassing technique would have been well suited to an abortion scenario. So why did Christie not use it?

Christie supposedly told Evans that Beryl's stomach was 'septic poisoned', giving that as his excuse for Beryl dying in the abortion. If it wasn't true, from where else could Evans have come up with such an expression?

Beryl's body was wrapped in a blanket and tablecloth. Christie wrapped his wife's body and one of his last three victims in a blanket. Beryl's body was found without knickers, as were Christie's last three victims. Beryl's body was doubled over, as were Christie's last three victims. The last three victims, though, could have been doubled over because there was limited space in the kitchen alcove. The ligature was not with Beryl's body, as was the case with Christie's wife and his last three victims. Beryl's body was concealed as were all of Christie's victims – buried in the garden, placed under the front room floorboards or placed in the alcove which was then papered over. Whereas the murder of Beryl Evans was short on the hallmarks of a Christie murder, the disposal of her body did have the characteristics of a Christie disposal. But would that suggest that Christie himself took Beryl's body to the wash-house, or would it be more likely that Christie and Evans together put her body there?

Why would Christie have taken the risk of killing Beryl on a day when his wife and the workmen were actually in the house?

Why would Christie have run the risk of Timothy Evans going straight to the police after he had discovered that his wife was dead? Certainly, if the police had found Beryl's body in the immediate aftermath of her being killed, a pathologist would have been able to fix the time of death quite accurately and Evans – at work – would have been cleared. Christie would have been caught with the 'body still warm'.

According to his 'Merthyr 2' statement, Evans looked at her body in the bedroom shortly after he came home from work. In a later interview with DC Evans, he said that he helped Christie carry her down to Mr Kitchener's first floor flat. So, if Christie strangled Beryl, how could Evans have failed to notice the weal on his wife neck?

If Christie had:

- been some time upstairs murdering Beryl;
- kept intercepting Evans at the bottom of the stairs;
- regularly gone upstairs to tend to the baby when Evans was at work;

How did Mrs Christie not notice and become suspicious of Christie's antics and lengthy absences?

How could Evans have been so naive as to allow Christie to take control, despite Christie having been responsible for his wife's death?

If Christie was responsible, with or without Evans' assistance, for the bodies being in the wash-house, was this a temporary hiding place? Did Christie plan to move the bodies elsewhere, that plan having to be put on hold because he developed fibrositis?

Was it part of Christie's plan to cover up his killings of Beryl and the baby and to get Evans to sell up and leave 10 Rillington Place? Was it part of his plan to 'fit up' Evans for the killings?

Was it really significant that Evans cut up and disposed of the wife's clothing but kept the baby's clothing and equipment?

If Christie murdered Beryl and the baby, what did he expect would be the outcome of persuading Evans to leave? Would he have ever thought that Evans would go to his family in South Wales? Would he not have expected him to go somewhere where he would not be known so there would be no need to say anything about his wife and child? Did he not anticipate that the disappearance of the Evanses would, sooner or later, cause suspicion such that the police would come to search 10 Rillington Place?

If Christie told Evans to clear out of London, why did he not tell him to go nowhere near his family and that he would need to stay incognito for some time until any fuss over Beryl's disappearance had died away?

If Evans believed the baby was still alive and with the couple in East Acton, then his visit back to 10 Rillington Place on Wednesday 23rd November was understandable. But if Evans knew the baby was already dead, what was the purpose of his trip back to see Christie? Evans left Wales on 21st November for London. He did not see Christie till the late afternoon of 23rd November. What was he up to on Tuesday 22nd and the morning of Wednesday 23rd?

Did Christie learn on that visit that Evans was staying with his family in South Wales? If so, would Christie not have told him to get away from his family altogether?

Did Christie mishandle Evans unexpectedly turning up at 10 Rillington Place on 23rd November?

By the time Evans returned, had Christie already worked out

that it was best for him to leave the bodies in the wash-house? Ideally, they would not have been found and would mummify, but if they were found, the blame could fall on Evans.

Despite having supposedly killed nobody, what broke Evans' nerve so that he went to the police on 30th November?

Evans received £40 from Mr Hookway on 14th November for his furniture. To him that was some eight weeks' wages. How did he manage to spend virtually all of it in just over two weeks?

If Christie knew the bodies were in the wash-house, would he not have ensured, as discreetly as possible, that the police covered the wash-house once they came searching 10 Rillington Place? While the bodies remained undiscovered, there was always the risk that Chief Superintendent Barrett or Chief Inspector Jennings would have ordered the back garden to be dug up.

The killing of the baby

The only excuse for killing the baby came from Evans. He told Sergeant Trevallian, 'it was the constant crying of the baby got on my nerves' and he told Donald Hume, 'it was because the kid kept crying.'[32] Why, though, could the baby not have been passed to Ethel Christie or Evans' mother for immediate care with Evans claiming Beryl had left him?

Did Ethel Christie have any idea that her husband had killed Beryl Evans and/or the baby, and did she cover up for him?

Was Ethel Christie getting suspicious, and was this why the baby had to be killed?

Was it possible that Geraldine was strangled on the same day as her mother? Was this why she was not overheard crying on Wednesday 9th and Thursday 10th when her father was away at work?

Other issues not necessarily dependent on who killed Beryl

Why was Beryl Evans' body doubled-up? Why was it wrapped in a blanket and tablecloth and tied up into a bundle?

How would the effects of rigor mortis have impacted the timings of when Beryl's body could have been doubled up and then moved around the house? How would rigor mortis have impacted on Evans' statements?

Why was Beryl's body wrapped up and Geraldine's not wrapped? Why was the clothing on Beryl Evans' body dishevelled when Dr Teare commenced his post mortem?

Why were both Beryl's and the baby's stomachs empty at the time they were murdered?

If Christie moved Beryl's body to the wash-house before Evans left on 14th November, would he not have got Evans to assist him?

Could Christie's fibrositis, that started on Saturday 12th November, have been caused by something other than moving Beryl's body?

With fibrositis which was severe enough to have him referred to a specialist at St Mary's Hospital, how could Christie have moved Beryl's body to the wash-house after Saturday 12th?

If the bodies were moved to the wash-house by Christie or by Christie and Evans together, what was the long-term intention for a more permanent disposal of the bodies? Why, though, were the bodies not moved on?

When he departed 10 Rillington Place on Monday 14th November, why did Evans go to his family in Merthyr Vale? Why didn't he go somewhere else where he would not be known?

Was Christie prevented from getting rid of the baby's clothing and equipment because Ethel knew about them?

Evans claimed he went to the police at Merthyr Tydfil on 30th November because he was concerned about the safety of his daughter. So, why did DC Evans, who interviewed him and took down his statements, have to force Evans to disclose the child's supposed whereabouts?

When Evans went to the police and told them he had disposed of his wife's body, he must have realised the police would find the body sooner or later. But did he not have sufficient knowledge to understand that they would find out exactly how she had been killed?

Why did Evans, in the first instance, give the police a story that was misleading? Why would he have wanted to protect Christie?

If, before being interviewed at Notting Hill, Evans believed that his wife had died in a failed abortion and his baby was being cared for by a young couple in East Acton, why, when he found out that Christie had strangled his wife and daughter, did Evans confess? Would the natural reaction not have been to vehemently accuse Christie?

Could the circumstances of Evans' protracted period in custody and the shock of learning how his wife really died and that his daughter had been strangled as well, have laid him open to being 'brainwashed' into making a false confession?

Mrs Probert claimed that when she saw her son in prison on 4th December, he told her that the police had kept him up until 5a.m. on Saturday 3rd making him confess. Why did Evans' defence team at his trial not make a big issue out of that? Mr Morris needed to get the confession discredited. He had to show the jury it was not voluntary or that it was impossible. But he did neither.

Evans told his mother that Christie had done it. 'Get Christie. He's the only one who can save me now.' What did Evans mean when he said Christie could save him?

According to Mrs Ashby, Evans told her that Christie told him he should confess and he (Christie) would see to it that it would be all right. This implies Evans had something to confess. When, though, would Christie have said such a thing to Evans?

Why after Evans made the confession at Notting Hill to

Detective Chief Inspector Jennings and Detective Inspector Black and then confirmed it in other interviews with police, prison staff and doctors, did Evans wait 13 days until 15th December to withdraw it?

Do we know for sure whether it was Evans' tie, Christie's tie or Kitchener's tie around the baby's neck? Was there anything significant in the knot used?

Could Geraldine have been strangled with some other ligature? Did Christie put the tie around the baby's neck at a later time to implicate Evans?

Why did the police not seek to interview Evans further, once inconsistencies in his 'Notting Hill confession' came to light, especially with regard to the issue of how and when Beryl's body could have been moved to the wash-house? They had, though, charged him on 3rd December, so they were not entitled to interview him further.

Why did the police effectively force the plasterer and the labourer to alter their statements to make them more compliant with Evans' confession, rather than take their original statements at face value?

The prosecution service withheld key statements from the defence, including the statements (and timesheets) of the workmen and Mrs Vincent. They were entitled to do so if the Crown was not going to use them in its case. Why, though, did the defence not realise that the workmen had to have been important and request their statements anyhow?

If Evans told Father Francis on the evening before he was executed that he was innocent, why didn't the priest get his church to make this known?

Did Christie frame Evans for his crimes?

References Chapter 2

1. Dr Teare could not be that precise as to when Beryl and Geraldine were killed – J Eddowes, p117

2. Mrs Evans wanted to get rid of the child she was carrying – Evans' 'Merthyr 1' statement, J Eddowes, pp 46-7; Mrs Christie's first statement, J Eddowes, p193; Christie's first statement, J Eddowes,p202

3. Beryl Evans seen morning/lunchtime of Tuesday 8th November 1949 – Mrs Christie's first statement, J Eddowes, p194; Christie's first statement, J Eddowes, p202; Mr Jones' second statement, J Eddowes, p200

4. Evans working 8th, 9th and 10th November 1949 at Lancaster Food Products – Evans' 'Merthyr 1', 'Merthyr 2' and 'Notting Hill 2' statements; Christie's first and second statements; Mrs Christie's evidence, Trial of Evans, Jesse, p42. Evans sacked, Introduction, Jesse, p v

5. Christie visited Dr Odess on 8th November 1949. Dr Odess' records did not state whether he attended his morning or evening surgery – Brabin, p146

6. In a letter to Mrs Lynch, Evans' mother states Tim told her that Beryl and the baby have gone to Brighton - Trial of Evans, Jesse, p46

7. Evans tells the Christies on 9th November that Beryl and the baby have gone to Bristol – Evans' cross-examination, Trial of Evans, Jesse, p79; Mrs Christie's first statement, J Eddowes, p194; Christie's first statement, J Eddowes, pp 202-3

8. Rags torn up – Evans' 'Merthyr 2' statement, Trial of Evans, Jesse, p51; DC Evans interview with Evans on morning of 1st December, Trial of Evans, Jesse, p52

9. Baby's things left with Christie till recovered by the police – Evans' 'Merthyr 2' statement, Trial of Evans, Jesse, p52; Christie's first statement, J Eddowes, p203

10. Evans sold furniture to Mr Hookway – both Evans' Merthyr statements and his 'Notting Hill 2' statement, Trial of Evans, Jesse, p48, pp 51-2, pp 56-7; Christie's first statement, J Eddowes, p203

11. Evans in Merthyr – Evans' examination and cross-examination, Trial of Evans, Jesse, pp 70-1, p79; Mrs Lynch's court testimony, Trial of Evans, Jesse, p45

12. Evans sold wife's wedding ring and told DI Black he had done so – Brabin, p79

13. Evans relaxed in Merthyr Vale and spoke fondly of Geraldine – Brabin, pp 44-52

14. Evans return visit to see Christie on 23rd November – Christie's and Evans' evidence at Evans' trial – Trial of Evans, Jesse, p20, pp 70-1

15. On returning from London, Evans gave the Lynches a new story about what had happened to Beryl and Geraldine – Mrs Lynch's evidence, Trial of Evans, Jesse, p45

16. Mrs Probert's letter to Mrs Lynch – Exhibit 5 read out in court, Trial of Evans, Jesse, p46

17. Both Evans' Merthyr statements read out in court during DC Evans' examination – Trial of Evans, Jesse, pp 46-8, pp 48-52

18. Police search of 10 Rillington Place on 1st December 1949 – Brabin, pp 21-2; Introduction, Jesse, p xiv

19. Bodies found in the search of 10 Rillington Place on 2nd December 1949 – DCI Jennings' evidence, Trial of Evans, Jesse, p53

20. Dr Teare's post mortem reports on Beryl and Geraldine Evans – Camps, pp 226-8

21. Evans brought back from Merthyr to London – Brabin, pp 64-7

22. Evans brought back to Notting Hill Police Station. Bundles in the interview room and comments from DCI Jennings – evidence of DCI Jennings and DI Black, Trial of Evans, Jesse, pp 53-4, pp 59-60

23. Evans' 'Notting Hill 2' statement – Exhibit 9, Trial of Evans, Jesse, pp 54-7

24. Evans charged with murdering his wife – Brabin, pp 79-80

25. Evans partially repeats his confession to Dr Matheson on being remanded to Brixton Prison – Brabin, pp 87-90; Scott Henderson Report, Appendix II, Jesse, p312

26. Evans' mother visits him in prison on 4th December 1949 – Brabin, p91

27. Hume's 1958 account of speaking with Evans at Brixton Prison as they both awaited trial – Hoskins, pp 42-44

28. Evans withdraws confession on 15th December 1949 – Introduction, Jesse, pp xx-xxi

29. Evans' magistrate court appearances on 15th and 22nd December – Introduction, Jesse, p xxi; Brabin, p97

30. Withholding of workmen's statements from the defence – Furneaux, p70

31. Transcript of Evans' Trial – Trial of Evans, Jesse, pp 1-117

32. Evans tells Trevallian and Hume baby killed because it would not stop crying – J Eddowes, p67; Hoskins, p43

Chapter 3

Evans' Statements to the Police at Merthyr

Evans made four key statements to the police – two in Merthyr Tydfil ('Merthyr 1' and 'Merthyr 2') and two at Notting Hill ('NH1' and 'NH2'). These statements are extremely important and are set out in full in this chapter and chapter 5, with commentary and debate. As Evans could not read or write, all the statements were written down by police officers and read back to him before he signed.

First Statement – Merthyr, Wednesday 30th November[1]

In 'Merthyr 1' Evans claimed to have disposed of his wife down a drain at 10 Rillington Place.

Made to Detective Sergeant Gough and Detective Constable Evans, Merthyr Tydfil Central Police Station, 3.20 p.m. to 5.10 p.m.

'About the beginning of October, my wife, Beryl Susanna Evans, told me that she was expecting a baby. She told me that she was about three months gone. I said, "If you are having a baby, well you've had one, another one won't make any difference."

Commentary – Dr Teare confirmed in his post mortem that Beryl Evans was about 16 weeks pregnant at the time of her death.[2]

'She then told me she was going to try and get rid of it. I turned round and told her not to be silly, that she'd make herself ill. Then she bought herself a syringe and started syringing herself. Then she said that didn't work and I said, "I'm glad it won't work."

Commentary – There was evidence of old bruising on the anterior wall of the vagina according to Dr Teare. This could have been consistent with Beryl having tried to induce an abortion using a syringe. [2] *Ludovic Kennedy, in his book* Ten Rillington Place – *see Chapter 14 – took issue with what Dr Teare supposedly said. He argued that, at the magistrate's hearing on 15th December 1949, Dr Teare said that the bruise in Beryl's vagina 'could have been caused by an attempt at forced intercourse or in a struggle.' Kennedy referenced this to the* West London Observer, *16th and 23rd December 1949.* [3] *He claimed that 'here was the vital missing link between Evans' claim that Christie had done it, and the reason why he had done it.'* [4] *Dr Teare countered Kennedy, stating that he 'said nothing in the Magistrates' Court about post mortem penetration or intercourse.'* [5] *The eminent pathologist, Professor Keith Simpson, who was present when Dr Frances Camps performed a second post mortem on Beryl Evans in 1953, and saw the bruising in question, stated that Dr Teare did say what Kennedy quoted but that Dr Teare later thought the bruising 'had more probably been a self-inflicted injury caused by a syringe.'* [6]

Kennedy also criticised Dr Teare for not taking a vaginal swab for testing. He claimed 'had he done so, he would almost certainly have found traces of Christie's spermatozoa.' [7] *Professor Keith Simpson, castigated Kennedy for his accusation against Dr Teare, stating 'I doubt if a more reckless over-statement can be found in all the millions of words written about the Evans-Christie case.'* [8] *In a footnote to his account of the Evans-Christie case in his 2002 book* Thirty-Six Murders & Two Immoral Earnings, *Kennedy backtracked: 'Dr Teare, the pathologist, found bruising in the wall of Beryl's vagina. In my book I said that if he had taken a swab from there, he would probably have found traces of Christie's sperm. I now think this unlikely.'* [9]

'Then she said she was going to buy some tablets. I don't know what tablets she bought because she was always hiding them from me. She started to look very ill and I told her to go and see a doctor and she said she'd go when I was in work but when I'd come home and ask her if she'd been she'd always say that she hadn't.'

Commentary – Mrs Christie's first witness statement to the police on 1st December 1949 aligned with Evans but went further in terms of Beryl wanting the baby aborted and her looking very ill.[10]

'On the Sunday morning that would be the sixth of November she told me that if she couldn't get rid of the baby she'd kill herself and our baby Geraldine. I told her she was talking silly.'

'She never said no more about it then, but when I got up Monday morning to go to work she said she was going to see some woman to see if she could help her. Who the woman was she didn't tell me and that if she wasn't in when I came home she'd be up her grandmother's.'

'Then I went to work. I loaded up my van and went on my journey. About 9 o'clock that morning I pulled up at a transport café between Ipswich and Colchester. I can't say exactly where it is, that's the nearest I can give. I went up to the counter and ordered a cup of tea and breakfast and I sat down by the table with my cup of tea waiting for my breakfast to come up and there was a man sitting by the table opposite me. He asked me if I had a cigarette I could give him. I gave him one and he started talking about married life. He said to me, "You are looking pretty worried, is there anything on your mind?" Then I told him all about it. So he said, "Don't let that worry you I can give you something that can fix it." So he said, "Wait there a minute, I'll be back," and he went outside. When he came back he handed me a little bottle that was wrapped up in brown paper. He said, "Tell your wife to take it first thing in the morning before she has any tea, and then to lay down on the bed for a couple of hours and that should do the job." He never asked no money for it. I went up to the counter and paid my bill and carried on with my journey.'

Commentary – This whole story of meeting a man in a transport café and obtaining a substance to induce an abortion gives the impression of having been made up. Why would Evans so readily have given away such intimate information to a complete stranger? Why would the stranger not want money for the treatment? In any case, Evans admitted this story was untrue right at the start of his 'Merthyr 2' statement. So, what else did Evans fabricate?

'After I finished my work I went home, that would be between seven and eight. When I got in the house I took off my overcoat and hung it on the peg behind the kitchen door. My wife asked me for a cigarette and I told her there was one in my pocket, then she found this bottle in my pocket and I told her about it.'

'Then I had my tea and sat down and read the papers and listened to the wireless. We went to bed at ten o'clock.'

Commentary – these two sentences were omitted by Ludovic Kennedy in his book Ten Rillington Place.[11] *That Evans could read at all did not fit his argument.*

'I got up in the morning as usual at six o'clock to go to work. I made myself a cup of tea and made a feed for the baby. I told her then not to take that stuff when I went in and said, "Good morning" to her and I went to work, that would be about half past six.'

Commentary – Evans sidetracked into describing what was his likely daily routine. He did that in other parts of 'Merthyr 1' and in 'Merthyr 2' and 'NH2'. The sidetracking did not seem to be because he was fabricating. He did have remarkable recall.

'I finished work and got home at half past six in the evening. I then noticed that there was no light in the place. I lit the gas and it started to go out and I went in the bedroom to get a penny and I noticed my baby in the cot. I put the penny in the gas and went back in the bedroom and lit the gas in the bedroom. Then I saw my wife laying in the bed. I spoke to her but she never answered me, so I went over and shook her, then I could see she wasn't breathing.

Then I went and made some food for my baby. I fed my baby and I sat up all night.'

Commentary – If a husband came home and found his wife lying on the bed and not breathing, his immediate reaction would be to seek help. Evans could have sought the help of the Christies, the ambulance service or his family who lived nearby. A normal husband would not just leave her there, feed the baby, sit up all night and do nothing. According to this story, Evans had done nothing wrong as Beryl's death was through her own misadventure.

'Between about one and two in the morning I got my wife downstairs through the front door. I opened the drain outside my front door, that is No. 10 Rillington Place, and pushed her body head first into the drain. I closed the drain then I went back into the house. I sat down by the fire smoking a cigarette.'

Commentary – Evans could not have opened the drain. Beryl's body was not put in the drain. Around the time Evans was supposed to be moving his wife's body to the front drain, both Christie and Mrs Christie stated they heard movements overhead that were likened to furniture being moved.[12]

'I never went to work the following day. I went and got my baby looked after. Then I went and told my governor where I worked that I was leaving. He asked me the reason and I told him I had a better job elsewhere. I had my cards and money that afternoon then I went to see a man about selling my furniture.'

Commentary – Evans' employers confirmed that he continued to work until the evening of Thursday 10th November. Evans drew the £5 that his wife should have collected from his employer the previous day. There was a row with his boss, Mr Adler, about how the money would get to Mrs Evans. Mr Adler was already dissatisfied with Evans' missed deliveries and summarily sacked him. Evans was to collect what was owing to him and his cards next day. Evans no longer had access to a van.[13] Evans was silent on the important matter of just how he 'got my baby looked after.'

'The man came down and had a look at my furniture and he offered me £40 for it. So I accepted the £40 for it. He told me he wouldn't be able to collect the furniture until Monday morning.'

'In the meanwhile I went and told my mother that my wife and baby had gone for a holiday. I stopped in the flat till Monday. The van come Monday afternoon and cleared the stuff out. He paid me the money. Then I caught the five to one train from Paddington and I come down to Merthyr Vale and I've been down here ever since. That's the lot.'

Commentary – Mrs Christie and Christie both referred to Evans selling his furniture in their statements. Christie quoted the amount Evans received as £60. Evans' mother, Mrs Probert, in her letter to Mrs Lynch (received 30th November 1949) confirmed that the furniture had gone from Evans' flat. [15]

(Signed) T.J. Evans

DC Evans took down Evans' statement and afterwards commented on what happened. Evans took a long time over his statement. (Evans' mother had said Evans spoke quickly when truthful and slowly when lying.) DC Evans believed he was a 'terrible liar' and he was 'telling a cock and bull story'.[16] The following critical inter-action took place between DC Evans and Timothy Evans, after Evans made his first Merthyr statement - as set out in Sir Daniel Brabin's 1966 report.

'DC Evans was anxious about the baby referred to in the statement and he thought Evans was unconcerned about her and said so. The officer became annoyed with Evans and asked about the whereabouts of the child. The answer was evasive. Evans said that she was somewhere in London with friends. When pressed for fuller details, Evans said that he had told his aunt, Mrs Lynch, with whom he had been staying, that the baby was with some friends from Newport, and it was the police officer's view that he was expected to believe this also. The officer said that Evans did not want to talk about the child at all. Eventually Evans said that the child had been handed over to Reginald Christie who lived at 10 Rillington Place. Evans was put under arrest on suspicion of having committed a felony.[17]

The Merthyr police then contacted the Metropolitan police advising on what Evans had stated, including that the child had been handed over to Reginald Christie. The Notting Hill police followed up these leads.

Debate: Questions and Implications arising from Evans' 'Merthyr 1' statement

Why did Evans go to the Merthyr police on the afternoon of 30th November 1949 and tell them he had put his wife's body down the drain?

Did the letter Mrs Lynch received that morning from Evans' mother trigger it? In that letter Mrs Probert:
- warned Mrs Lynch Evans had been lying to her,
- stated she had not seen Evans in three weeks and Beryl and the baby in four,
- added that Evans had told her Beryl and the baby had gone to her father in Brighton,
- wanted to find out about the furniture which had disappeared from his flat,
  Commentary – for which she stood as guarantor.
- indicated she now disowned him,
- mentioned he had packed up a good job,
- stated that his name stank and people wanted to see him to recover what he owed them.[15]

Did this letter, which Mrs Lynch read to him at the breakfast table, coming on top of him having gone back to Rillington Place to meet Christie on 23rd November, make Evans realise that his position was now untenable? His standing with the Lynches was now undermined. There would be big trouble if he tried to return to his family and his creditors in west London. Perhaps seeing Christie again had alarmed him. With no income and the £40 he got for the furniture running out, he could no longer stay with his aunt, but he had nowhere else to go. His world had closed in.

If he had not killed his wife and he believed the baby was either still alive or knew Christie had strangled the child, it was time to go to the police and sort it all out. What Evans later told Mr Christmas Humphreys at his trial, 'Well, I was getting worried about my daughter', made sense. But if he was a killer, he was naive in not realising he was endangering his own life in going to the police.

If he went to the police because he was concerned about his daughter, why was that not right up front in what he told the Merthyr police? His first words to the police were not about the welfare of the baby. They were recorded as 'I have disposed of my wife. I put her down the drain.'[18] In actual fact this was a lie. In the first statement that was then taken, he only mentioned the baby in the context of feeding her, seeing her in the cot and arranging for her to be looked after. There was no expression of concern for the baby's current welfare.

Firstly, consider Evans' 'Merthyr 1' statement from the point of view that he had killed his wife and/or his daughter.

Why make a statement that would arouse the police's suspicions, uncover the fact that his wife and the baby were missing and quickly reveal Evans' account to be untrue? The police would inevitably find that his wife's body was not in the drain, but

that his wife and daughter had been missing for some time. This would set in motion a search that would sooner or later lead to Beryl's body being found. They would ascertain that Beryl did not poison herself and the child she was carrying had not been interfered with. They would find she had been strangled. On top of this,

Evans had fled 10 Rillington Place.

Evans had effectively opened the Pandora's box that could very well take him to the gallows. If Evans was a killer, it remained difficult to understand why he initially gave the police such a concocted story. Further, the idea that Evans did concoct the story to alert the police as a prelude to then trying to put the blame onto Christie implied mental subtlety well beyond Evans' capabilities. While the police considered Evans 'quite worldly'[19], the Principal Medical Officer at Brixton Prison who assessed his sanity, considered him 'an inadequate psychopathic personality with schizoid traits… tends always to want to get his own way and who will act without any foresight, regardless of possible consequences to himself.'[20]

Secondly, consider Evans' first statement from the point of view that he did not kill his wife and he believed Geraldine was still alive and being cared for in East Acton.

When Evans went to the police, did he consider that his wife had died sort of accidentally, albeit in an illegal abortion, but the baby was safe. His only offence was that he had conspired in covering up his wife's death.

The story about his wife taking pills to induce an abortion but instead they poisoned her could indeed have been an attempt to cover for Christie's supposed failed abortion.

The story that Evans disposed of his wife's body in the drain could reflect that he left her body to be disposed of by Christie and Christie told him that was what he would do with her.

The accounts of Evans covering up Beryl's killing by telling his mother that his wife and child had gone on holiday and of him selling up and leaving 10 Rillington Place were substantially true. But if his prime concern was the current welfare of his baby, he did not raise that in the statement. As already stated, Geraldine was only mentioned in terms of her being fed, of her being in her cot and of Evans getting her looked after.

Even if he had told the police that his wife had killed herself trying to abort her second child and he had disposed of the body and arranged for the child to be looked after, why did he not say next that he was now very concerned over the child's safety and welfare? That would have got the main message – the child's welfare – across and still covered for Christie. That he didn't do it this way could well suggest that he knew the child's welfare was not the issue.

This opens the door to another point of view from which Evans first statement can be considered: that Evans had not killed his wife but was a passive, even unwitting, participant in a joint enterprise with Christie in which Geraldine was strangled. This would seem to be more consistent with the fact that Evans expressed no concern at all for the welfare of his child because he knew the baby was already dead. Evans, though, would not consider he was responsible for the child's death as he knew nothing of the concept of joint enterprise in English criminal law.

On balance, 'Merthyr 1' appears most consistent with Evans not knowing that his baby was already dead.

The Notting Hill police, after further persistence from DC Evans, followed up on the information received from the Merthyr police. They replied that it required three men to open the drain at Rillington Place and there was no body in the drain,[21]

When Evans was told there was no body in the drain and that they did not believe he could have opened it, he provided a second statement ('Merthyr 2').

Second Statement – Merthyr, Wednesday 30th November [22]

The 'Merthyr 2' statement heavily involved Christie in his wife's death and the baby being cared for. Evans, though, did not make accusations of murder against his neighbour.

Made to Detective Sergeant Gough and Detective Constable Evans, Merthyr Tydfil Central Police Station, 9.10 p.m. to 11.50 p.m. Wednesday 30th November 1949.

'The only thing that is not true in the statement I made to you this afternoon is the part about meeting the man in the café and about disposing of my wife's body. All the rest is true.'

Commentary – but there was more that was not true, particularly how his wife was supposed to have died. While some threads of 'Merthyr 1' were pulled through, 'Merthyr 2' was radically different and far more comprehensive.

'As I was coming home from work one night, that would be about a week before my wife died, Reg Christie, who lived on the ground floor below us, approached me and said, "I'd like to have a chat with you about your wife taking these tablets. I know what she's taking them for, she's trying to get rid of the baby. If you or your wife had come to me in the first place I could have done it for you without any risk." I turned around and said, "Well I didn't think you knew anything about medical stuff!" So he told me then that he was training for a doctor before the war. Then he started showing me books and things on medical. I was just as wise because I couldn't understand one word because I couldn't read. Then he told me that the stuff that he used one out of every ten would die with it. I told him that I wasn't interested so I said goodnight to him and I went upstairs.'

Commentary – Christie did have an old St John's Ambulance Brigade Handbook confirmed by himself and Ethel Christie at Evans' trial.[23] This raises the question of how Evans, who could not read, knew that if Christie hadn't shown it to him?

The police looked into whether Mrs Christie and Christie were abortionists. If Mrs Christie had been, why did she not offer an abortion to Beryl? The police searched the Christies' flat in December 1949 and found no abortion paraphernalia.²⁴ Only an old syringe came to light, a likely find in many homes in the immediate post-war years.

'When I got in my wife started talking to me about it. She said that she had been speaking to Mr Christie and asked me if he had spoken to me. I said "Yes" and I told her what he had spoke to me about. I turned round and told her that I told him I didn't want nothing to do with it and I told her she wasn't to have anything to do with it either. She turned round and told me to mind my own business and that she intended to get rid of it and that she trusted Mr Christie. She said he could do the job without any trouble at all.

'On the Monday evening, that was the seventh of November, when I came home from work my wife said that Mr Christie had made the arrangements for first thing Tuesday morning. I didn't argue with her, I just washed and changed and went to the K.P.H. [Evans' favourite local pub] until 10 o'clock. I came home and had supper and went to bed. She wanted to start an argument but I just took no notice. Just after six I got up the following morning to go to work. My wife got up with me. I had a cup of tea and a smoke and she told me, "On your way down tell Mr Christie that everything is all right. If you don't tell him I'll go down and tell him myself." So as I went down the stairs he came out to meet me and I said, "Everything is all right." Then I went to work.'

Commentary – Setting up the abortion worked in with details of domestic routines did give the impression of authenticity.

'When I came home in the evening he was waiting for me at the bottom of the staircase. He said, "Go on upstairs I'll come behind you!" When I lit the gas in the kitchen he said, "It's bad news. It didn't work!" I asked him where was she, He said, "Laying on the bed in the bedroom." Then I asked him where was the baby? So he said, "The baby's in the cot." So I went in the bedroom, I lit the gas, then I saw the curtains had been drawn. I looked at my wife and saw that she was covered over with the eiderdown. I pulled the eiderdown back to have a look at her. I could see that she was dead and that she had been bleeding from the mouth and nose and that she had been bleeding from the bottom part. She had a black skirt on and a check blouse and a kind of a light blue jacket on. Christie was in the kitchen.'

Commentary - Evans' description of how he found his wife was in accordance with Dr Teare's post mortem on one key point. In his post mortem report, Dr Teare described what Beryl Evans' was wearing when she died and it was closely aligned to what Evans described in 'Merthyr 2'. Dr Teare reported that Mrs Evans' face and neck were bloated and swollen and that there was 'some exudation of sanguineous fluid from the mouth and nostrils.' This was out of line with Evans' description in 'Merthyr 2'. Dr Teare did not report on any blood from the bottom part, which he certainly would have done had there been any. The pathologists who conducted the second post mortem on Beryl's exhumed body in 1953 confirmed Dr Teare's findings.[25]

At his trial, Evans changed the narrative in respect of the bleeding from his wife's mouth, nose and bottom part. Whereas in this statement, he pulled the eiderdown back and could see she had been bleeding, under examination from his counsel, Malcolm Morris, Evans stated that his wife was wrapped in the eiderdown and he did not move it; she was lying on her right and there was blood on the pillowslip and on the bottom of the eiderdown.[26] *Whereas Evans' 'Merthyr 2' statement was inconsistent with Dr Teare's findings, his trial evidence was adjusted to a possible fit.*

As Evans stated later in this statement, the eiderdown and, presumably, the pillowslip were cut up and put in the sacks given to the man who took them away before Evans left 10 Rillington Place.[27]

If this account was true, why did Evans not realise Christie had been deceiving him when he saw the blood – and swelling and bruising – on Beryl's face? If Evans had gone to the police then, the post mortem would have been able to determine that Beryl died when Evans was away at work, implicating Christie.

There are lines of argument that suggest Evans' account here was fabricated. When Evans came home, Christie should have been away seeing his doctor. Christie supposedly went to see Dr Odess at his evening surgery on that Tuesday.[28] Leaving that aside, Evans had Christie in the kitchen when he went to view his wife's body. Christie could not allow Evans to view the body without him being present to control what Evans could see and provide explanations. Evans, though, did state seeing a lot of detail of his wife's injuries, but how could he not have noticed the strangulation weal on her neck?

'I went over and picked my baby up. I wrapped the baby in a blanket and took her in the kitchen. In the meanwhile Mr Christie had lit the fire in the kitchen. He said, "I'll speak to you after you feed the baby." So I made the baby some tea and boiled an egg for her, then I changed the baby and put her to sit in front of the fire. Then I asked him how long my wife had been dead. He said, "Since about three o'clock." Then he told me that my wife's stomach was septic poisoned. He said, "Another day and she'd have to have gone to hospital." I asked him what he had done but he wouldn't tell me. He then told me to stop in the kitchen and he closed the door and went out.'

Commentary – again Evans is very detailed on what he did caring for the baby and in relating his conversation with Christie. Would he have been able to invent the part about septic poisoned and her having to have gone to hospital?

'He came back about a quarter of an hour later and told me that he had forced the door of Mr Kitchener's flat and had put my wife's body in there. I asked him what he intended to do and he said, "I'll dispose of it down one of the drains!" He then said, "You'd better go to bed and leave the rest to me." He said, "Get up and go to work as usual in the morning," and that he'd see about getting someone to look after my baby. I told him that it was foolish to try to dispose of the body and he said, "Well that's the only thing I can do or otherwise I'll get in trouble with the police." He then left me.'

Commentary – again Evans was very detailed on what happened and his conversation with Christie. But, according to his trial evidence, a lot was left out of the account of how his wife's body was moved down the stairs from the second-floor bedroom to Mr Kitchener's first floor flat. Steered through his evidence by Mr Morris, Evans stated that, while in his kitchen with the door closed, he heard Christie puffing and blowing on the stairs. He opened the door and saw Christie shifting Beryl's body down the staircase. Evans helped Christie carry the body into the kitchen of Mr Kitchener's flat. Evans did not see his wife's body again.[29] This raises the question – why did Evans leave out that he moved his wife's body, if 'Merthyr 2' was the truth?

'Before I went to bed I took the eiderdown and one blanket off the bed and put them in a cupboard in the bedroom.'

Comment – Why did Evans make this curious comment? Was it that the eiderdown and blanket were stained with blood?

'I got up next morning about six o'clock. I made myself a cup of tea and made the baby some breakfast and fed her and changed her and put her back into her cot. Christie had told me that he was going to look after the baby that day so I went to work. I saw Christie before I went and he told me that he would slip up and feed the baby during the day. I had wanted to take the baby to my mother the night before but he said not to as it would cause suspicion straight away. He also told me in the morning that he knew a young couple over in East Acton who would look after the baby and he'd go over and see them.'

Commentary – If Christie was caring for the baby when Evans was at work would he really have reduced the baby's crying? The baby must have been missing her mother and, at thirteen months old, the baby's crying would have been quite loud. How did Mrs Christie not hear the crying and realise that something was wrong? She did state that she needed to be part way up the stairs to hear the baby crying. Furthermore, if Christie was involved over the period, Tuesday 8th to Thursday 10th November, he would have been up and down the stairs to the second floor, tending to Beryl, talking to Evans and tending to the baby. So, if this was Christie's behaviour, how did he disguise it from his wife?

Mrs Christie did state that she spoke to Evans late on Wednesday 9th November and he told her that 'she [his wife] had gone away with the baby to stay with friends in Bristol.' [31] *At his trial, Evans admitted under cross-examination that he had lied to Mrs Christie and others. But he added, he 'did it on the advice of Mr Christie.'* [32]

The risk for Christie and Evans must have been enormous. Mrs Christie could easily have ventured up the stairs - curious that her husband kept going up or because she became aware of incessant crying. On the stairs her suspicion could have been confirmed and she would then have gone on up to check what was going on. She would have found the baby alone in her cot and Beryl missing. She would have tended to the baby and raised the alarm.

There was no credible evidence that Mrs Christie covered up for her husband and Evans in the aftermath of Beryl Evans' killing.

'When I came home from work on that Wednesday night at about five or six, Christie told me that the young couple from East Acton would be in Thursday to take the baby. I fed the baby that night and was playing with her by the fire when Christie came in. He said, "In the morning when you get up feed the baby and dress her then put her back in the cot, the people will be here just after nine in the morning to fetch her." He said, "I've told them to knock three knocks and I'll let them in." He also told me to pack some clothes for the baby. I did all that in the morning before I went to work. I saw him as I was going out that morning about half past six and told him what I had done.'

Commentary – The plan was heavily flawed. How, in the early morning, were two strangers, knocking three times and taking away the baby and her things, not going to be noticed by Mrs Christie and the neighbours? Worse, Mrs Christie had been told just the evening before that Beryl and the baby were in Bristol. [31]

Supposing Christie deceived Evans with the plan to clear his way to kill the baby, to either eliminate the risk she offered of the early detection of Beryl's killing or simply because he was a psychopath. Dr Teare reported that the baby's stomach was 'quite empty' when she was killed. The expectation would have been that it would have taken some two to two and a half hours for a thirteen-month-old child's stomach to empty after a feed. Thus Evans would have fed the baby before he went to work on Thursday 10th November and Christie would have left her crying in the cot for over two hours after Evans left before killing her. Would he have done that?

But what could Christie do with the child's body to ensure Evans did not come across it? Perhaps he also hid Geraldine's body in Mr Kitchener's flat, but well away from Beryl's body that was supposedly left in the kitchen.

What happened to the clothes that Evans was supposed to have packed? Were they in Kitchener's flat with the baby's body until Christie could dump them? Were they with the baby's things that were eventually recovered by the police?

'About half past five that evening I came home. I went upstairs and as I got in the kitchen, he came up behind me. He told me that the people had called and took the baby with them and to pack the rest of her things and he had a case and would take them over to East Acton with the pram and her chair later in the week. I then asked him how did he dispose of my wife's body. He said he put it down one of the drains. That's all he said to me then he went downstairs.'

Commentary – Why wouldn't the couple in East Acton have wanted the pram and chair when they collected the child on the Thursday morning?

Why was Evans not suspicious that Christie did not collect the pram and high chair from him later in the week and take them away? Instead, later in this statement, Evans stated that the pram, small chair and a case of baby clothes were given to Christie on Monday 14th November, just before Evans departed Rillington Place.

'Later that evening I went around to see my mother, Mrs Thomasina Probert, at No. 11, St. Marks Road, London, W.11. She asked me where Beryl and the baby was. I told her they had gone away on a holiday.'

Commentary – Evans' mother, Mrs Probert, confirmed in her letter to Mrs Lynch, that Evans had told her Beryl and the baby had gone to Brighton. [35]

'When I left my mother's place that night l went up to the K.P.H to have a drink. I didn't go to work on the Friday as I had finished there on Thursday. On that Thursday evening Christie said, "Now the best thing you can do is to sell your furniture and get out of London somewhere." I just said, "All right."

Commentary – Evans did not mention that he had been sacked after work on the Thursday.

If Christie was involved in the killings, it made good sense to get Evans to leave his flat. Christie could then tell anyone following up on what had happened to the Evanses that they had gone away. There would be no need to search 10 Rillington Place or the garden.

'On the Friday I went up to see a man in Portobello Road about selling my furniture. He came down on the Friday afternoon and said it was worth £40. He told me he would pick it up on the following Monday. On the Friday I went to the pictures and the pub, then went home to sleep. On the Saturday I did the same thing. On Sunday afternoon I went to see a rag dealer. I met him outside a café in Ladbroke Grove, that's where he lives. I told him that if he came down to my place on the Monday there was quite a lot of rags he could have.'

'I got up about six o'clock on the Monday morning and ripped up all my wife's clothes and the eiderdown and cut up the blanket. The man came around just after nine o'clock and he took about two sacks full and I didn't take nothing off him for them.'

'About three o'clock the furniture van came. They cleared all the furniture out and the bed clothes and lino and the furniture man paid me £40 which I signed for. The only things left in the house then was the vases, a clock, some dishes, saucepans and a bucket and the case with the baby's clothes, her pram and small chair. Christie had all that stuff. He asked me where I was going to go and I told him I didn't know. Then I got my case, I took it up to Paddington, left it in the luggage department until half past twelve that evening.'

'I went to the pictures and a pub and then I went to Paddington again and picked up my case about half past twelve that evening and caught the five to one train to Cardiff. I got into Merthyr Vale about twenty to seven in the morning, then went to 93 Mount Pleasant, and I've been there ever since.'

Commentary – Evans left out that he returned to London on Wednesday 23rd November when he visited 10 Rillington Place and met Christie. He never mentioned the visit in any of his four statements. He mentioned at his trial he did return on 23rd November to see Christie and find out about his daughter. Evans stated that Christie told him he should wait two or three weeks before he should see her, 'to give her time to settle in.' [36] *Christie claimed that when he called, Evans said he had been looking for work but had been unsuccessful. Christie claimed Evans told Mrs Christie that his own wife 'was all right but she had walked out on him,'* [37] *Mrs Christie stated that she only heard about Evans' visit from her husband.* [38]

(Signed) T.J. EVANS

'This statement was made to me between 9.10 pm and 11.50 pm

on Wednesday 30th November 1949, at the Criminal Investigation Department, Central Police Station, Merthyr Tydfil. It was read over to Evans in the presence of Detective Sergeant Gough before he signed it as being true.

(Signed) G. H. EVANS. D/Cons. 53 (Signed)

G. H. GOUGH. D/Sgt.'

Debate: Questions and implications arising from Evans' 'Merthyr 2' statement

'Merthyr 2' was triggered by the Metropolitan Police reporting back to the Merthyr Police that there was no way Evans could have opened the drain outside 10 Rillington Place and, in any case, there was no body down the drain. 'Merthyr 1' was exposed as false, so Evans volunteered a second statement.

Firstly, consider 'Merthyr 2' from the standpoint that Evans had killed his wife. Evans distanced himself from the deed and implicated Christie in her death. The account was plausible, subtly blending domestic detail and fabricated events. But would a man so lacking in education have been able to compose such a fiction that was consistent and plausible?

Secondly, consider 'Merthyr 2' from the standpoint of joint enterprise in killing the child. Evans substituted an account of Christie arranging to place Geraldine with the young couple in East Acton when Evans would have been there to see Christie strangle the child on the evening of Wednesday 8th November. Evans would have wanted to distance himself from the child's murder rather than admit he stood idly by. Again, though, would a man who was lacking in education have been able to compose such a fiction that was consistent and plausible?

Thirdly, consider 'Merthyr 2' from the standpoint that Evans did not kill his wife and he believed Geraldine was still alive. Again, plausible. It would become the basis of Evans' defence at his trial. Christie had manipulated Evans, but Evans had not killed anyone. He was only guilty of covering up his wife's death.

Evans' mother stated that, 'when Tim was lying he was very hesitant; if he was speaking the truth he would go straight on.'[39] The words, timing and word rate for the three main statements were:

'Merthyr 1': 982 words taken down and read back to Evans in 110 minutes. Indicative rate of 9 words per minute;

'Merthyr 2': 1,744 words taken down and read back to Evans in 160 minutes by DC Evans. Indicative rate of 10.9 words per minute;

'NH 2': 2,017 words taken down and read back to Evans in 80 minutes by DI Black. Indicative rate of 25 words per minute.

Prima facie, 'NH2' was more reliable than either of the Merthyr statements. Of course the words per minute rates could well have been affected by the different police interviewing techniques at Merthyr and Notting Hill and the scribing abilities of DC Evans and DI Black. In any case, there should have been no police questioning at Notting Hill given the voluntary nature of the statement.

References Chapter 3

1.   Evans' first Merthyr statement – J Eddowes, pp 46-9

2.   Dr Teare's post mortem report on Beryl Evans – Camps, pp 226-7

3.   Kennedy's exaggerations on Dr Teare – Kennedy 10RP, p136

4.   Kennedy's vital missing link – Kennedy 10RP, p137

5.   Dr Teare countered Kennedy – J Eddowes, p117

6.   Simpson clarified Dr Teare – Simpson, p196

7.   Kennedy criticised Dr Teare for not taking a sperm sample – Kennedy 10RP, p101

8. Simpson castigated Kennedy – Simpson, p196

9. Kennedy footnote – Kennedy 36 Murders, p25

10. Mrs Christie's first statement – J Eddowes, pp 192-3

11. Evans reading papers omitted by Kennedy – Kennedy 10RP, p88

12. Christies hear bumps overhead – Christie's second statement, J Eddowes, p205; Mrs Christie's second statement, J Eddowes, p195

13. Evans loses his job on 10th November – J Eddowes, pp 30-1

14. Christies' statements confirm Evans sold his furniture – J Eddowes, p194 and pp 205-6

15. Mrs Proberts' letter to her brother's sister in which, among other things, she exposed the mystery over the disappearance of Evans' furniture – J Eddowes, p44

16. DC Evans comments on taking down Timothy Evans' first statement – Oates, p62

17. DC Evans presses Evans for whereabouts of child and Evans' arrest – Brabin, pp 5-6

18. Evans first words to the Merthyr police – Introduction, Jesse, p viii

19. Police view of Evans' capability – Oates, p72

20. Dr Matheson's view on Evans' sanity – Brabin, p90

21. Metropolitan Police inform Merthyr Police of the difficulty of opening the drain and there being no body – Brabin, pp 6-8

22. Evans' second Merthyr statement – J Eddowes, pp 50-4

23. Christie and Mrs Christie both confirm Christie had a St John's Ambulance Brigade handbook – Trial of Evans, Jesse, pp 25-6 and p43

24. Police check whether the Christies were abortionists – Oates, p77 (his reference, National Archive MEP03/3147)

25. Camps confirms Dr Teare's findings following 1953 exhumation and second post mortem – Camps, pp 44-5

26. Evans changes account of blood on wife's body – Trial of Evans, Jesse, p64-5

27. Evans cuts up clothes and bedding and gives materials away – Later in 'Merthyr 2'

28. Christie at Dr Odess' evening surgery on Tuesday 8th November – J Eddowes, p26

29. Evans changes account of moving wife's body to Mr Kitchener's flat – Trial of Evans, Jesse, p66

30. Mrs Christie needed to be part way up the stairs to hear the baby crying – Mrs Christie's second statement, Eddowes, pp 195-6

31. Evans tells Mrs Christie, late Wednesday 9th November, Beryl and the baby have gone to Bristol – Mrs Christie's first statement, J Eddowes, p194

32. Evans admits lying about Beryl and Geraldine – Trial of Evans, Jesse, p80

33. Dr Teare's post mortem report on Geraldine Evans – Camps, pp 227-8

34. Two to two and a half hours for Geraldine's stomach to empty – Bonner JJ, Vajjah P, Abduljalil K, et al. 'Does age affect gastric emptying time?'

35. Mrs Probert in her letter to Mrs Lynch stated Evans told her Beryl and the baby had gone to Brighton – Mrs Probert's letter, Brabin, pp 45-6

36. Evan's account of his return to 10 Rillington Place on 23rd November – Trial of Evan, Jesse, pp 70-71

37. Christie's account of Evans' return on 23rd November – Christie's first statement, J Eddowes, p203

38. Mrs Christie only knew of Evans' visit as Christie told her about it – Mrs Christie first statement, J Eddowes, p194

39. Evans' mother on when Evans was lying and when he was telling the truth – J Eddowes, p154

Chapter 4

Post Mortems

Dr Robert Teare (1911-79) was the Home Office pathologist who performed the post mortem examinations on Beryl and Geraldine Evan at Kensington Mortuary on the afternoon of 2nd December 1949. Dr Teare along with Professor Keith Simpson and Dr Francis Camps were 'the 'three musketeers' who performed the medical analysis on the victims of suspicious deaths in the London area in the years following World War Two.[1]

Dr Robert Teare

Mrs Evans' father, Mr William Thorley, identified the bodies.[2] Chief Inspector Jennings attended.

Dr Teare's reports were as follows:[3]

POST MORTEM REPORTS ON BERYL
AND GERALDINE EVANS

Post mortems performed by Dr R. D. Teare

BERYL EVANS, age 19 years, date 2.12.49, at Kensington. Identified by Chief Inspector Jennings. Post mortem commenced at 3 p.m.

EXTERNAL EXAMINATION:

Well-nourished adult woman, 5 ft. 2 in. in height, estimated weigh 7½ stones. The body is dressed in a blue woollen jacket, a spotted cotton blouse and a black dress. It has been tied up in a table cloth and rough blanket. Decomposition is at its worst in the face and neck which are bloated and swollen with some exudation of sanguineous fluid from the mouth and nostrils. Parchment decomposition is seen particularly on the right side of the chest and arm and there are some small patches of mould on the chest. There are numerous maggots about the mouth and left breast. There are a series of abrasions 3½ inches long on the right side of the throat, varying from I¼ inches in width to ⅜ inch. On the left side of the back of the neck is another group of abrasions, 2½ inches long by I¼ inches broad at its widest. These abrasions fade away to decomposition. There is a small abrasion ⅜ inch in diameter 1¼ inches to the left of the mid line immediately above the collar bone. There is a bruise 1½ inches in diameter on the inner aspect of the left thigh, 4 inches above the knee. There is a bruise 2½ inches long by 1 inch wide on the inner aspect of the left calf immediately below the knee.

There is considerable swelling of the right eye and the upper lip due to bruising. Petechial haemorrhages are seen on the right side of the chin and the point of the chin.

INTERNAL EXAMINATION

The *skull* is intact. The meninges are intensely congested.

Circulatory system. The right side of the heart is widely dilated and contains fluid blood. The left ventricle is normal in size and the myocardium is perfectly healthy. No congenital abnormality or organic disease is found.

Respiratory system. Petechial haemorrhages are seen on the surfaces of the lungs and of the epiglottis. There is deep bruising of the neck on the right side of the voice box.

Intestinal system. The liver is intensely congested. The stomach contains mucus only.

Genito-urinary system. The kidneys are perfectly healthy. The uterus contains a male foetus 6¼ inches in length, of about 16 weeks' gestation. The membranes are intact and there is no evidence of interference. There is an old scar in the posterior wall of the vagina and beside this is a little ante mortem bruising.

Conclusions. She was a healthy woman.

Cause of death. Asphyxia due to strangulation by a ligature.

GERALDINE EVANS, age 14 months, date 2.12.49, at Kensington. Identified by Chief Inspector Jennings. Post mortem commenced at 4.30 p.m.

EXTERNAL EXAMINATION:

The body of a well-nourished baby girl. It is not wrapped but is dressed in the normal clothing for a baby of this age. Height of child is 33½ inches. Decomposition is most advanced in the upper part of the body, the face being bloated and swollen but the lower part of the body is not seriously affected.

A tie is extremely tightly tied around the neck. The circumference of the ligature is 6½ inches.

INTERNAL EXAMINATION:

Skull is intact. The brain is very decomposed and the meninges congested.

Circulatory system. A few petechial haemorrhages are seen on the posterior surface of the heart, the right side of which is widely dilated. No congenital abnormalities or organic disease is found in the heart.

Respiratory system. There is definite bruising in the muscles around the upper part of the voice box and the base of the tongue. Petechial haemorrhages are seen on the surfaces of the lungs which are a little collapsed and very congested throughout.

Intestinal system. The liver is congested. The stomach is quite empty. There is no inflammation of the intestines.

Genito-urinary system. The kidneys are perfectly healthy.

Conclusions. This was a well-developed and perfectly healthy child.

Cause of death. Asphyxia due to strangulation by ligature.

Further explanations by
Dr Teare concerning Beryl Evans[4]

The ligature that had been used to strangle Beryl Evans was not found upon the body. The abrasions on the neck indicated that the strangler had attacked from behind.

Commentary – If Evans had strangled his wife in a temper, he would have been much more likely to have done it from the front with his bare hands than from behind with a rope.

Dr Teare thought that the ligature had been a rope of ½ inch to ¾ inch diameter. He could not exclude the possibility that a twisted nylon stocking might have been used in that, being twisted, the grooves in the pressure mark which tend to be seen when looser ligatures are used, would not appear. He thought, however, that a twisted stocking would produce narrower marks than the ones found.

Commentary – in none of Christie's four victims in 1952-3 did the pathologist, Professor Camps, indicate the type of ligature used.[5]

Additional findings and explanations:

1. On the left front of the neck, just above the collar bone, there was an abrasion which Dr Teare thought could have been made by the hand of an assailant grasping the victim's throat, or by the victim's own fingernails when trying to pull something away from her throat.

2. There was a bruise 1½ inches in diameter on the inner aspect of the left thigh 4 inches above the knee and another 2½ inches long by one inch wide on the inner aspect of the left calf immediately below the knee. The mark on the thigh was large for a thumb mark although a thumb which dwelt and moved in

that area might have caused it. Although Dr Teare had not seen similar marks produced in such cases, he accepted that these marks were at least consistent with a man trying to force Beryl Evans' left leg with his right hand and right knee. The bruising of the left thigh and calf had not produced the kind of marks that Dr Teare had seen in cases of forced intercourse.

3.   There was considerable swelling of the right eye and upper lip.

4.   Dr Teare thought that these findings were consistent with a struggle having taken place.

The considerable swelling of the right eye and upper lip recorded in Doctor Teare's post-mortem examination report was not adduced when Dr Teare's deposition was taken at the Magistrates Court, nor was it mentioned at Evans' trial when Dr Teare was asked less than thirty questions. The condition of Beryl Evans' face at the first post mortem showed signs of blood, being the fluid of decomposition lying over and beyond the area of the mouth. There was no evidence of any fresh haemorrhage at or immediately before death. If there had been blood anywhere which had been wiped away it would have come from the mouth. The upper lip was markedly swollen and turned upwards virtually touching the nose. The lip had taken this shape and position in order best to accommodate the gases and fluids of decomposition. Dr Teare thought that the facial injuries had been caused by one blow with the back of a hand or by the less likely cause of two blows with a fist, and that when inflicted there would have been little if any blood. He thought this because in the decomposition he could not see any gross laceration of the lips.

Dr Teare was of the opinion that the swelling caused by the blow or blows would account for about half that seen after decomposition. He thought that after receiving the blow Beryl Evans must have lived for some time for the swelling to develop. He was not prepared to provide a precise time but his estimate was that the blow or blows probably occurred twenty minutes before death.

In 1953, Dr Teare commented to Professor Camps that 'the post mortem changes did not seriously interfere with his examination of the bodies and the diagnoses of the causes of death. It was still possible to see the petechial haemorrhages on the serous surfaces and the pregnant uterus was in perfect condition.'[6]

Importantly, Dr Teare found nothing of note that indicated an abortion had been attempted on Beryl Evans. He did not mention the presence of spermatozoa, something he would have followed up on if there had been any indication of its presence. He did not mention carbon monoxide poisoning; again something which would have been obvious (distinct pinkishness) if it had been present.

Challenges by Ludovic Kennedy in his book Ten Rillington Place

In 1953, when it came to light that Christie had killed two women during the war and four more in 1952-3, a number of MPs and authors argued that Evans had to be innocent of killing his wife and daughter in 1949. One line of their argument was that Dr Teare had overlooked vital evidence that would have implicated Christie. That, despite the fact that Teare's findings had been confirmed in 1953 by Professor Camp when he conducted second post mortems on Beryl and Geraldine.

The criticism of Teare was fully developed in Ludovic Kennedy's 1961 book, *Ten Rillington Place*. That book is considered in Chapter 14 (Volume 2). Nevertheless, it is appropriate to deal with Kennedy's criticisms of Dr Teare's findings in this chapter, alongside his reports.

According to Kennedy, Christie killed Beryl Evans. He gassed her using his own contraption. He then inserted something into her such that she resisted and struggled. He savagely hit her in the face and then strangled her. 'All this must have taken a matter of seconds.' Kennedy then had Christie having intercourse with her.[7]

Kennedy gave the following account of Dr Teare attending 10 Rillington Place and his summary of Teare's post mortem findings. 'At the same time the body of little Geraldine was found hidden under some wood behind the door with the tie that had strangled her still knotted round her neck. Dr Donald Teare, the Home Office pathologist, was sent for, and when he arrived the package containing Beryl's body was opened. At this time there was no smell from the bodies: the weather during November had been very cold and, as one pathologist put it, "refrigeration conditions were perfect." After a cursory examination the bodies were taken to the mortuary. Dr Teare found that both bodies had been dead about three weeks and that death in both cases had been caused by asphyxiation due to strangulation by a ligature. Beryl's throat and neck were deeply bruised, her right eye and upper lip were badly swollen and there was bruising inside her vagina. Dr Teare thought of taking a swab of Beryl's vagina, but in his own words, 'while I suggested it at the time, others thought it unnecessary'. Had he done so, he would almost certainly have found traces of Christie's spermatozoa.'[8]

Kennedy's account of the murder of Beryl Evans was far from consistent with the post-mortem evidence on the following counts.

- There was no evidence to support Kennedy's contention of carbon monoxide poisoning. Carbon monoxide has 'an affinity for haemoglobin which is about 300 times greater than that of oxygen.'[9] Had Beryl been subjected to London coal gas – which had a carbon monoxide concentration of around 15% in 1949[10] – the signs of gas poisoning would have been quickly evident. Dr Teare at the original post mortem would readily have noticed the distinct pink colouration of CO poisoning. He didn't. Again, at the second post mortem in 1953, no evidence of carbon monoxide was detected in Beryl's body.[11]

- Both post mortems reported on severe swelling and bruising on the right side of Beryl's face. Teare mentioned there was no haemorrhaging from the wound.[12] The skin though was not broken. There is a time lapse between a person being physically injured and consequential bruising actually appearing. This delay between injury and bruising is vital and beneficial to us – it means a surgeon is able to do his work. It also means that in order for bruising to have formed, Beryl must have been struck at least 20 minutes before she actually died. Kennedy's account had Christie striking her and strangling her in a single frenzy. Clearly not so.

- Both post mortems identified an anterior bruise to the back of the vagina and a bruise on the inside of her left thigh. It has been argued that the vaginal bruising could well have been caused by her own attempt to procure an abortion by using a syringe. There was virtually no evidence of Beryl being molested sexually or of any attempt to procure an abortion. At the first post mortem, Dr Teare did not take a swab of Beryl's private parts. Had he noticed or even suspected the presence of spermatozoa, he most certainly would have done so.

Kennedy also attempted to diminish Dr Teare in his book by criticising him for the evidence he supposedly gave at the Magistrates' Court hearings after Evans had been charged.

Kennedy quoted from the brief Evans' solicitors gave to Evans' counsel. 'The evidence given by Dr Teare appears to be open to the comment that his expert opinion travelled beyond justifiable inference from his examination of the corpse in so far as he purports to suggest that there might have been an attempt at sexual penetration after death. The case is sufficiently horrible without disgusting surmises of this nature being introduced into the minds of the jury... If anything of the sort occurred, it would presumably have been evidence of sadistic mania. There is no other evidence of that nature during the prisoner's life history.'

After this section in the main narrative, Kennedy wrote, 'Here was the vital, missing link between Evans' claim that Christie had done it and the reason why he had done it. Here, so to speak, were Christie's fingerprints and, had what is now known about Christie been known then, this in itself would have been enough for Evans to have been released from Brixton Prison and for Christie to have taken his place. But at the time, Evans' guilt seemed so certain that it never occurred to anyone that there had been sexual penetration after death.'[13]

Dr Teare strongly refuted Kennedy's misrepresentation at the time Kennedy's book was published. However, Professor Simpson, who took part in the second post mortem on Beryl Evans, was most succinct in countering Kennedy's assertion that Teare's comments implied Christie's guilt. In his autobiography, *Forty Years of Murder,* he wrote: 'Ludovic Kennedy commented, "Here, so to speak, were Christie's fingerprints... in the light of what we know now, it pins the crime fairly and squarely on Christie." It does nothing of the kind, as Mr Justice Brabin made clear, because Teare never said what was attributed to him. In the magistrates' court he repeated what he had written in his autopsy report on Beryl. "There is an old scar in the posterior wall of the vagina and beside this is a little ante mortem bruising." The Latin phrase "ante mortem" is rarely used outside the medical profession, but post mortem is part of the English language. When we do not hear a sentence completely we automatically fill in the blanks from what we assume to be the sense, and familiar words are more likely to suggest themselves than the esoteric. Baillie Saunders, the solicitor's clerk who drafted the brief to counsel, was over eighty when he listened to Teare's evidence before the magistrate, an age when it is not unusual to be a little hard of hearing. So the misunderstanding is easily explained: the coincidence was eerie.' [14]

In 2002, Kennedy wrote a book titled *Thirty-six Murders and Two Immoral Earnings*. In Chapter 2 he returned to the Evans and Christie case. In the chapter, Kennedy did not reiterate the description of the murder of Beryl Evans he gave in *Ten Rillington Place*. Instead, he fell back on one of Christie's versions of how he was supposed to have murdered Beryl:

'In admitting the crime three years later, this is one of several statements that Christie made about it: She brought the quilt from the front room and put it down in front of the fireplace (in the kitchen). She lay on the quilt; she was fully dressed. I got on my knees and found I was not physically capable of having intercourse. I turned the gas tap on, and as near as I can make out I held it close to her face. When she became unconscious, I turned the tap off. I was going to try again to have intercourse with her but it was impossible. I think that's when I strangled her.., then I left her where she was and went downstairs.' [15]

Then Kennedy wrote, 'In the interval between killing Beryl and writing the above, Christie seems to have quite forgotten the reason for his visiting her - the promised abortion. Nor does he mention the matter of the blood on her face or on the "bottom part", or the piece of tubing he must have attached to the gas tap. Everything must be speculation now, but my guess is that to convey verisimilitude he probably inserted some blunt instrument like a spoon into Beryl's vagina. Then, having attached a piece of rubber tubing (which he had already used on Muriel Eady), he turned on the gas ("Just a whiff to make you comfortable, my dear") so that Beryl became panic-stricken and struggled. But Christie, not to be denied another victim, began hitting her savagely about the face drawing blood which he may even have smeared on her bottom part to convince Evans that he had at least attempted an abortion.' [15]

Kennedy's newly concocted version of how Christie was supposed to have killed Beryl, mingling Evans' 'Merthyr 2' statement and Christie's 'confession', was further at odds with the actual evidence. There was no gas. There was no blood around the bottom parts. There was no time for bruising and swelling to have formed. Dr Teare never mentioned that there was blood from the blow to the face.

Kennedy had impugned Dr Teare's professional integrity in his 1961 book. In his book, *Thirty-six Murders*, he admitted in a footnote he had been wrong. 'Dr Teare, the pathologist, found bruising in the wall of Beryl's vagina. In my book I said that if he had taken a swab from there, he would probably have found traces of Christie's sperm. I now think this unlikely.'[16] Kennedy had undermined his own 'Christie's fingerprints' contention.

The post mortem evidence was vital. For Beryl Evans, the evidence showed that she was struck in the face at least twenty minutes before she was strangled. The strangler was behind her. The pregnancy was not interfered with, nor was she sexually molested. Beryl had not eaten for some time before she died, given her empty stomach. She had not been gassed. The body had to have been doubled up before or after rigor mortis. Clearly the post-mortem evidence did not point to a Christie style murder. Does the facial injury, a while before she was strangled, indicate that the killing was not premeditated?

For Geraldine, the evidence showed that the defenceless child was strangled and that she had not eaten for some time before she died. It was a cold-blooded killing.

References for Chapter 4

1. Dr Teare and the three musketeers – Simpson, p27

2. William Thorley identified the bodies – Trial of Evans, Jesse, p14

3. Beryl and Geraldine Evans post mortems 1949 – Appendix IX to 'Medical & Scientific Investigations in the Christie Case' by Francis E. Camp published by Medical Publications Limited, 1953

4. Dr Teare's explanations of his post mortem findings on the body of Beryl Evans – Brabin pp 59-61

5. Professor Camps did not identify what ligatures were used in the strangling of Christie's last four victims – Camps pp 24-40

6. Dr Teare confirmed to Dr Camps that post mortem changes did not affect his post mortems – Camps p228

7. Kennedy's account of how Christie killed Beryl Evans – Kennedy 1ORP pp 64-65

8. Kennedy's distorted account of Dr Teare's post mortem on Beryl Evans – Kennedy 1ORP pp 100-101

9. CO affinity for haemoglobin 300 times that of oxygen – Camps p156

10. London coal gas having 15% concentration of CO – Camps p164

11. CO not found in Beryl Evans' body in 1949 or 1953 – Camps p165

12. No haemorrhaging where Beryl had been struck in the face – Brabin, p61

13. Kennedy's interpretation of Dr Teare's supposed evidence at the West London Magistrates Court on 15th December 1949 – Kennedy 10RP pp 136-138

14. Simpson countered Kennedy's attempt to manipulate Teare's words to imply Christie's guilt – Simpson p205

15. Kennedy's new, concocted version of Beryl Evans' killing – Kennedy 36 Murders pp 24-5

16. Kennedy's retraction of his Christie's 'fingerprint' accusation relegated to a footnote – Kennedy 36 Murders p25.

Chapter 5

The Evans' confession to the Police at Notting Hill

Police visited 10 Rillington Place on Wednesday 30th November 1949. Having lifted the drain with difficulty, they found nothing. Nevertheless, Detective Inspector Black made an initial search of the property and garden (by torchlight). Nothing obvious was found and the garden had not been disturbed. Beryl Evans and the baby were missing; Christie stated that the Evanses had gone away.[1]

Overnight, first statements were taken from Christie and Mrs Christie.

Chief Inspector Jennings and Inspector Black made a more detailed search of 10 Rillington Place on the afternoon of Thursday 1st December, including searching for the Christies' having abortion paraphernalia. The wash-house was overlooked. Then Inspector Black and Sergeant Corfield were ordered to go to Wales and bring Evans back to London. He was to help inquiries concerning a stolen briefcase found in his flat and the disappearance of his wife and child.[2]

On the morning of Friday 2nd December, Chief Superintendent Barrett and Chief Inspector Jennings revisited 10 Rillington Place. The police, with the Christies, opened the wash-house door and found the body of Beryl Evans hidden behind wood under the sink and the body of Geraldine hidden behind the door. CS Barrett conveyed the findings to Inspector Black at Merthyr. Interviewing of Evans concerning the stolen briefcase was stopped. The bodies were removed to the mortuary at Kensington and Dr Teare carried out post mortems. Both Beryl and Geraldine had been strangled.

Evans was told he was being taken back to London in connection with further enquiries about the briefcase. Evans, Black and Corfield travelled back from Cardiff to London; the train arriving at Paddington at 9:30 p.m. Chief Inspector Jennings met the train and Evans was taken back to Notting Hill police station, arriving at 9:45 p.m.

Evans was taken into an office. Two piles of clothing were sitting on the office floor. One was Beryl's clothing together with the blanket, green tablecloth and cord she was wrapped in. The other was the baby's clothing with a tie on top. The tie had a distinctive knot and had been cut at the back to release it from the baby's neck.[3]

Jennings told Evans, 'I am Chief Inspector Jennings in charge of this case. At 11.50 a.m. today I found the dead body of your wife Beryl Evans concealed in a wash-house at 10 Rillington Place, Notting Hill, also the body of your baby daughter Geraldine in the same outbuilding and this clothing was found on them. Later today I was present at Kensington Mortuary when it was established that the cause of death was strangulation in both cases. I have reason to believe that you were responsible for their deaths!'[4] Evans answered 'Yes.' Evans picked up the tie and was crying.[5]

The Chief Inspector then cautioned Evans and Evans made a verbal statement which each officer recorded in his own notebook. Inspector Black commented that he wrote down what was said by Jennings and Evans. He wrote quickly, abbreviating words as necessary so that nothing would be missed.[6]

Commentary - When Evans saw the pile of his wife's clothing, with a cord on top, and the pile of his baby's clothing, with a cut tie on top, and then heard DCI Jennings' accusation, he may well have thought that Jennings knew it all. Jennings, though, was not as informed as Evans may have believed. But Evans was disorientated. There was considerable controversy concerning Evans' two Notting Hill statements. The first statement, 'NH1', was a short admission. The second statement, 'NH2' was a longer confession. Why did 'NH2' differ so much from 'Merthyr 2'? If Evans did not kill his wife and/or daughter, it made absolutely no sense for Evans to confess to both murders at Notting Hill.

First Notting Hill Statement ('NH1'), 2nd December 1949[7]

To Chief Inspector Jennings and Inspector Black Notting Hill
Police Station
Circa 9.45 p.m. Friday 2nd December 1949

'She was incurring one debt after another and I could not stand it any longer so I strangled her with a piece of rope and took her down to the flat below the same night whilst the old man was in hospital. I waited till the Christies downstairs had gone to bed, then took her to the wash-house after midnight. This was on Tuesday 8th November. On Thursday evening after I came home from work I strangled my baby in our bedroom with my tie and later that night I took her down into the wash-house after the Christies had gone to bed.'

Chief Inspector Jennings' notebook showed his entries. On page 3 he had written '9.45 pm on 2.12.49 at F.H. Stn. saw Evans', followed in the Chief Inspector's handwriting by the statement made by Evans. At the end was Evans' signature, the time and the date - '9.55 p.m. 2/12/49' - all written in Evans' hand.

Chief Inspector Jennings said that he wanted the time of signature recorded and that Evans looked at his wristwatch to check the time. Inspector Black could say no more than that he had a vague recollection that Evans had a rather large new-looking wristwatch.

Commentary – In a terse statement of just 105 words, Evans had confessed to killing his wife and, two days later, his daughter. On the night each was killed, the body was taken to the wash-house. 'NH1' is, in effect, a resume of Evans' next statement, 'NH2'.

Already issues arose. Why did Evans go from having Christie responsible for his wife's death and Christie having arranged for his child to be looked after in 'Merthyr 2' to taking all the blame and effectively exonerating Christie in this 'NH1' statement? If his 'Merthyr 2' statement was near the truth, he knew from what Jennings told him and the piles of clothing that Christie had betrayed him. The natural reaction of that betrayal had to have been to repeat 'Merthyr 2' but with the bitterness towards Christie ramped up?

In the first instance, Evans incriminated himself by stating he strangled his wife using a rope. Jennings in his opening remarks did not mention any ligatures. He only said the victims had been strangled. And there was only a cord on top of the wife's pile. Evans further incriminated himself by stating that it was he who took the bodies to the wash-house. Jennings, though, did say that was where they were found.

There already was an inconsistency that the police never returned to. The rope used to strangle Beryl was missing and never found.

Alternatively, could Evans have suffered an emotional collapse, perhaps brought about by exhaustion, the piles of clothes he saw on the interview room floor and fear? He had been with the police and under arrest for two days. He had been abruptly brought to London. He stated at his trial, 'Well, when I found out about my daughter being dead I did not care what happened to me then.' He also stated at his trial that 'I was frightened at the time…Well, I thought if I did not make a statement the police would take me downstairs and start knocking me about.' [8]

Evans, after saying that he was glad to get that off his chest, followed on with his second statement.

Second Notting Hill Statement ('NH2), 2nd December 1949[9]

To Chief Inspector Jennings and Inspector Black Notting Hill
Police Station
9.55 p.m. to 11.15 p.m. Friday 2nd December 1949.

'I have been cautioned by Chief Inspector Jennings and told that I am not obliged to say anything unless I wish to do so and that anything I say will be taken down in writing and may be used in evidence. (Signed) T. J. Evans.'

'I was working for the Lancaster Food Products of Lancaster Road, W.11. My wife was always moaning about me working long hours so I left there and went to work for the Continental Wine Stores of Edgware Road. I started at 8 a.m. and finished at 2 p.m., and the job was nice there. In the meanwhile my wife got herself into £20 debt, so I borrowed £20 off the Guv'nor under false pretences, so he gave me the £20 which I took home and gave it to my wife. I asked her who she owed the money to but she would not tell me; so a week later I got sacked. I was out of work then for two or three weeks. In the meanwhile I had been driving for two or three days a week. I was earning 25s. to 30s. a day. This was for the Lancaster Food Products. I used to give her this money and she was moaning she was not getting enough wages, so one of the regular drivers at the Lancaster Food Products left so the Guv'nor asked me if I would like my regular job back at a wage of £5 15s. a week. I was doing quite a lot of overtime for the firm, working late, which I used to earn altogether £6 to £7 a week. Out of that my wife used to go to the firm on a Friday and my Guv'nor used to pay her £5 what she used to sign for. Perhaps through the week I would have to give her more money off different people from which I used to borrow it. I used to pay them back on a Friday out of my own pocket. I had to rely on my overtime to pay my debts and then I had a letter from J. Brodericks telling me I was behind in my payments for my furniture on the hire purchase. I asked her if she had been paying for the furniture and she said she had; then I showed her the letter I had received from Brodericks, then she admitted she hadn't been paying for it. I went down to see Brodericks myself to pay them £1 a week and ten shillings off the arrears, so then I left the furniture business to my wife. I then found she was in debt with the rent. I accused her of squandering the money, so that started a terrific argument in my house. I told her if she didn't pull herself together I would leave her so she said, "You can leave any time you like," so I told her she would be surprised one day if I walked out on her. One Sunday early in November, I had a terrific row with her at home so I washed and changed and went to the pub dinner time. I stopped there till two o'clock. I came home, had my lunch, left again to go out, leaving my wife and the baby at home, because I didn't want any more arguments. I went to the pictures – A.B.C., Lancaster Road, known as Royalty, at 4.30 p.m. I came out when the film was finished, I think about 7.15 p.m. I went home, sat down and switched the wireless on. I made a cup of tea. My wife was nagging till I went to bed at 10 p.m. I got up at 6 a.m. next day, made a cup of tea. My wife got up to make a feed for the baby at 6.15 a.m. She gets up and starts an argument straight away. I took no notice of her and went into the bedroom to see my baby before going to work. My wife told me that she was going to pack up and go down to her father in Brighton. I asked her what she was going to do with the baby, so she said she was going to take the baby down to Brighton with her, so I said it would be a good job and a load of worry off my mind, so I went to work as usual so when I came home at night I just put the kettle on. I sat down, my wife walked in so I said, 'I thought you was going to Brighton?' She said, 'What, for you to have a good time?' I took no notice of her. I went downstairs and fetched the pushchair up. I came upstairs she started an argument again. I told her if she didn't pack it up I'd slap her face. With that she picked up a milk bottle to throw at me. I grabbed the bottle out of her hand, I pushed her, she fell in a chair in the kitchen, so I washed and changed and went out. I went to the pub and had a few drinks. I got home about 10.30 p.m. I walked in she started to row again so I went straight to bed. I got up Tuesday morning and went straight to work.'

Commentary – In the opening part of 'NH 2', Evans gave a quite detailed account of the mounting indebtedness he and his wife were incurring. Evans blamed it on her. She blamed Evans for not providing her with enough wages. The sourness between him and his wife intensified with her threatening to go off to Brighton. Their ongoing arguments escalated to mild violence on the evening of Monday 7th November. There was, though, no mention of Beryl being about four months pregnant and her being desperate to terminate the pregnancy.

This opening part has all the hallmarks of being Evans's own account. Only some phraseology gives the impression of having been tightened by Inspector Black while he was recording 'NH 2'.[10]

'I came home at night about 6.30 p.m., my wife started to argue again, so I hit her across the face with my flat hand. She then hit me back with her hand. In a fit of temper I grabbed a piece of rope from a chair which I had brought home off my van and strangled her with it.'

Commentary – This implied that hitting his wife across the face, her retaliation and Evans strangling her were all one transaction. This does not work. Given the bruising seen on Beryl's face at her post mortem, she had to have been struck at least twenty minutes before she was strangled.[11] At Evans' trial, Dr Teare was not examined or cross examined on the issue of ante mortem bruising.[12]

There was also the issue of Evans strangling his wife with a rope from behind, when if a strangulation was performed in a fit of temper, the expectation would be that it was done with bare hands front-on.

In 'Merthyr 2', Evans mentioned drawing back the eiderdown and looking at Beryl's body. He also mentioned helping Christie take her body to Mr Kitchener's flat. So, whether he struck Beryl and strangled her as in 'NH2', or whether Christie struck her and strangled her as implied in 'Merthyr 2', how could Evans have failed to mention that her face was bruised and swollen? In 'Merthyr 2' Evans spoke of blood around her face and on the pillowslip, but Dr Teare did not identify a laceration that could have caused that.

If 'NH2' was true, the fact that Evans stated he struck his wife fitted into his account of the escalating argument that led to him strangling his wife.

'I then took her into the bedroom and laid her on the bed with the rope still tied round her neck.'

Commentary – The rope was not around Beryl's neck when her body was found in the wash-house. If Jennings and Black were orchestrating the confession, and had guided Evans to state that he hit his wife, wouldn't they have made Evans include a clarification on when he removed the rope and what he did with it?

'Before 10 p.m. that night I carried my wife's body downstairs to the kitchen of Mr Kitchener's flat as I knew he was away in hospital.'

Commentary – If Jennings and Black were orchestrating the confession, wouldn't they have made sure the statement addressed why Evans did that and how he was able to enter Kitchener's flat? This, though, reflected what Christie, with Evans' help, did in 'Merthyr 2'.

'I then came back upstairs. I then made my baby some food and fed it, then I sat with the baby by the fire for a while in the kitchen. I put the baby to bed later on. I then went back to the kitchen and smoked a cigarette. I then went downstairs when I knew everything was quiet, to Mr Kitchener's flat (kitchen). I wrapped my wife's body in a blanket and a green table cloth from off my kitchen table. I then tied it up with a piece of cord from out of my kitchen cupboard.'

Commentary – Beryl's body was indeed found wrapped in a green tablecloth and a blanket and tied with cord.[13] Did Evans going down to Kitchener's flat to wrap the body when it was quiet, correspond to the overhead noises – thuds, like moving furniture – that both Mr and Mrs Christie stated they heard in their second statements?[14]

Again, if Jennings and Black were orchestrating the confession, wouldn't they have got Evans to explain why the body was doubled up?[15]

'I then slipped downstairs and opened the back door, then went up and carried my wife's body down to the wash-house and placed it under the sink. I then blocked the front of the sink up with pieces of wood so that the body wouldn't be seen. I locked the wash house door. I come in and shut the back door behind me. I then slipped back upstairs. The Christies who live on the ground floor were in bed. I went into the bedroom to see if my daughter was asleep. When I looked in the cot she was fast asleep so I then shut the bedroom door and laid on the bed all night fully dressed until it was time to get up and go to work.'

Commentary – There have to be serious doubts over this part of Evans' statement. Evans would have had to carry a doubled-up body, albeit wrapped and tied, but weighing 107 pounds,[15] down a flight of stairs, along the passageway outside the Christies' bedroom, through into the yard. He would then have to have opened the wash house door which required foreknowledge to do so, manoeuvre the body under the sink and build a screen from wood pieces. And where did those wood pieces come from? All this in the dark and without making any noise! Any noise would certainly have brought Christie out of the bedroom to see what was going on.

There was also the obstacle of the Larters' workmen still renovating and using the wash-house on and after 9th November when, according to 'NH2', Beryl's body was already in it.[16]

Would it not be more likely that Evans, or Christie and Evans together, moved Beryl's body from Kitchener's flat to the wash-house sometime over the weekend of 12th-13th November? This would explain why Evans was able to be so detailed on how the body was concealed, notwithstanding what DCI Jennings had told him about it. Was Evans just shifting the timing and, perversely, leaving out Christie's involvement? The moving of Beryl's body would have had to be done when Ethel Christie was out of the house - for instance, shopping or visiting the laundry.

'I then got up, lit the gas and put the kettle on. I made my baby a feed and fed it. I then changed her and put her back into the cot wrapping her up well so that she would not get cold, then went to the kitchen and poured myself out a cup of tea. I then finished my tea and slipped back into the bedroom to see if the baby had dropped off to sleep. It was asleep so I went off to work. I done my day's work and got home about 5.30 p.m. that Wednesday evening.'

Commentary - Evans left the baby unattended for some 10–11 hours! Again, if Jennings and Black were orchestrating the confession wouldn't they have wanted to pursue this issue? What was he thinking of neglecting the baby in this way? Did he take any steps to ensure the baby's crying – which must have been loud at thirteen months - was not overheard by the Christies or the workmen, so that the fact that his wife was missing would not be found out? Could the baby get out of the cot or tip it over?

'I come in, lit the gas, put the kettle on and lit the fire. I fed the baby, had a cup of tea myself, sat in front of the fire with my baby. I made the baby a feed about 9.30 p.m. I fed her then I changed her, then I put her to bed. I come back into the kitchen, sat by the fire until about twelve o'clock, then went to bed. I got up at 6 a.m. next day, lit the gas, put the kettle on, made the baby a feed and fed it. I then changed and dressed her. I then poured myself a cup of tea I had already made. I drank half and the baby drank the other half. I then put the baby back in her cot, wrapped her up and went to work.'

Commentary – Evans was there to care for the baby during the evening and night of Wednesday 9th/Thursday 10th November. He did not refer to speaking to Mrs Christie, telling her that Beryl and the baby had gone to Bristol.[17]

Then for the daytime of 10th November the baby was again left alone for 10-11 hours. The same issues mentioned in the previous comment apply again.

If Jennings and Black were orchestrating Evans' confession, why all the repetition of Evans feeding and caring for the baby?

'I done my day's work and then had an argument with the Guv'nor then I left the job. He gave me my wages before I went home. He asked me what I wanted my wages for. I told him I wanted to post some money off to my wife first thing in the morning. He asked where my wife was and I told him she had gone to Bristol on a holiday. He said, "How do you intend to send the money to her?" I said, "In a registered envelope." He paid me the money so he said, "You can call over tomorrow for your cards."

'I then went home, picked up my baby from her cot in the bedroom, picked up my tie and strangled her with it.'

Commentary – Absolutely no reason given for strangling the baby. Again, if Jennings and Black were orchestrating the confession, they would have wanted the motive for the killing clearly stated.

'I then put the baby back in the cot and sat down in the kitchen waiting for the Christies downstairs to go to bed. At about twelve o'clock that night I took the baby downstairs to the wash- house and hid her body behind some wood. I then locked the wash-house door behind me and came in closing the back door behind me. I then slipped back upstairs and laid on the bed all night, fully clothed.'

Commentary – Same modus operandi for disposing of the child's body as for disposing of the wife's body. The body of the child would have been easily manageable compared to that of his wife.

Whereas Evans stated he placed his wife's body under the sink hidden by pieces of wood, he only stated that the baby's body was hidden by wood. He did not state where in the wash-house he had placed the body. In this regard, Jennings had only told Evans that his wife's body had been concealed in the wash-house and the baby's body was found there too.[18]

'I got up the following morning, washed, shaved and changed, and then went to see a man in Portobello Road about selling my furniture. I don't know his name. During the same afternoon he came to my flat, looked at it and offered me forty quid for it. I told him I would take £40 for it and then he asked me why I wanted to sell it. I told him I was going to Bristol to live as I had a job there waiting for me. He asked me why I wasn't taking the furniture with me. I told him my wife had already gone there and had a flat with furniture in it. He then asked me if it was paid for. I said it was. He said he would call Sunday afternoon to let me know what time the driver would call on Monday for it. I said I would wait in for him. Between 3 and 4 p.m. on Monday this man took all the furniture, all the lino, and he paid me £40 which I signed for in a receipt book. He handed me the money which I counted in his presence. I waited till he went, then picked up my suitcase which I took to Paddington. The same night I caught the 12.55 train from Paddington to Cardiff and made my way to 93 Mount Pleasant, Merthyr Vale, where I stayed with my uncle, Mr Lynch. The rest I think you know. I have been asked to read this statement myself but I cannot read. It has been read over to me and is the truth.

(Signed) T. J. Evans.'

Commentary – Significantly, in the confession, there was no mention of Beryl's pregnancy or her wanting an abortion. There was no mention of Christie being involved. Everything, including his departure, was down to Evans.

Debate: Questions and Implications arising from Evans' 'Notting Hill 2' statement

The fact that Evans went to the police meant he had a sense of guilt. At worst, he was guilty of being a dual killer; at the least, he was guilty of covering up his wife's murder. But, with reference back to Chapter 2, how could Evans' statements shift from one extreme scenario to the other? Whereas Evans' 'Merthyr 2' statement was Scenario 8 with Christie being the double murderer and Evans a stooge, the 'NH2' statement was Scenario 1 with Evans the double killer and Christie having no part.

Perhaps Evans could not handle the reality of how his wife and daughter really died. Perhaps he felt cornered given Jennings' scene setting and accusation and the knowledge that the evidence contradicted his Christie abortion statement. All this coming on top of the strain of his period in police custody and the train journey back to London. The underlying sense of guilt became overwhelming and he was prepared to bear all the blame, true or not. As he said at his trial, 'When I found out about my daughter being dead I was upset and I did not care what happened to me then.'[19]

Numerous authors who have advocated Evans' innocence, most notably Ludovic Kennedy, have argued that Evans was worn down into making his confession.[20] Jennings and Black effectively controlled the confession, providing Evans with all the information he needed and persuading him to agree to how they interpreted what Evans said. It was notable that Kennedy's accusation that Jennings and Black 'did pervert the course of justice'[21] was made in 2002, by which time Jennings and Black were probably deceased.[22]

Certainly Jennings and Black put pressure on Evans right at the start of the Notting Hill interview, most notably having the piles of Beryl's and the baby's clothing placed on the floor of the interview room. There was also the tie at the top of the baby's pile.

Then there was the scene setting and accusation from Jennings.[23] Although never reported, could Jennings have made Evans aware that no abortion had been attempted on Beryl? Jennings would have known this, for as he told Evans, he was at the mortuary when the post mortems were carried out. Given what Evans had said in his 'Merthyr 2' statement, an examination for an attempted abortion would have been at the forefront of Dr Teare's mind. Jennings had the evidence to dismiss the 'Merthyr 2' abortion account and perhaps as Evans spoke he made that clear.

To accuse Jennings and Black of perverting the course of justice, by composing the confession for Evans, by providing him with all the information he needed and by browbeating him into conforming with their view, does not work. The confession read as voluntary and not forced. On the one hand, it unfolded with so much unnecessary detail. On the other hand, there were a number of key issues senior police officers would never have left out if they were steering the statement. For example, the confession left out the reason why Evans murdered the child and the reason why Evans decided to put the bodies in the wash-house. Further, it also had glaring absurdities. For example, how could Evans have left the baby unattended, and without her mother, for some ten hours on each of two consecutive days and nobody in the 'dolls' house' heard her crying?

With 'NH2' there were big inconsistencies. How would Evans have been able to move his wife's body to the wash-house at the time and in the manner he stated? The idea that he moved her relatively heavy, doubled-up body at dead of night, in the dark, down a narrow flight of stairs and past two sides of the Christies' bedroom, without making noise to disturb them, was highly implausible. We don't even know if Evans had the knack needed to open the wash- house door. Furthermore, Larters' workmen still using the wash-house on 9th November, after Evans was supposed to have hidden Beryl's body under the sink, was a big problem. The police took statements from the workmen, but then got the workmen to "correct" them.[16] These inconsistencies are considered in more depth in chapter 8.

If Evans had not killed his wife and he believed Geraldine was still alive, then there are questions over whether Evans would have had all the information he needed to make his confession, even allowing for what he saw on the floor of the interview room and what DCI Jennings said to him. If he, or he and Christie, had moved his wife's body to the wash-house at a later time than Evans stated, he could have known her body was placed under the sink and hidden with pieces of wood. But if Evans had nothing to do with Beryl's body being moved to the wash-house, how would he have been so precise on where and how Beryl's body was hidden unless the police told him?

At Evans' trial, DCI Jennings was adamant that Evans was told nothing about where in the wash-house Beryl's body was placed or how it had been concealed.[24] DI Black, though, agreed that Jennings had told Evans that his wife's body was under the sink and concealed behind some timber.[25]

If the confession wasn't Evans' idea but driven by DCI Jennings and DI Black, why didn't Evans or his counsel make strong claims that Evans had been manipulated into making the confession?

After he had made the confession on 2nd December, Evans backed it up on at least three occasions:

- He admitted to Sergeant Trevallian, who was keeping observation on him on 3rd December, that he strangled the baby. Evans told Trevallian that the constant crying of the baby got on his nerves and he just had to strangle it as he could not put up with the crying.[26]

- On the journey to his first magistrates' court hearing on 3rd December 1949, Evans told DI Black, 'after I killed my wife I took her wedding ring from her finger and sold it to Samuels at Merthyr for six shillings.'[27]

- When remanded to Brixton prison, Evans was initially interviewed by the Principal Medical Officer, Dr Matheson. Matheson's notes of the interview record that Evans admitted killing his wife. Evans mentioned that Beryl was incurring debts and she was jealous of the baby. There was rowing. 'She kept at it until Tuesday 8.11.49 and he killed her. It all happened in a fit of temper. He came home from work, a row started over debt, he lost his temper and strangled her. He put her body in the wash-house.' Dr Matheson also noted, 'baby disposed of on Thursday 20.11.49 (sic).'[28]

On the other hand, Evans made declarations that he had not killed his wife and baby:

- To his mother and other members of his family he pinned the blame for both killings on Christie.[29]

- He told the psychopath Donald Hume, when they were in the same hospital ward at Pentonville, that Christie, had 'murdered her [his wife] and also the child. It was because the kid kept crying... Christie had gone into a bedroom and strangled the child with a piece of rag while he [Evans] looked on.'[30]

- After he was convicted, Dr Quinn, Medical Officer at Brixton Prison, interviewed Evans. Asked why he had confessed, Evans replied that he did not know, 'it was a mistake.' Dr Quinn considered, 'if such a young man had learned for the first time that his baby was dead and had been strangled, he might, under the stress of emotional shock, make a confession which was not based on reality.'[31]

- The Senior Medical Officer at Pentonville, Dr Coates, saw Evans in February 1950. Evans told Coates that Christie had committed the murders.[32]

- A prisoner officer at Brixton, following Evans' conviction, stated that Evans said Christie had 'shopped him'.[33]

- At the Statutory Inquiry set up to decide if there was any mental encumbrance to Evans' execution going ahead, Evans again denied the killings. A member of the panel, Professor Curran, reported, 'Evans explained his confession as being due to shock on hearing of his daughter's death and thereafter not caring what happened and that, he said, was how he came to make his long statement.' Evans also stated, 'the only thing that sticks in my mind is that I am in for something I have not done. The police caught me for a statement when I was upset. I say Christie done it.'[34] There was no suggestion from Evans in the record of the Inquiry that he made his statement because the police had put the words into his mouth.

From whatever standpoint, there are problems with Evans' confession. But in 1949, before Christie's was exposed as a serial strangler, Evans' 'NH2' confession appeared entirely plausible. The relationship between himself and his wife was deteriorating because of the couple's dire and worsening financial situation. Then there was another child on the way. The constant rowing, mentioned in their statements by the Christies, Mrs Probert and Evans himself, had already escalated into violence.

Furthermore, the Notting Hill confession fitted the post mortem evidence that Beryl had been beaten in the face and then, later, strangled. The post mortem evidence did not fit Evans' ' Merthyr 2' statement. Beryl did not die as the result of a failed abortion by Christie. And if Evans had killed his wife surely he also killed his daughter.

References Chapter 5

1. Police investigations at 10 Rillington Place over the evening of Wednesday 30th November 1949 and overnight into Thursday 1st December 1949 – Brabin, pp 14-20

2. Police continue searching 10 Rillington Place and Black and Corfield sent to Wales – Brabin, pp 21-3

3. Summary of events from Evans' 'Merthyr 2' statement to his 'Notting Hill 1' statement – Brabin, pp 55-70

4. Jennings' opening remarks to Evans at Notting Hill – Brabin, pp 69-70

5. Evans reaction on seeing the piles of clothing – DI Black evidence, Trial of Evans, Jesse, p60; J Eddowes, pp 59-60

6. Caution and note taking – Brabin, p70

7. Evans' first Notting Hill statement – J Eddowes, p60

8. Evans' reasons for making his confession to the Notting Hill police – Trial of Evans, Jesse, p72

9. Evans' second Notting Hill statement – Trial of Evans, Jesse, p 54-7

10. Inspector Black wrote down 'NH 2' – J Eddowes, p61

11. Implications of bruising on Beryl Evans – Brabin, pp 60-61

12. Dr Teare not asked about Beryl's bruised face at Evans' trial – Trial of Evans, Jesse, pp 14-5

13. Beryl Evans' body doubled up, wrapped in a blanket and a tablecloth and bound with cord – Brabin, p56

14. Both Mrs Christie and Christie mention thud in the night overhead in their second statements – J Eddowes, p195, p205

15. Beryl Evans' weight at death, 107 pounds – post mortem report, Camps, p226

16. Statements of Larters' workmen doing renovations to the outhouses and ground floor of 10 Rillington Place up to Friday 11th November 1949 – J Eddowes, pp 196-201

17. Evans tells Mrs Christie, late Wednesday 9th November, Beryl and the baby have gone to Bristol – Mrs Christie's first statement, J Eddowes, p194

18. What Jennings told Evans before Evans made his Notting Hill statements – Brabin, pp 69-70

19. Evans did not care what happened to him – Trial of Evans, Jesse, p72

20. Jennings and Black manipulated Evans' confession – Kennedy 36 Murders, pp 29-33

21. Jennings and Black pervert the course of justice – Kennedy 36 Murders, p33

22. Dates of the deaths of Jennings and Black not found. Both though retired from the Metropolitan Police in 1963, thirty-nine years before Kennedy's accusation against them.

23. At the start of the Notting Hill interview Jennings told Evans what was found in the wash-house, how Beryl and Geraldine were killed and that he had reason to believe Evans was responsible – Brabin, p70

24. Jennings denied telling Evans where in the wash-house Beryl's body was hidden and how it was concealed – Trial of Evans, Jesse, p58

25. DI Black did agree that Evans was told where in the wash-house Beryl's body was hidden and how it was concealed – Trial of Evans, Jesse, p60

26. Evans admission to Sergeant Trevallian – Brabin p76

27. Evans tells DCI Black he sold his wife' wedding ring – Brabin, p79

28. Evans' interview with Dr Matheson at Brixton Prison – Brabin, pp 88-9

29. Evans denied killings to his family – Brabin, pp 91-6

30. Evans denied killings to Donald Hume – Hoskins, p43

31. Evans told Dr Quinn he did not know why he confessed – Brabin, pp 174-5

32. Evans in interview with Dr Coates blamed Christie – Brabin, p176

33. Evans told a prison officer that Christie 'shopped him' – Brabin, p176

34. At the Statutory Inquiry Evans denied the killings. The police had caught him for a statement when he was upset – Brabin, pp 178–181

Christie's Confessions in 1953 to Killing Beryl Evans

Before considering how Timothy Evans' trial unfolded, it is necessary to move forward in time to 1953. Following the discovery of a further six bodies at 10 Rillington Place, Christie was arrested. While under arrest, he eventually confessed to murdering Beryl Evans.

Christie's Confession

On 27th May 1953, at a meeting with a psychiatrist, engaged by his defence, and his solicitor, Mr Arthur, Christie admitted killing Mrs Evans. As the defence team, led by Mr Derek Curtis Bennett QC, was building its case on insanity, Christie was encouraged to admit the killing in a voluntary statement to the police. Accordingly, Christie made a third statement to the Police on 8th June 1953.[1] The part of the statement – actually most of it – that related to the killing of Mrs Evans is reproduced as follows:

'In August 1949, there was a terrific row upstairs on the top floor between Mr and Mrs Evans and a blonde who was living with them. My wife told me afterwards that a woman who lives in Lancaster Road, overlooking the back of 10 Rillington Place had told her that she had seen Mr and Mrs Evans fighting at their open kitchen window and that Mr Evans appeared to be trying to push his wife out of the window. I think it was Mrs Hyde who told my wife this. I think Mrs Swan saw it from her garden next door. Mr Evans' mother called while the fight was in progress. After the row had quietened down, Evans' mother told the blonde to pack up and clear out. I was in my front room when I heard this shouted. I also heard Evans say that if she (the blonde) went he would go with her. Evans, his mother and the blonde were at the first floor coming down the stairs, when I heard this said. The mother went out and Evans and the blonde went back upstairs. As the mother went out she said to us, me and my wife, that she was going to throw the blonde out there and then.

That evening Evans went out with the blonde and he was carrying a suitcase. He came back alone later. The next day Mrs Evans told my wife that she was going down to the Police Court to get a separation from her husband. My wife and I had a chat and we agreed between us that if they did separate we would adopt the baby, but Mrs Evans told my wife that if they did separate his mother would take the baby. At a later period, Mrs Evans told me that her husband was knocking her about and that she was going to make an end of it, meaning that she was going to commit suicide.'

Commentary – the rows between Tim and Beryl Evans and the problem with Lucy Endecott were confirmed by other witnesses, especially by Lucy Endecott herself. [2]

'One morning shortly after this, it would be early in November, I went upstairs and found Mrs Evans lying on a quilt in front of the fireplace in the kitchen. She had made an attempt to gas herself. I opened the door and window wide because there was a lot of gas in the room. There was a gas pipe at the left-hand side of the fireplace with a tap about 2 feet 6 inches from the floor at the level of the top of the kitchen fireplace. There was a piece of rubber tubing from the tap to near her head. She was lying with her head towards the window. She was fully dressed and was not covered over with anything. When I opened the door and window she started coming round. I gave her a drink of water. I do not know what she said, but a little while after she complained of headache, and I made her a cup of tea. My wife was downstairs but I did not call her or tell her. Mrs Evans asked me not to tell anyone. Mr Evans was out and I don't know if there was anyone else in the house. I had a cup of tea too because my head was thumping as I had got the effect of it (the gas) too. After a little while I went downstairs.'

Commentary – there was nothing else that gave any support for the episode. Evans never mentioned her being distressed when he returned from work on Monday 7th. According to 'Merthyr 1', she found the bottle of pills in his pocket which she would take next day with fatal results. According to 'Merthyr 2', she told him she and Christie arranged for the abortion first thing on Tuesday morning. According to the Notting Hill confession, they argued with her picking up a milk bottle to throw at him and him pushing her into a chair. [3]

Odd, too, that Mrs Evans had the length of rubber tubing and she put it next to her head.

'The next day I went upstairs again, I couldn't say if it was the morning or afternoon. I think it was about lunchtime. She still said she intended to do away with herself. I am certain that there was a small fire in the grate in the kitchen when I found Mrs Evans the day before, and that's why I rushed to open the window.'

'When I went up to Mrs Evans at lunchtime the next day she begged me to help her to go through with it, meaning to help her commit suicide. She said she would do anything if I would help her. I think she was referring to letting me be intimate with her. She brought the quilt from the front room and put it down in front of the fireplace. I am not sure whether there was a fire in the grate. She lay on the quilt. She was fully dressed. I got on my knees but found I was not physically capable of having intercourse with her owing to the fact that I had fibrositis in my back and enteritis.'

Commentary – Christie was not suffering from fibrositis on Tuesday 8th November. He did not go to see his doctor with back pain until Saturday 12th November. [4]

We were both fully dressed. I turned the gas tap on and as near as I can make out, I held it close to her face. When she became unconscious I turned the tap off. I was going to try again to have intercourse with her but it was impossible, I couldn't bend over. I think that's when I strangled her. I think it was with a stocking I found in the room. The gas wasn't on very long, not much over a minute, I think. Perhaps one or two minutes. I then left her where she was and went downstairs. I think my wife was downstairs. She didn't know anything about it.'

Commentary - Mrs Evans was not gassed. There was no carbon monoxide poisoning. There was no time in this account for the facial bruising to form. [5]

'Evans came home in the evening about six o'clock. It was dark when I heard him come in. I went to my kitchen door and called him.

I spoke to him in the passage and told him that his wife had committed suicide, that she had gassed herself. I went upstairs with him. We went into the kitchen and Evans touched his wife's hand, then picked her up and carried her into the bedroom and put her on the bed. It was dark, there were no lights on in the kitchen or the bedroom. I feel certain it was a stocking I strangled her with. I didn't tie it round the neck. I just wound it round the neck. Before I went downstairs, I think I took the stocking off and threw it in the fireplace. I think there was a fire in the grate. I did not feel any effects of the gas.

After Evans lay his wife on the bed, he fetched the quilt from the kitchen and put it over her. I then lit the gas in the centre of the room, the front room, which is used as the bedroom. I told Evans that no doubt he would be suspected of having done it because of the rows and fights he had had with his wife. He seemed to think the same. He said he would bring the van down that he was driving and take her away and leave her somewhere. I left him and went downstairs. I think this was on a Tuesday and on the following Friday Evans sold his furniture, and after my wife had given him some dinner he left saying he was going to Bristol.'

Commentary – there were some similarities with Evans' 'Merthyr 2' statement as to what happened when Evans came home.

'At that time, I was under the impression that he had taken his wife away in his van. I didn't go into the bedroom that day until Evans came home in the evening. I can't recollect seeing the baby there. I think Evans told me the next day that he had fed the baby. Evans called at the house some days later, but only stayed a few minutes. I had my coat on ready to go to the Doctor's and we left the house together and both got on a No.7 'bus. I paid the fares, I got off the bus near the Doctor's, and Evans stayed on the bus to go to Paddington.'

Commentary – Christie's new account of what happened between Beryl's killing and Evans going to the police on 30th November was entirely different from what he stated in his three statements in December 1949. [6]

'Early in December, police called at the house and said they were making inquiries about Mrs Evans. There were three officers - Detective Sergeant Corfield, Detective Byers, and I think, Inspector Black. They told me they had got Evans in Wales and that he had made a statement that he had put his wife down a drain. They said they had already had the drain up before they came to the door. They asked me to go to Notting Hill Police Station to make a statement, and I went with them in a car. I stayed there from 11 p.m. till five in the morning. When I got back I found they had taken a statement from my wife. They left a policeman there all night and came again next day and made a search. They found something in the out house and asked my wife to go to the outhouse (wash-house). She told me afterwards that they had pointed to a bundle and asked her if she knew anything about it. She said she did not and they asked her to touch it to see if she knew what it was. She said she touched it but didn't know what it was and she had never seen it there before. An officer told us soon after that they had found a body.'

Commentary – Christie's account of the police searches at 10 Rillington Place was corroborated.[7]

'When I left Evans in the bedroom on that Tuesday evening he did not know that his wife had been strangled. He thought she had gassed herself. I don't know when he first found out that his wife had been strangled. I never mentioned it to him.'

Commentary – Supposedly Evans, alone, managed Beryl's body from the Tuesday evening. How could Christie have thought Evans did not notice the weal around her neck caused by the ligature?

'I never had intercourse with Mrs Evans at any time. We were just friendly acquaintances nothing more. I went up that first afternoon to have a cup of tea as she had previously asked me once or twice. I believe it was a couple of days previously that she had asked me to go up and get some sugar she had saved up for me. When I was up there she said she had just made a cup of tea and asked me to have one. I had a cup of tea with her then and she told me to come up any time I wanted a cup of tea.'

Commentary – summing up and padding.

'The wash-house was a communal one, but actually it was only used for keeping rubbish and junk in. There was no key to it and the lock was rusted and broken and not usable. It could be opened and shut by turning the handle but could not be locked. The wash-house was only used for getting water to rinse out pails or put down the lavatory.

I had some shoring timber and old floorboards from my front room which had been left behind by the work people and I asked

Evans to take it to the yard for me as I could not carry it owing to my fibrositis. He took it to the yard and I suggested he put it in the wash-house out of the way. I saw it in the wash-house afterwards and some of it was stacked in front of the sink. I don't think it was possible to get to the tap after the timber was put in there.'

Commentary – Christie was clever here. Although having confessed to killing Mrs Evans, he reinforced that he was not involved in hiding her body and he also distanced himself from the child's murder.

'I feel certain I strangled Mrs Evans and I think it was with a stocking. I did it because she appealed to me to help her commit suicide. I have got it in the back of my mind that there was some other motive, but I am not clear about it.'

Commentary – summing up yet again. Christie never provided the other motive.

'I don't know anything about what happened to the Evans' baby. I don't recollect seeing the baby on the Tuesday or at any time afterwards.'

Commentary – Christie never formally stated that he had anything to do with Geraldine's death. He denied killing her at his trial. [8]

At this stage, though, comments are needed on what was right and what was wrong with Christie's confession.

What was right?

Christie's confession included three matters that were also mentioned three and a half years earlier by Evans in his 'Merthyr 1' and 'Merthyr 2' statements.

- Evans' 'Merthyr 1' statement had Beryl killing herself with pills to induce an abortion. Christie's confession had Beryl trying to kill herself and seeking Christie's help.

- On the day Beryl was killed, Evans' 'Merthyr 2' statement had Christie accosting him at the foot of the stairs as Evans came back from work to tell him it was bad news. That same day, Christie's confession has him meeting Evans at the foot of the stairs to tell him his wife had committed suicide.

- In 'Merthyr 2' and Christie's confession, Evans and Christie held a conversation covering what happened, and planning what needed to be done next.

Three other matters which were correct:

- Dr Teare examined the weal around Mrs Evans' neck and his opinion was that the ligature was more likely to have been a rope but it could have been a twisted stocking.[9]

- There was no sexual interference with Mrs Evans, nor was her pregnancy interfered with. This was confirmed by Dr Teare in his post mortem.[10]

- Christie's description of the layout of the top floor flat was accurate. But then, he and his wife lived in it for a year before they moved down to the ground floor flat in December 1938.

What was wrong?

Nine matters:

- How come Christie turned up at the Evans' flat on Monday 7th November and entered of his own accord at the very moment that Mrs Evans was unconscious and the gas was on?

- When Christie was supposedly killing Beryl – around lunchtime on Tuesday 8th November – the builders had said she had been seen late that morning going out of the building with the baby in the pram and another woman.

- Why would Mrs Evans have had a length of rubber tubing to fit to the gas tap and, even if she did, what happened to it? The police mentioned nothing about finding rubber tubing when they searched the flat on 1st December 1949.

- Would a mother have attempted to gas herself, simply leaving her child uncared for?

- There was a story that circulated, firstly during the 1953 Scott Henderson Inquiry, that Mrs Evans had left her child, wearing a yellow suit, with a neighbour on Tuesday 8th November. The story, though, petered out.[11] Even supposing she did, Evans never mentioned how he knew the child needed collecting or that he ever did so.

- Why would Christie have stated that he could not have intercourse with Mrs Evans as he could not bend down because of his fibrositis and enteritis? He did not go to see Dr Odess complaining of back pain until Saturday 12th November.

- There was no carbon monoxide poisoning detected in Mrs Evans' body by Dr Teare in his December 1949 post-mortem or by Dr Camps and his colleagues at the second post-mortem in May 1953.

- Christie made no mention of striking Beryl across the face prior to supposedly killing her, nor of a delay of at least twenty minutes that would have been needed between the blow and her death to allow bruising and swelling to develop. If, again supposedly, Evans had struck his wife the previous evening or that morning, Christie did not mention what would have been a very significant temporary disfigurement to Beryl's face at the time of his second visit.

- If Christie had killed Beryl Evans, it is inconceivable that he would have left Evans to dispose of the body. Christie had a low opinion of Evans and he would never have taken the risk of leaving Evans to do such a task. He would, at least, have directed what was to happen.

Whether or not he killed Mrs Evans, was Christie clever enough to realise he could not confess to her murder along the same lines as Evans had implied in 'Merthyr 2'? Had he done so, then if Evans' 'Merthyr 2' was now shown to be 'true' for Beryl's killing, why would it not have been true for what happened to Geraldine as well? If Christie deemed 'scoring' Beryl's murder would help his insane defence, he still needed his account to be at odds with Evans'. Otherwise, he would be laying himself wide open to immediate accusations that he really did kill the baby.

Christie's confession is considered further in Chapter 11 of volume II in the context of the other six bodies that were found at 10 Rillington Place in March 1953 and in the context of his special 'guilty but insane' defence.

References Chapter 6

1. Christie confessed to murdering Beryl Evans – Trial of Christie, Jesse, pp 159-162

2. Lucy Endecott confirmed Christie's opening – J Eddowes, pp 13-7

3. Evans' different accounts of what happened when he came home from work on Monday 7th November – Trial of Evans, Jesse, pp 47-8, pp 49-50, p55

4. Christie went to his doctor with back pain on Saturday 12th November – Brabin, pp 38-9

5.   Mrs Evans not subjected to gas. No time for bruising to form – Camps, pp 226-7

6.   Christie's 1949 statements – J Eddowes pp 201-7

7.   The police search – Brabin, pp 7-8, pp 14-8, p21-2, pp 55-6

8.   Christie repeats he did not kill Geraldine at his trial – Trial of Christie, Jesse, p192

9.   Dr Teare thought ligature a rope or twisted stocking – Brabin, p59

10. Dr Teare's post mortem report on Beryl Evans – Camps, pp 226-7

11. Story of Beryl leaving Geraldine, in a yellow suit, with a neighbour on 8th November – Brabin, pp 223-5

Chapter 7

Mrs Ethel Christie

A biography of Ethel Simpson has already been set out in Chapter 1. At the time of the murders of Beryl and Geraldine Evans she was 51 years old and had been living with her husband in the ground floor flat at 10 Rillington Place for eleven years. According to Christie, 'he and Ethel lived happily enough.'[1]

Photographs of Ethel Christie as a young woman

Photographs of the mature Ethel Christie

Ethel's role in what happened at 10 Rillington Place in November 1949 has been the subject of much speculation. At one extreme, she knew what was going on and covered up for her husband. Ethel was more cunning and deceitful than she appeared. At the other extreme she was totally unaware of what was happening. The statements she made after the bodies were found and her evidence at Evans' trial were reliable. Ethel was well-meaning and honest.

In trying to determine what Ethel did or did not know, it is firstly necessary to consider the two statements she made to the police on 1st and 5th December 1949.

First statement[2]

Statement of Witness.

Notting Hill Police Station 'F' Division. 1st December 1949

Name: Mrs Ethel Christie. Age 51.

Address: 10 Rillington Place, W11.

Occupation: Housewife.

Commentary - This statement was taken after Evans had given his 'Merthyr 2' statement implicating Christie in the fatal abortion and in getting the baby fostered, but before the bodies of Beryl and Geraldine were found.

'I am the wife of John Reginald Christie, and I reside with him at the above address. We have no children. We occupy the ground floor which consists of a bedroom, living room and a kitchen. The first floor is occupied by Mr Kitchener who lives on his own, and until about three weeks ago the top floor was occupied by Mr & Mrs Evans and their fourteen months old daughter. The Evans family have been in occupation of their part of the premises since twelve months ago last April 1949. I didn't know them before they came to us, but since they have been here I have been on very friendly terms with them, particularly Mrs Evans.'

Commentary – The Evanses moved to 10 Rillington Place at Easter 1948. There is nothing to suggest that the Christies and the Evans' family did not get on well, with Mrs Christie looking out for Geraldine when Beryl Evans had to 'pop out' on errands. Mrs Christie stated as such in the last part of her statement.

'About two months ago Mrs Evans told me that she was then two months pregnant and that she did not want another baby. She told me that she had already taken various pills that had been recommended to her by different people in an endeavour to secure this miscarriage, and that she had purchased a syringe with this object in view. Two of the people she mentioned were her mother-in-law, whose name I cannot remember, I know it's not Evans because Mr Evans was a son of her first marriage, and a Mrs Lawrence, who lived at 8 Rillington Place. She did not discuss what they told her to do. I advised Mrs Evans to stop trying to procure her miscarriage, but she seemed determined to go on with it, and even spoke of going somewhere for an illegal operation. She mentioned about the operation sometime after she had told me of the various pills she was taking to secure her miscarriage. The exact words she used were, "She would have an operation but that it costs money". I have an idea she mentioned going to Praed Street near St Mary's Hospital for the operation, but she never told me the address where she intended to go.'

Commentary – This account of Beryl's attempts to get rid of the new baby was consistent with Evans' 'Merthyr 1' statement. Mrs Christie's view that Beryl was four months pregnant was confirmed in Dr Teare's post mortem.

Suggestions were made that Mrs Christie undertook 'back street' abortions. If she did, why did she not offer the service to Mrs Evans? When the police searched 10 Rillington Place in early December 1949 for instruments of abortion, they found only an old and perished syringe that belonged to Mrs Christie. [3]

'All the time the Evanses have lived at our address there have been frequent quarrels, some of which my husband and I have heard when their voices were raised, although we have not heard what was actually said. After some of these quarrels Mrs Evans would tell me that she had rowed with her husband over his lying to her, his associating with other woman and financial matters. The last time I heard them quarrel was on or about Sunday 13th November 1949, when they were shouting at each other and appeared to be having a violent quarrel. It lasted all day on and off.'

Commentary – Mrs Christie was consistently a week out on her timings.

The rowing between Tim and Beryl Evans was well documented elsewhere. The rowing over 'the blonde', Lucy Endecott, staying in the Evans' flat in August 1949 was brought to an end when Evans' mother, Mrs Probert, and the police became involved and Lucy was told to leave.[4] The row on Sunday 6th November was confirmed by Evans in his 'NH2' statement.

'I saw Mrs Evans the following morning and she looked terribly ill, she did mention that a friend of hers called Joan had made trouble between her and her husband, and that Joan was coming round that morning, and that she (Mrs Evans) did not want to see her. After Mrs Evans told me this she went back upstairs, and shortly after Joan came but Mrs Evans locked herself in her kitchen and refused to see her. I don't know where Joan lives, but her husband is the son of the people who keep a paper shop near the railway bridge in St Mark's Road. That afternoon Mrs Evans went out and asked me to keep an eye on her baby daughter who was in bed. She said she would not be long. However, she had not returned at 5:30 p.m. but her husband came in and my husband and I went to the pictures.

We got home about nine o'clock, but I don't know whether Mrs Evans had returned home. I did not see her.'

Commentary – Joan Vincent initially timed her visit when the door to the Evans' kitchen was held against her to Monday 7th November. It was years later that she switched the timing to lunchtime on Tuesday 8th.[5] *Some authors switching the time, allowed the door being held against her incident to coincide with the time Christie was supposedly killing Beryl.*

'I think I saw Mrs Evans go out with her baby about diner time the next day. It was in the pram.'

Commentary – Christie, too, stated that he saw Mrs Evans going out with the baby in the pram around the same time.[6] *Furthermore, one of the workmen, Mr Jones, stated that he saw Mrs Evans going out with the baby in the pram and another woman around 10.00 a.m. that morning.*[7]

'As far as I know she did not speak to me, and she certainly made no mention of going away for good. I do remember Mr Evans coming in at about 10:30 p.m. on the Wednesday, because the floorboards were up in the passage and I shone a light so that he would not fall over when he came in. I asked where his wife was and he told me that she had gone away with the baby for a month to stay with friends in Bristol. He did not mention any address. I remarked that she had not told me she was going, and he then said she would be writing to me. This she has not done. I didn't really believe his wife had gone to Bristol because Evans had told me on a number of occasions that his wife was going away on holiday to different parts of the Country. However, I did think she may have left him as a result of the quarrels and gone to her father in Brighton. I don't know his address. The reason I thought this was because she had frequently told me that she would leave him, as she could not stand his behaviour to her any longer.'

Commentary – In his statements and confession, Evans did not mention speaking to Mrs Christie on the late evening of 9th November. However, at his trial he admitted he lied to his boss, Mrs Christie and his aunt about the whereabouts of his wife and daughter, claiming Christie told him to tell anyone who asked that they had gone on holiday.[8]

'I have not seen or heard of Mrs Evans since, and I don't think she has been in the house, otherwise I should have heard her or the baby.'

Commentary – Mrs Christie's comments would imply that while she would have expected Beryl to have told her she and the baby were going away, she had her own interpretation of Beryl not doing so. In any case, nothing happened thereafter to suggest to Ethel that Beryl's and the baby's departure was other than legitimate.

'Mr Evans remained at our address until Monday 21st November 1949, and whilst he was there he sold the furniture. He had previously told me on the weekend after I last saw his wife that he was going to sell up their home and join his wife at Bristol.'

Commentary – Consistent with Evans' statements and confession.

'I did not see Evans after this, but my husband saw him when he came to the front door on the following Wednesday, 23rd November 1949, at about 6 p.m. I was in the house but I did not go to the door. My husband afterwards told me that he said his wife had walked out on him. Also that he had spent all his money that he had got for his furniture and could not get a job anywhere. My husband then told him off for telling us so many lies.'

Commentary – Mrs Christie's timing for this event was correct. Evans and Christie both confirm Evans saw Christie, but not Mrs Christie on Wednesday 23rd November. Mrs Christie was clear that she could only provide a 'hearsay' account of what her husband told her took place.

'I have seen nothing to suggest that Mrs Evans had had a miscarriage at our address and I cannot think why Evans should suggest that she had and that my husband knew all about it.

We were both on friendly terms with him whilst he was at our address. I do know that he was always telling lies. We have never had any friction with him.'

Commentary – Clearly a response to being told by the police what Evans had alleged in his 'Merthyr 2' statement against her husband.

This statement has been read to me and it is true.'

[Signed] E. Christie

Statement taken, read over and signature witnessed by Philip Fensome, Detective Sergeant 'F' Division on 1st December 1949, at 10 Rillington Place, W.11. *(Ethel is a week out)*

For all the incidents in Mrs Christie's statement that could be confirmed from other sources, such confirmation existed. For the incidents that could not be confirmed there was nothing controversial. There was no reason to consider her first statement other than truthful.

Second Statement[9]

Statement of Witness.

Notting Hill Station 'F' Division. 5th December 1949.

Name: Mrs Ethel CHRISTIE. Age: 51.

Commentary – this statement was taken after Evans had confessed and he had appeared in the Magistrates' Court charged with having killed his wife.

'Since making my statement to the Police on 1st December 1949, I have remembered one or two points which I think I ought to mention to you. On the night of Tuesday 8th November 1949, my husband and I went to bed between 10 p.m. and 10.30 p.m. During the night I woke up and heard what seemed to me that someone overhead was moving furniture. I also heard a kind of thud somewhere, but could not place it as I was half asleep. It woke my husband up, and he spoke to me about the noise. I remember it was the Tuesday, 8th November 1949, as it was on the Monday 7th November 1949 that Mrs Evans told me of the row she had had with her husband on the day before, Sunday 6th November 1949. I did not pay much attention to the noise as I thought they were getting ready to move out silently as the landlord's agents had taken out a summons against them for arrears of rent, I knew they were heavily in debt.'

Commentary – The account of the thud in the night was also given by Christie.[10] This was at the time, according to his Notting Hill confession, that Evans was wrapping up his wife's body in Mr Kitchener's flat before taking it down to the wash-house.

If Evans' confession was true, it was incredible that the Christies' heard the wrapping going on in Kitchener's flat but nothing of the really difficult manoeuvre of the body being brought down the stairs, along the passage right outside their bedroom door and into the yard.

Was it possible that Christie made the story up to cover his tracks and got his wife to comply with it? How, though, would Christie have known that Evans had stated in his confession that he had moved Beryl's body to the wash-house that particular night?

Was it possible that Evans simply visited his wife's body in Mr Kitchener's flat in the early hours of 9th November and the Christies' overheard that visit?

'After 8th November 1949 I did not hear the baby cry at all. It would be possible for the baby to cry without my hearing it because Evans occupied the top floor of the house which is two floors and I spent most of my time in our kitchen which is situated on the ground floor at the back of the house. When Mrs Evans has gone out and asked me to give an ear for the baby, I have had to go up part of the stairs to listen, otherwise I would not hear it. The middle floor is rented by a Mr Kitchener who is almost blind and lives by himself. His kitchen is situated immediately at the top of the stairs on the first floor. Mr Kitchener was away from here for some weeks in the eye hospital at Marylebone Road, suffering from cataract until 17th November 1949, when he returned home.'

Commentary – Mrs Christie not overhearing Geraldine after her mother was killed had to be a contentious issue. But if the baby was still alive on the top floor through to Thursday 10th November, Ethel's explanation was credible. Under normal circumstances, she had to go part way up the stairs to hear any crying. She would not have gone onto the stairs, if she had no reason to do so. Furthermore, if Ethel was mainly in her kitchen at the back of the house, she was as far away as possible from the baby. The Evans' bedroom was two floors up and at the front of the house.[11] And the workmen never mentioned overhearing Geraldine crying either.

'At 8.15 p.m. 2nd December 1949, I attended Notting Hill Police Station where Chief Inspector Jennings showed me one black skirt and one pale blue coatee and one green table cover which I identified as property belonging to Mrs Evans. I was also shown a child's pink woollen coat, a white flannelette dress, a white woollen dress and one pair of plastic knickers which I identified as Geraldine Evans' clothing.

The small outbuilding, which is a disused wash-house situated in my back yard, is used for storing wood and other things because the copper is out of order. This building has an outside door which we usually lock at nights. Since 7th November 1949, we have been using this place daily for the purpose of getting water for rinsing the slop pail when emptying it in the lavatory which is situated next door. We had some wood in there in front of the sink and in the corner behind the door but I never saw anything unusual there or any smell.'

Commentary – basic description of the wash-house and how it was used. Mrs Christie said it was locked in the evening. The lock was broken. But it was effectively locked if the door was closed. A spindle was needed to lift the latch and this was kept indoors.

This statement has been read over to me and it is true.

[Signed] E. Christie

Statement taken by Chief Inspector Jennings, written down, read over and signature witnessed by James N. Black, Detective Inspector 'F' Division.

As with Mrs Christie's first statement, there was support for what she stated. Mrs Christie's second statement can be deemed truthful.

The two statements contribute nothing to any supposed 'cover up' for her husband.

Evidence at Evans' trial[12]

At Timothy Evans' trial, Mrs Christie was called to give evidence by the prosecution. Mr Christmas Humphries, for the Crown, examined her on three matters:

- The bump in the night (8th/9th November). Mrs Christie likened it to furniture being moved about.

- Her speaking to Evans on the Wednesday (9th November) evening. She had put the light on for him when he came in and asked him about Beryl and the baby. Evans told her they had gone away to Bristol. She told him that Beryl never came to tell her she was going.

- Evans giving up his job on Thursday 10th November. Mrs Christie said he was angry about that.

Mr Morris, for the defence, cross-examined her asking questions on eight issues:

- Her husband's interest in medical matters. Mrs Christie replied that his interest was only in first aid. She repeated this a number of times throughout the cross-examination.

- Christie trying to learn more about medical matters but his learning being interrupted by some accident around the beginning of the last war. Mrs Christie did not know of any such accident.

- When the floorboards were up in the passageway. She stated they were up on Thursday night to Friday. They were not up on the Wednesday.

- Other times Mrs Christie saw Mr Evans. She saw him on Monday 7th and a number of times on Friday 11th after he had lost his job.

- When she last saw the baby. Mrs Christie did not see the baby on Wednesday 9th or afterwards.

- Had she a particular reason for saying that the bump in the night was on 8th November? Mrs Christie replied that her husband had been up to see his doctor that evening. He always went up on Tuesday evenings.

- Had she seen Evans when he returned on 23rd November? She only heard him.

- Whether Evans inquired about the baby's welfare. Mrs Christie replied 'No.'

Mr Humphreys re-examined:

- Had she or Christie gone into the Evans' flat after hearing the bump in the night? Mrs Christie replied 'No.'

- Whether Christie could feed a baby? She said he knew how to give a bottle.

Mrs Christie's responses mainly confirmed what she had already told the police in her statements. She dismissed Mr Morris' attempts to get her to agree that Christie's medical learning had been curtailed by an accident.

As with her statements, Mrs Christie's evidence in court could not be faulted. She never corroborated her husband's health problems other than mentioning his habit of visiting his doctor on Tuesday evenings.

She never mentioned his enteritis or fibrositis. The questioning in court did not bring out that she was covering up for her husband.

Accusations levelled at Ethel Christie

There were authors on the Evans/Christie case who argued that Ethel was aware of what was happening at 10 Rillington Place during the second week of November 1949. Also, that she protected her husband in the aftermath.

Ludovic Kennedy was the most extreme in developing an argument that Mrs Christie knew her husband was involved in an abortion on Mrs Evans and she covered up for him.

Commentary - this is the subject of chapter 14 of Ludovic Kennedy's book, Ten Rillington Place.

On page 98, Kennedy imagined Christie walking home after having given a statement to the Notting Hill police before the bodies in the wash-house were discovered. Kennedy wrote, 'His confidence must have been slightly shaken by finding a policeman on guard outside his front door and even more shaken at hearing from his wife that an independent statement had been taken from her while he was away. But he need not have worried: he had briefed her too well. Her sole object was to protect her husband from any suspicion of his unsuccessful 'abortion' which she genuinely believed he had performed on Beryl. To this end she made two distinct pronouncements. The first was designed to show that there had been an abortion but it was done by another hand than Christie's. Mrs Evans determined to go on with it and even spoke of going somewhere for an illegal operation...The exact words she used were 'She would have an operation but it would cost money. I have an idea she mentioned going to Praed Street near St Mary's Hospital for the operation, but she never told me the address she intended to go.'[13] The second pronouncement, according to Kennedy, was a totally gratuitous piece of information about Mrs Vincent visiting Mrs Evans on Monday 7th November and Mrs Evans not wanting to see her. Mrs Christie's reason for stating that was, 'to protect her husband, whom she knew was desperately worried about Mrs Vincent's visits, and whom she believed was performing an abortion on Beryl at the time of Mrs Vincent's arrival.'[14]

Commentary – Kennedy's story that Christie had briefed his wife and her statements being aimed to deflect suspicion that her husband had performed an unsuccessful abortion on Beryl, had to be considered in terms of Kennedy having to discredit the evidence of Ethel Christie. Her statements did nothing to allay Evans' confession.

John Eddowes, in his book, *The Two Killers of Rillington Place*, countered Kennedy's story. 'If Christie had killed Beryl and Geraldine, she'd have noticed his absences upstairs, both times followed by the discovery of a body. She would almost certainly have known something if Christie was going upstairs to abort Beryl, and would then have been presented with a dead body, followed by another absence of her husband upstairs, followed by another dead body. She had left Christie before for his criminality, she came from a thoroughly decent family (Black and Jennings both considered her a completely truthful person), and there seems no doubt she'd have gone to the police this time round. She was not a particularly stupid woman, and it is unlikely that she was 'gullible enough to believe anything anyone told her', as Ludovic puts it. [15]

Mrs Vincent made statements to the police on 1st and 7th December concerning her visits to see Beryl in early November 1949.

In her second statement she timed the visit at which the kitchen door at the Evanses' flat was shut when she was sure someone was inside, as 10.30 a.m. on Monday 7th November. She also said she met Mrs Christie in the hall when she was leaving.[16] This totally matched what Mrs Christie said in her first statement.

In 1953 Mrs Vincent wrote to Mr Baker, who was investigating the Evans-Christie case for the Daily Mirror. She then claimed that the day the kitchen door was held against her was Tuesday 8th November and her next visit was on the following day. Christie intercepted her but while they were talking she supposedly saw the baby's pram and high chair in the Christies' front room.[17] But they were not there at that time; Evans did not pass them to the Christies until he left on Monday 14th November.

Kennedy's accusation against Mrs Christie based on Mrs Vincent moving the date of her visit to Beryl forward a day was not credible. Her timing made a month after the event had to be far more reliable than the altered timing Mrs Vincent gave over three years after the event!

It is most likely that Ethel was not in league with Christie or Evans over the murders of Beryl and Geraldine Evans. In any case, she would never have allowed the baby to be killed. Ethel would have looked after Geraldine until the child could have been placed elsewhere, probably with Mrs Probert. If Ethel even suspected that the bundle under the sink in the wash-house was Beryl's body, she would have hung back from touching it when the police asked her to do so on 2nd December.

There is nothing in Mrs Christie's statements, her trial evidence or her actions that indicated she was covering up for her husband over the murders.

Christie committed his first two murders in 1943 and 1944 when Ethel was away visiting her relatives in Sheffield. He successfully hid those killings from her.

During 1952, Mrs Christie was supposed to have told a fellow tenant, Joan (or Pat) Howard, 'I am convinced that my husband had something to do with those two murders.'[18] Did Christie find out about his wife's thinking and decide that she had to be killed? Or was it simply that he wanted his wife out of the way?

Christie claimed he had strangled his wife as a mercy killing because she was choking and in severe distress after having overdosed on his phenobarbitone pills. But the post mortem revealed Ethel had not taken any phenobarbitone. It was, of course, for the murder of his wife that Christie was tried, convicted and executed.

References Chapter 7

1.   Reg and Ethel lived happily enough – Christie's articles in the Sunday Pictorial of June/July 1953

2.   Ethel Christie's first statement to the police, 1st December 1949 – J Eddowes pp 192-5

3.   Search of 10 Rillington Place for instruments of abortion – Brabin p22

4.   Rows between Tim and Beryl over Lucy Endecott – Brabin pp 26-7

5.   The changed timings of Joan Vincent having the door held against her when visiting Beryl Evans – J Eddowes pp 125-7

6.   Christie claimed in his second statement of 5th December to have seen Beryl outside around 1 p.m. on Tuesday 8th November – J Eddowes p204

7.   Mr Jones, in his second statement, altered the timing of when he last saw Beryl going out with the baby and another woman. He moved it back a day from Wednesday 9th to Tuesday 8th November – J Eddowes p200

8. Evans confirms at his trial that he did lie to Mrs Christie and others about his wife and child going on holiday – Evans' trial, Jesse p80

9. Ethel Christie's second statement to the police, 5th December 1949 – J Eddowes pp 195-6

10. In his second statement of 5th December 1949, Christie also heard thud in the night – J Eddowes p205

11. Layout of the Evans' flat – Furneaux p19

12. Mrs Christie's evidence at Timothy Evans' trial – Evans' trial, Jesse pp 41-5

13. Ludovic Kennedy's book had Mrs Christie deflecting Mrs Evans' abortion to outside 10 Rillington Place – Kennedy 10RP p9

14. Ludovic Kennedy considered Mrs Christie mentioning Mrs Vincent's visit was to protect her husband – Kennedy 10RP pp 98-9

15. John Eddowes' counter to Kennedy's accusations of Mrs Christie's collusion – J Eddowes p32

16. Mrs Vincent had door held against her and talked to Mrs Christie on Monday 7th November – Brabin pp 40-1

17. Mrs Vincent in a 1953 letter to Mr Baker changed her visits to see Beryl to 8th and 9th November – Brabin p42

18. Ethel tells Ms Howard she was convinced her husband had something to do with the murders of Beryl and Geraldine Evans – Oates p101 (Oates related it to a Home Office record in the National Archive).

Chapter 8

The Bodies in the Wash-House

The wash-house was a small four foot by four foot outbuilding at the rear of 10 Rillington Place.[1]

Left: Rear of 10 Rillington Place: the one-storey extension comprised the wash-house and toilet. Right: looking into the wash-house

Inside the wash-house, as the second picture shows, the back left was taken up with a disused copper. To the right of that was the sink, shown in the picture as covered with planks. On the wall above the sink there was a tap. The door opened inward. As can be seen, the wash-house was used for storing wood and old paint pots. Mrs Christie stated the tap was used to get water, such as for rinsing slop pails.[2] The weather in November 1949 was cold so it offered some degree of refrigeration.

Kensington Borough Council identified a schedule of remedial work that was needed for the outbuildings and ground floor of 10 Rillington Place. The landlord's agent engaged the local building firm of Larter & Sons to carry out the work. They did so between 31st October and 14th November 1949.[3]

Drawing on the statements given to the police by the builders, Evans and the Christies, the timetable of events relating to the wash-house repairs and the workmen's other involvement at 10 Rillington Place is summarised in the following table. For context, selected other events are included.

Date	Activity
Monday 31st October	Repair work at 10 Rillington Place commences in the afternoon. Manger, Mr Phillips, stated 'work was carried out to the external front bay.'[4]
Tuesday 1st November	Work continued on the external front bay. [4]
Wednesday 2nd	Work continued on the external front bay. [4]
Thursday 3rd	Per manager, Mr Phillips, work commenced on removing the defective roof over the wash-house and toilet and replacing it with a new reinforced concrete roof. [4] In their first statements, both the Plasterer, Mr Willis, and the Labourer, Mr Jones confirmed they had started removing the wash-house and water closet roof.[5,6]
Friday 4th	Plasterer and labourer worked on the wash-house roof. [4]
Saturday 5th	Plasterer and labourer continued working on the wash-house and toilet roof. [4] The labourer stated, 'we completed the laying of the concrete at midday and then went home.' [6]
Sunday 6th	No workmen on site. [4]
Monday 7th	No workmen on site – inclement weather. [4]
Tuesday 8th	Manager, Plasterer and Labourer all confirmed that work was carried out on cementing the roof/plastering the ceiling of the wash-house.[4,5,6 -] (continued over...)

Tuesday 8th	Labourer's second statement – He 'cleaned up the wash-house thoroughly and left the floor clean' not on the afternoon of Friday 11th November (as given in his first statement),' but on looking back it was the day that we removed the timber shores ...... which I now recollect as Tuesday 8th November 1949.'[7]
	Plasterer only mentioned the shores in the context of four of them and the tools being all he saw in the wash-house from the morning of Wednesday 9th November.[6]
	The Manager stated that the shores were 'removed' on Tuesday 8th.[4] (Removed could be either taken down or taken down and taken out of the wash-house?)
	Labourer first statement – he claimed to see two young women and the baby on the morning of Wednesday 9th November.[6]
	But in his second statement the Labourer brought the timing of this sighting forward to the morning of Tuesday 8th November.[7]
	Evans' 'Merthyr 2' statement – he returned home to find his wife dead following Christie's failed abortion and he assisted Christie in moving her body to Mr Kitchener's flat.[8]
	Christie's first statement – claimed to have seen Mrs Evans going out into the street.[9]
	Christie second statement – expanded on the sighting of Mrs Evans. Was at around 1 p.m. and she had the baby with her. Visited Dr Odess between 5.30 p.m. and 6.45 p.m. He and his wife wakened in the night by a heavy thud overhead.[10]
	Ethel Christie second statement – stated she heard noises in the night, like furniture being moved and coming from overhead.[2]
	Evans' 'Notting Hill Confession' – took wife's body to the wash-house, placed it under the sink and hid it with pieces of wood.[11]
Wednesday 9th	Manager's statement – 'Plasterer completed the ceiling of the wash-house during the morning ... and there was nothing unusual in there when he left, otherwise he would have told me.' His men moved on to work in the ground floor front room.[4]
	Plasterer first statement – 'I completed plastering the ceiling of the wash-house about the middle of the morning... I did no further work in the wash-house but we kept the tools in there and I was constantly in and out until the job was finished.'[5]
	Labourer second statement – adjusted forward by one day, to around 10.00 a.m. Wednesday 9th November, his sighting of the dark, short and fairly thick set young man coming downstairs.[7]

Thursday 10th	Plasterer and labourer working in the front room.[4]
	Workmen getting tools from the wash-house.[5]
	Carpenter worked in the hall.[12]
	Evans' 'Merthyr 2' statement – couple from East Acton collected Geraldine, as arranged by Christie.[8]
	Evans' 'Notting Hill Confession' – strangled his baby and took the body down to the wash-house in the night, hiding it behind some wood.[11]
Friday 11th	Carpenter worked in the hall.[12]
	Plasterer and labourer completed their work at 10 Rillington Place.[4]
	Plasterer's first statement – 'during the morning, we cleared the shores and tools out of the wash-house and when we left the place was completely bare.'[5]
	Plasterer's second statement – 'I feel now that it would have been quite possible for anything to have been under the sink in the corner with timber in front of the sink, as we left some old wood flooring behind for the tenants to use as firewood.'[13]
	Labourer's first statement – 'after completing the work... I personally swept out the wash-house and also cleaned out the copper which was in it. There was definitely nothing whatever in the wash-house or the copper.'[6]
	Labourer's second statement – he had thoroughly swept out the wash-house on Tuesday 8th – the day the shores were removed. On Friday 11th, at the end of the work, he just picked up spare materials and tools from the wash-house.[7]
Saturday 12th	Manager's statement – Carpenter spent 4 hours at 10 Rillington Place replacing boards in the hall.[4]
	Christie has his back strapped.[14]
Sunday 13th	
Monday 14th	Manager's statement – Carpenter completed his work to the hall floor which took him up to 10 a.m.[4]
	Furniture dealer called and took away Evans' furniture. Geraldine's pram, chair and a suitcase were left in the Christies' front room. Evans vacated his flat and left for South Wales.[11]

Christie, in his third statement to the police (8th December 1949),[15] made reference to the workmen and the wash-house. His statement mostly agreed with the workmen, but there were some differences:

- Christie and the workmen both had the timber shores in the wash-house being knocked down on 8th November.

- Christie had the work in the wash-house finished on 8th November but the workmen stated they did not finish their work there until Wednesday 9th.

- Christie had the workmen taking all their tools to the front room on 8th November but the workmen stated they kept their tools in the wash-house until they left on Friday 11th.

Commentary – both could be correct. The workmen could easily have operated just taking the tools they needed at the time to the front room, leaving the rest in the wash-house.

- Christie and the builders were in agreement as to when the plasterer, labourer and carpenter all ceased working at 10 Rillington Place.

- Christie stated that the builders kept their cement and sand outside the front of the house and they did all their mixing there. The labourer mentioned he was mixing outside the front on Tuesday 8th.

- Christie mentioned planks left outside to be taken away which was confirmed by the workmen.

- Christie did not mention scrag ends being given to him for firewood by Mr Anderson on 14th. Anderson later identified some of that wood in photographs of the wash-house.

Only Evans provided accounts of how Beryl Evans' body was disposed of. In his 'Merthyr 1' statement, he put her body down the drain on the night she poisoned herself.[16] In an interview with DC Evans following his 'Merthyr 2' statement, Evans said that he assisted Christie in taking Beryl's body to Mr Kitchener's flat. Evans did not see it again.[17] In his Notting Hill confession, on the night after Beryl was killed, he wrapped and tied up his wife's body in Mr Kitchener's kitchen. He then 'carried my wife's body down to the wash-house and placed it under the sink. I then blocked the front of the sink up with pieces of wood so that the body would not be seen.'11 According to Christie's 1953 confession, Evans took his wife's body to the bedroom on the evening she died and Christie did not see it again.[18]

Only Evans gave an account of what happened to the baby's body. In his Notting Hill confession he stated that he returned home after losing his job on the Thursday evening and killed the child. 'At about twelve o'clock that night [he] took the baby downstairs to the wash-house and hid her body behind some wood.'11 Christie in his confession did not mention seeing the baby on Tuesday 8th

November or afterwards. He only mentioned Evans feeding her.[18]

But was it possible for Evans to have put the bodies in the wash-house when he stated he did? A series of questions need to be considered:

- Why was the wash-house chosen to dispose of the bodies?
- Who moved them there and when?
- What wood was used to hide the bodies and when did it become available?
- Why were the bodies not discovered before the police found them on 2nd December?

Why use the wash-house for the disposal of the bodies?

The wash-house was effectively under the Christies' control. Christie used it as a store; Ethel used it to obtain water. They had to have noticed if the layout had been changed or if there was a bad smell.

If Evans was acting alone in needing to dispose of his wife's and his daughter's bodies, why would he have considered putting them in the wash-house? If he killed Beryl, he may well have intended to take her body away from 10 Rillington Place in his van. But when he was unexpectedly sacked on the evening of Thursday 10th, he needed an alternative hiding place. His options would have been under the floorboards in his own flat, under the floorboards in Kitchener's flat, or the wash-house. If Evans killed Geraldine, it would not have been difficult to take the tiny body from the house and hide it at a remote location where, hopefully, it would not be found.

For Evans, on his own account, to put the bodies in the wash-house and then leave 10 Rillington Place to go and stay with his family in South Wales made no sense. He would have lost control of the bodies. In due course the bodies would have been discovered and Evans would have been arrested. Would Evans have been that irrational; unable to understand the consequences of his actions?

At his trial in 1953, Christie stated that for both of his wartime victims, Ruth Fuerst (1943) and Muriel Eady (1944), he temporarily stored their bodies in the wash-house.[19] He later buried both bodies in the back garden. So Christie already had 'a track record' for holding bodies in the wash-house.

In 1953 Mr John Scott Henderson conducted an Inquiry into whether there had been a miscarriage of justice in the Evans case. This Inquiry is the subject of Chapter 12 (volume II). Mr Scott Henderson interviewed the labourer, Mr Jones. Jones stated that he spoke to Evans, in the presence of Christie, on the morning of Wednesday 9th November 1949. Evans, while offering him a smoke, asked 'when do you reckon you will finish this job?' Jones replied, 'We want to get out of here by Friday if we can.'[20] This implied that Evans and Christie were both keen to know when the wash-house would be clear of the workmen.

If Christie by himself, or with Evans, took Beryl's body to

the wash-house, it would appear more likely than not that it was Christie's idea that the wash-house should have been used to hide the body until it could be moved to a more permanent grave.

Who moved them there and when?

Evans on his own

In the night of 8th/9th November both Christie and Mrs Christie stated they were woken by a thud and the noise of furniture moving overhead.[2,10] If Evans was making such a noise moving his wife's body upstairs then the noise would have been far worse if he was taking her body all the way to the wash-house. He was hardly physically strong enough to carry his wife's doubled-up body. He would have had to roll it down the stairs and drag it along the ground floor passageway and yard. There would have been such a racket that the Christies would have come out of their bedroom to see what was going on.

Furthermore, as mentioned above in the table, the plasterer and the labourer kept visiting the wash-house through to the afternoon of Friday 13th to get tools. Since the wash-house was only four foot by four foot, they could hardly have failed to notice the sink being blocked off with pieces of wood.

It is almost certain that Evans did not dispose of his wife's body in the manner he confessed he did.

For the same reason he could not have moved Beryl's body to the wash-house during the night of 8th/9th November, he could not have done so on any other night before he left on Monday 14th.

To move the body after the workmen had finished, during daytime or in the evening, Evans would have needed both Christie and his wife out of the house for some time. Christie did go to see his doctor with a strained back on Saturday 12th. Mrs Christie may have gone shopping at the same time. They might have gone together to the pictures. Even so, how would Evans have known that he had the house to himself for sufficient time to ensure he would not be caught in the act?

While a way for Evans, acting alone, to have taken his wife's body to the wash-house can be concocted, it remains most unlikely that he did so.

Christie on his own

Christie went to see his doctor on Saturday 12th November with a back strain. It was so severe that Dr Odess strapped him up and referred him to a consultant at St Mary's Hospital, Paddington. When he was examined at St Mary's a week later the severe back strain/fibrositis was confirmed.[21] If Christie, by himself, moved Beryl's body from upstairs to the wash-house, he could only have done so after the workmen had stopped using the outbuilding but before he incurred the back strain. This leaves a very short time window, running from the evening of Friday 11th to the morning of Saturday 12th. It would have been most unlikely that Ethel and Evans would both have been out of the house for some time in that time window. And the carpenter was working in the hall on Saturday morning.

The idea that Christie's back strain eased sufficiently to allow him to move Beryl's body from Kitchener's flat after Evans had left on Monday 14th hardly works. Mr Kitchener came back from hospital on Thursday 17th November.

According to DC Evans' questioning of Evans at Merthyr on 1st December, Christie was puffing and blowing simply moving Beryl's body to Kitchener's flat.[22] So how was Christie, weakened by enteritis and, later with fibrositis, supposed to have taken Beryl's body to the wash-house?

But, with Evans still in residence and knowing that his wife's body was in Kitchener's flat, why would Christie have ever sought to move her body on his own?

Evans and Christie together

Hiding Beryl's body in the wash-house had to be the principal concern. She weighed 7½ stone. That the baby was not hidden under the sink with her mother suggested that it was more likely she was placed in the wash-house at a different time.

Evans and Christie had to rethink taking Beryl's body away in Evans' van when Evans was sacked on Thursday 10th and lost the van. They had to decide how to hide her body within 10 Rillington Place. They could not leave the body too long in Mr Kitchener's flat as there was always the danger that Mr Kitchener might suddenly return from hospital. Christie may well have told Evans that Beryl's body would be safe in the wash-house as a temporary hiding place. The workmen would be clear of the wash-house by Friday evening, so the body could be moved over the weekend. It is unlikely that the move could have been made on Saturday morning as the carpenter, Mr Anderson, was working in the hall for four hours and the plumber was in the house for an hour as well. More likely Beryl's body was moved in the afternoon. Even if Ethel was not in the habit of going shopping on a Saturday afternoon, Christie could well have arranged for her to go out and get something he needed for his enteritis.

Once 'the coast was clear', Christie and Evans together could quickly move Beryl's body and hide it in the wash-house. But during the move Christie may well have severely strained his back. He went to see Dr Odess on Saturday 12th November. The doctor observed a strained back/fibrositis 'consistent with his having carried an unusually heavy weight a day or two before.'[23] Dr Odess strapped him up and referred him to a specialist at St Mary's.

Perhaps after Evans and Christie together had hidden Beryl's body in the wash-house, Christie gave Evans an assurance that he would move the body on, into a drain. With his wife's body being permanently disposed of, or so he thought, and the baby being fostered, or so he thought, Evans could have been more content about leaving 10 Rillington Place.

In the event that Evans and Christie hid both bodies in the outhouse at the same time, Christie could have given an assurance that both bodies would be permanently disposed of down the drain. Again, Evans could have been reassured about leaving the house.

When did the wood become available?

The advocates of Evans' innocence made a big issue of the availability of the wood used to hide Beryl's body under the sink. It was claimed that because some of the wood would not have been available until after the night of 8th/9th November, Evans could not have killed his wife; Christie must have done it.

In 1953, in the report on his Inquiry, Mr Scott Henderson played down the importance of the wood not having been available on the night of 8th/9th. He considered, 'it is not certain the bodies were put there before 11th November.'[24]

The Scott Henderson Report was heavily criticised in Parliament. Some MPs argued that if the wood used to hide the body was not available until 14th November then Evans could not have put his wife's body in the wash-house, so he couldn't have murdered her.[25] Those MPs chose to set aside Scott Henderson's point that the body could have been put in the wash-house on 11th November or afterwards.

The question of the availability of the wood has been

exagger- ated since 1953, but it was not a real issue. It did not matter whether Evans, Christie or Evans and Christie together hid Beryl's body under the sink behind a stack of wood. If more wood had been given to Christie, it would have been the natural thing for him to add that new wood to the stack that was already there. The wash-house was far too small to have numerous stacks of wood. The fact that the carpenter identified wood that he had given Christie on the 14th November in the stack in front of the sink had no bearing on who put the body in the wash-house and when.

Why did the bodies remain undiscovered?

If Evans moved the bodies to the wash-house without the Christies' knowing, it is inexplicable that Christie did not find out.

But if Christie was involved in moving Beryl's body and, at the same time or maybe later, the baby's body, he could have protected them so they would not be found. He had the luck of November being particularly cold, so the bodies were partially refrigerated and did not smell.

Summing up on the wash-house

The police considered they had a water-tight case. They had nothing, other than Evans' 'Merthyr 2' statement, to link the killings to Christie. There was plenty of evidence pointing to Evans' guilt. There were stories of his violent rows with his wife. There was his flight to South Wales. He sold his wife's wedding ring in Wales. He came to the police and built a track record of lying to them. He confessed.

But If the police had to concede that one part of Evans'

confession was false, then could more of it have been fabricated? The confession could unravel. They were put on warning by the workmen that the bodies could not have been in the wash-house and hidden by wood until, at least, the afternoon of Friday 11th.

The police should have taken the workmen's accounts at face value and followed up with open minds. Instead, they chose to pressurise the workmen into altering their statements so they would be 'Evans' confession' compliant.[26] They should have 'proved' that Evans' confession fitted the facts, especially when the workmen's evidence cast doubt. Had they done so, their investigation might have dramatically changed course.

References for Chapter 8

1. Description of wash-house – Furneaux, p18

2. Ethel Christie's second statement – J Eddowes, pp 195-6

3. Larter & Sons engagement to do remedial work – Kennedy 10RP, pp 60-1

4. Statement of Mr Philips, Manager at Larter and Sons, in charge of work at 10 Rillington Place – J Eddowes, pp 207-9

5. First statement of Mr Willis, Plasterer – J Eddowes, pp 196-7

6. First statement of Mr Jones, Labourer – J Eddowes, pp 198-200

7. Second statement of Mr Jones – J Eddowes, pp 200-1

8. Evans' 'Merthyr 2' statement – Trial of Evans, Jesse, pp 49-52

9. Christie's first statement – J Eddowes, pp 201-4

10. Christie second statement – J Eddowes, pp 204-6

11. Evans' 'Notting Hill' confession – Trial of Evans, Jesse, pp 54-7

12. Carpenter, Mr Anderson, working on replacing flooring in the

hall – Brabin, p136

13. Second statement of Mr Willis – J Eddowes, p198

14. Christie saw his doctor and had back strapped on Saturday 12th November – Leading dates, Jesse, p xcvi

15. Christie's third statement to the police that covered the workmen's activities – J Eddowes, pp 206-7

16. In his 'Merthyr 1' statement, Evans put his wife's body in the drain – Trial of Evans, Jesse, p48

17. In an interview with DC Evans, Evans last saw his wife's body when he helped Christie take it to Kitchener's flat – Trial of Evans, Jesse, p52

18. In his 1953 confession to killing Mrs Evans, Christie last saw her body in the bedroom of Evans' flat. He last saw Geraldine when Evans was feeding her at the same time – Trial of Christie, Jesse, p161

19. Christie placed wartime victims' bodies temporarily in the wash-house – Trial of Christie, Jesse, pp 188-9

20. Evans asked Jones when the builders would be finished – J Eddowes, p76, Brabin, pp 133-4

21. Christie goes to see Dr Odess with back strain on 12th November 1949 – Introduction, Jesse, p lxxviii

22. DC Evans interview of Evans on the morning of 1st December 1949 – Trial of Evans, Jesse, p52

23. Dr Odess confirmed to Mr Scott Henderson that he diagnosed Christie with fibrositis on 12th November – Scott Henderson Supplementary Report, Jesse, p370 (para 17)

24. Mr Scott Henderson considered it was not certain when Evans

put his wife's body in the wash-house – Scott Henderson Report, Jesse, p315 (para 37)

25. Debate in Parliament on the Scott Henderson Report (29 Appendix 3, Jesse, pp 332 64 (July 1953)

26. Further interviews of the workmen on 8th December 1949 – Brabin, pp 130-5.

Chapter 9

The Evans Trial

Timothy Evans' trial was held at the No.1 Court at the Old Bailey and lasted into three days, 11th-13th January 1950. As trials go it attracted little press attention – just another squalid case of domestic murder in a poor neighbourhood.[1]

The trial was presided over by Mr Justice Lewis. Sir Wilfred Lewis had been called to the bar in 1908. Between 1930 and 1935 he was a junior Treasury counsel ('Treasury Devil') leading for the Crown in prosecutions. In 1935 he became a High Court judge. At the time of Evans' trial he was 68 years old. He died two months afterwards.[2]

Mr Justice Lewis   Mr Christmas Humphreys QC

The prosecution was led by Mr Christmas Humphreys, the son of the eminent barrister and judge, Sir Travers Humphreys. He was called to the bar in 1924 and appointed a junior Treasury counsel in 1934 and a senior Treasury counsel in 1950. He was 49 years old at the time of Evans' trial. Besides the Evans case, he led for the Crown in other *causes célèbres*, including Craig and Bentley (1952) and Ruth Ellis (1955). He became a judge in 1968. He retired in 1976 after controversy over the inconsistency of his sentencing. Christmas Humphreys was an eminent British Buddhist. He died in 1983 (aged 82).[2]

Counsel for the defence was Mr Malcolm Morris, who was called to the bar in 1937. He was deemed to have 'a beautiful speaking voice which he used to great effect with juries.' He was 36 years old at the time of Evans' trial. Although he was actually born in Bromley, Kent, he was deemed Welsh, and that was a consideration in him coming to defend Evans.

Mr Malcolm Morris QC

Morris would later be involved in some high-profile cases – Dr John Bodkin Adams (1957), Mick Jagger and Keith Richards (1967) and John McVicar (1971). He died in 1972 (aged 59).[2]

The prosecution chose to proceed on the charge of Evans having murdered Geraldine. There could be no defence of provocation.

However, they needed the judge to accept that the murders of Beryl and Geraldine were a linked transaction, so that evidence that covered both Beryl's and Geraldine's murders could be placed before the jury. If the judge had ruled that the evidence on Beryl's murder was inadmissible, the prosecution case may well have collapsed. For Geraldine's murder there was only Evans' confession and little else.

Even if the prosecution case on the charge of murdering Geraldine had collapsed, the prosecution could have returned with a charge of Evans having murdered his wife.

The defence alternatives were limited. The defence of insanity was ruled out; there was no medical evidence that Evans was insane.[3]

Morris would try to get the evidence pertaining to Beryl's murder set aside. However, 'Morris thought it unlikely that they would succeed in pinning it [the murder of Geraldine] on the neighbour [Christie], but Evans told him that this was what happened and that was what he wanted to say. Morris accepted the instruction as he was obliged to do and prepared his case professionally but not with any deep personal conviction.'[4]

The trial opened with Timothy John Evans being charged with the murder of Geraldine Evans on the 10th November 1949. He pleaded not guilty.

Right at the start of the trial, the jury was sent out as the judge and the prosecution and defence counsels debated whether evidence pertaining to the death of Beryl Evans should be admitted. Crucially Mr Justice Lewis allowed the evidence to be admitted, while noting Mr Morris' objection.[5]

Commentary – On the one hand, the killings were linked - both victims strangled, both bodies found in wash-house, the baby killed to prevent the killing of the mother coming to light. On the other hand, they were different - different age groups of victims, bodies not hidden together, different ligatures, different motives.

Prosecution case

Mr Humphreys, in his opening speech, summarised the prosecution's understanding of the case against Evans.[6] Essentially, Evans had got depressed because he lost his job and killed his wife, then killed the child.

Commentary – in actual fact Evans had not lost his job when he was supposed to have killed his wife. He had lost his job when he was supposed to have killed his daughter.

Evans lied about it and then lied in a series of statements including blaming his neighbour, Mr Christie. Mr Humphreys provided more detail on each of the principal events.

Commentary – already covered in preceding chapters of this volume.

Humphreys drew his argument to the confession Evans made to Chief Inspector Jennings. He then warned the jury that, after the judge's ruling, they would hear the facts relating to both killings but, 'You are concerned with the death of the baby.'

Mr Humphreys then called a series of prosecution witnesses. The initial witnesses formally described the scene of the crime and confirmed the identity of the victim, Geraldine Evans.

The first material witness was the pathologist, Dr Donald Teare.[7] Dr Teare had only six questions and two re-examination questions from Mr Humphreys. He confirmed that Geraldine had been strangled and a tie was found tightly tied around her neck. He confirmed that Beryl was 16 weeks pregnant and that the pregnancy had not been interfered with. He confirmed that she was strangled with a piece of rope.

Mr Morris' cross-examination of Dr Teare comprised only nine questions. He questioned Teare further on the possibility of the pregnancy being interfered with, but got nowhere.

Commentary – Mr Morris' probing for a chink of support for an attempted abortion had drawn a blank. Although he had not yet put forward the 'Merthyr 2' defence, a vital witness had already undermined it.

Morris did, though, establish that Beryl's stomach contained only mucus and she had not had a meal for three to four hours before her death.

Commentary – that made it possible for Evans to have strangled his wife after returning home from work on Tuesday 8th November, before they had had an evening meal, or for Christie to have murdered her earlier in the day before she had had lunch.

Then Mr Humphreys called Christie. The examination was bland, mainly aimed at establishing Evans' movements and what he said around the time of and immediately following the murder of his wife and child.[8]

A summary of the key elements is as follows:

- Christie was questioned about the layout of 10 Rillington Place. It was established that everyone living in the house had use of the backyard, the outside lavatory and the wash-house. Anyone wanting to use these facilities had to pass through a door (kept unlocked) at the end of the passageway between the Christies' kitchen and bedroom.

- Christie said that he last saw Mrs Evans and the baby on Tuesday 8th November.

- Around the middle of the night of Tuesday 8th/Wednesday 9th November, Christie said he and his wife heard 'a very loud thud', followed later by 'some movement which appeared to be upstairs'. He saw nothing from his bedroom window which overlooked the yard.

- Then there was a mix up over when Christie next saw Evans. In the confusion, which involved the judge trying to clarify, Mr

Morris interjected asking Christie to keep his voice up. Christie replied, 'I have a quiet voice; it is the reaction of gas poisoning in the last war'.

Commentary – Christie neatly took the opportunity to impose a positive character reference for himself. Morris must have been annoyed that this would be left unqualified in the jurors' minds for so long.

- Christie said he next saw Evans on Wednesday 9th November at about 10.30 p.m. His wife put the hall light on for him coming in. Christie overheard his wife ask Evans, 'Where's Beryl and the baby?' Evans replied, 'Oh, she has gone away to Bristol.' Mrs Christie said that she never told me she was going', to which Evans replied, 'she didn't tell his mother either but she will write.'

- Evans was seen again on Thursday 10th November at around 6.30 p.m. when he came in and went straight upstairs. About a quarter of an hour afterwards, Evans knocked on the Christies' kitchen door. Evans told the Christies that he 'had packed in his job' as he had failed to make deliveries down in Brighton. Christie added that Evans 'had prospects of a job in Bristol' and he 'may be going down at the weekend and, if the job comes off, then I shall settle down there.' Christie added he seemed 'angry, upset, really wild, as though he had had a terrific row.'

- Evans was seen yet again on Friday 11th November – Mrs Christie put the hall light on when he came in as the hall floorboards had been taken up. She wanted to know if Evans had heard from Beryl. Christie stated that Evans said that 'she [Beryl] is going to write to you.' He then said he 'would be selling his furniture … because he could not take it down to Bristol.'

- The furniture went on Monday 14th. A quarter of an hour after it had gone, Evans called, carrying a rather large suitcase. Evans said that he was going to Bristol and that he had received £60 for the furniture. He showed Christie a roll of banknotes. Evans then went.

- Christie next saw Evans on Wednesday 23rd November. Evans told him he had 'just come straight down from Wales. I've come from Paddington Station. I've not seen anybody. Beryl has walked out on me and I couldn't find a job.' He had tried in Bristol, Cardiff, Birmingham and Coventry. He had spent a lot on travel and only had about a couple of pounds left. Christie added Evans was anxious to leave to return to Wales and Christie went part way to Paddington with him.

- Christie, asked about his health, confirmed he was 'a rather sick man.'

That ended Mr Humphreys' examination and Day One of the trial.

Commentary – Mr Humphreys had guided Christie through, laying a series of markers for his eventual cross-examination of Evans.

At the opening of the second day, Mr Morris began his crucial cross-examination of Christie.[9]

- Christie denied knowing a young couple living in Acton. He had no friends in Acton. Morris went over the point again – seven more questions. He got a series of 'no' responses.

- Morris produced the tie that had been found around Geraldine's neck and had it handed to Christie. Christie stated he had seen the tie at the police station when he was asked to identify clothing on the floor that belonged to Mrs Evans and the baby. Christie was not certain whose tie it was, but it wasn't his.

- Morris kept going with questions on the tie. He wanted to know if Christie had connected the tie with Evans when he was at the police station, but Christie only said he had seen Evans wearing a striped tie. Morris fired more questions aimed at trying to get Christie to admit he told the police it was Evans' tie. Christie consistently answered that Evans did wear a striped tie. Morris pointed out that Christie was wearing a striped tie himself.

- He had Christie hold up the tie. Morris stated that it was not obviously striped. Christie replied 'Not a great deal, no.'

- Then Morris, even though the witness had not been undermined in the exchange concerning the striped tie, launched his first accusation that Christie was 'responsible for the death of Mrs Evans and the little girl; or, if that is not so, at least that you know much more about those deaths than you have said?' Christie replied, 'That is a lie.'

Commentary – Morris launched his attack after making no impression with the lines of questioning on the young couple in Acton and the striped tie. But why did he weaken his question and weaken the attack with the qualification 'if that is not so, at least that you know very much more about those deaths than you said.' The defence argument was that Christie did it, not that Christie knew about it. Furthermore, after Christie denied the accusation, there was no follow up. Morris turned to a new line of questioning.

- In response to questions on the relationship he and his wife had with Mrs Evans and on her pregnancy, Christie replied that he and his wife had discussed the fact that Mrs Evans looked really ill. They spoke to her and encouraged her to stop taking pills. That was in late October.

- Morris turned to a line of questioning drawn from 'Merthyr 2'. Christie confirmed that he did have a chat with Evans concerning his wife doing herself harm with the pills. Morris suggested that Christie told Evans, 'if you and your wife had come to me in the first place I could have done it for you without any risk.' Christie emphatically denied this and referred back to Evans needing to get rid of any more pills. Morris tried to fix this supposed chat to around a week before Beryl was murdered but Christie placed it the day after he and his wife had spoken to Mrs Evans.

- Morris tried to make out that Christie told Evans he had medical knowledge; that Christie was training to be a doctor before the war but had to give it up because of an accident. Evans said to him 'I didn't know you knew anything about medical stuff', or something to that effect. Christie replied that it was nonsense. He had first aid certificates and these hung in the front room and he had pointed them out to Evans.

- Morris tried to fix the timing of the accident at the beginning of the war. The judge intervened: 'which war?' Christie took the judge's lead to mention the wounds he received in the previous war. Morris re-timed his accident question to the beginning of the last war and Christie replied – 'No.'

Commentary – Mr Morris would raise Christie's supposed accident when cross-examining Mrs Christie, later.

- The cross-examination continued with more questions on Christie convincing Evans he had medical knowledge. Morris asked Christie if he remembered showing Evans medical books. Christie replied that he had 'a St John's Ambulance book; a small black book.' Morris asked if it had diagrams and Christie replied, 'diagrams of bones.' Morris asked, 'showing different parts of the body?' Christie replied: 'No – bones. There are one or two other details about the heart and the arteries and veins; there is a diagram of that.' Christie denied showing Evans a handbook.

Mr Morris then asked Christie, 'can you suggest why in the world I am able to ask a question about it; why Evans could have known that you had a book with diagrams in your flat?'

Mr Humphreys immediately interjected, 'how can he say that?' The judge asked Mr Morris if he was asking these questions following instructions, which allowed Morris to put the question another way, emphasising that the book had diagrams of the human body. Christie started his reply, 'well, it might have been obvious'... but he was then interrupted by Mr Humphreys, 'It is not for the witness to make hypotheses as to how something happened, or what somebody else might have known.'

Commentary – although Christie had fended off the implicit suggestion that he had used medical books to convince Evans of his competence to perform an abortion, Morris would still have left the jury with the impression that there could be some truth in it. How else would Evans have known he had a medical book, even if it was only a first-aid handbook?

- Having established that Christie knew Evans could not read or write, Mr Morris moved on to question Christie on what he was doing on Tuesday 8th November (the day Beryl Evans was murdered). In response to a series of questions, Christie stated that for most of the time he was in bed, sometimes in his pyjamas. He was in discomfort due to back pain. Other than his wife, he only saw the builders. He saw no one else.

  Morris, having emphasised Christie was now stating that he saw no one else on the Tuesday, asked, 'then I presume you did not see either of the Evanses?' Christie corrected himself, 'I did not – oh, on Tuesday? I beg your pardon; on Tuesday I had walked into the front room and I was near the bay windows and I saw Mrs Evans... that would be about lunchtime on Tuesday.'

  The judge intervened and established Christie thought she had the child with her.

  Morris tried to confuse Christie. 'I am just asking you, Mr Christie, how it is you said that yesterday [that he had seen Mrs

Evans going out] and you have forgotten that today?' Christie responded that he had been in severe pain all night; he had seen the doctor and had been prescribed pills.

The judge suggested Mr Christie would be more comfortable sitting down. He asked Christie if he was suffering from fibrositis and Christie replied, 'badly.'

Commentary - Morris left the issue of Christie being in severe discomfort, yet being able to come out of the bedroom to see Beryl through the front window. Despite correcting himself, Christie's responses would have seemed plausible to the jurors.

Christie was suffering from fibrositis while in the witness box, but on 8th November he was only suffering from enteritis.

• Continuing with questions on events on Tuesday 8th November, Morris asked about the presence of the builders. He wanted Christie to confirm that the builders had started working in the hall on that day and that the floorboards had been lifted. But Christie maintained the builders were not working in the hall on Tuesday 8th; they were working in the front room. Christie timed their working in the hall as starting on Wednesday 9th or Thursday 10th. He concurred that when they did so they took up the floorboards and walking on the planks left by the carpenter was noisy. Christie also said: 'There were planks on the top and anybody could have tripped over them. The planks were dangerous as they were not reaching the front door.'

Christie confirmed to the judge that the floorboards were up on Thursday and Friday, but not on Tuesday.

Commentary – Mr Morris appeared to be pursuing a line of questioning that would have discredited Evans' confession. If the floorboards were up on Tuesday, how could Evans have taken his wife's body to the wash-house? However, he got nowhere with Christie on this tack.

- Mr Morris asked about the events of the evening of Tuesday 8th. Christie stated that when he and his wife came back from the doctor's they heard a noise upstairs and presumed the Evanses were in. Morris suggested a different course of events. 'On that Tuesday evening, when Evans came in, you were waiting for him at the bottom of the stairs and you said to him, 'go upstairs, I will come up behind you' and you followed him up to the flat?' Christie repeated he was at the doctor's, so it would be impossible.

  Morris then shifted the timing of Evans coming in until after Christie returned from the doctor's. Christie replied, 'No.' Morris continued on regardless, 'it's bad news: it didn't work.' Christie replied, 'No.'

  Mr Morris: 'meaning the abortion had not worked?' Christie replied that he was feeling pretty bad. He went to bed and his wife brought him in some milk food, which she spilt.

  Morris then asked: 'Then Mr Christie – I will take this quite shortly – you would deny any suggestion you went into Evans' flat with him and there saw the dead body of his wife?' Christie gave an obvious answer, 'I definitely would.'

  Commentary - Whether Christie was in the hall to meet Evans when he came home from work on Tuesday 8th November or whether he was at the doctor's was crucial. But from the way Morris put his questions, the defence team did not appear to have checked up on whether or not Christie saw Dr Odess on Tuesday 8th November and, if so, at what time? What had to have been a crucial line of questioning had drawn another blank for Morris.

- The questioning turned to 'the thud in the night'. Christie said, 'it seemed loud; it rather startled us; it woke us up.'

  The judge intervened with a question on where the noise came from. Christie could not be definite.

Asked about looking out of the window, Christie replied that he could see nothing in the dark and lay down again.

Asked if the noise of furniture moving seemed to come from the floor above, Christie replied that he didn't know 'whether it was from the floor above or above that'.

Mr Morris drew to the point he was trying to make. 'If the movement appeared to come from the first floor, you would have been suspicious that something out of the ordinary was happening... because you knew that the first floor was empty?' Christie replied 'Yes.' Morris pointed out that Christie had never mentioned the noise of something moving when he gave evidence at the Magistrate's Court. Christie responded, 'Yes, I did mention it, I am certain.'

Commentary – Morris did not come back with a challenge to Christie on this. Why did he say that Christie didn't mention the noise at the magistrate's court and simply leave it at that when Christie said he did? Again, Morris moved on, having failed to catch Christie out.

• Asked if he saw Evans next morning, Christie replied that he saw him on his way out saying to him, 'good morning, you're early.'

Morris then launched into a second accusation against Christie – again drawing on Evans' 'Merthyr 2' statement. 'I'm suggesting to you that what happened then was that you carried the dead body of Mrs Evans, with Evans' help, down to Kitchener's flat on that evening.' Christie replied, 'that is absolutely ridiculous, because... at this time this fibrositis in my back was so bad, and I had been on a starvation diet, just milk food for several weeks because of the enteritis, I could scarcely bend.'

Commentary – unfortunately the defence team remained in the dark over the real state of Christie's health. Had they but known he was grossly exaggerating his health problems, Morris could have made headway by exposing the fact that Christie was not suffering from fibrositis on 8th November.

Mr Morris then made out, in response to an intervention from the judge, that 'Evans had helped Christie carry this body to Kitchener's flat and this witness said subsequently he would dispose of it down one of the drains.'

Commentary – Christie had said no such thing. But Mr Morris left 'the body down one of the drains' in the jurors' minds.

- Christie was asked a series of questions, again drawn from Evans' 'Merthyr 2' statement, trying to make out that Christie looked after and fed the baby while Evans was away at work. Christie denied that.

- Mr Morris returned to his initial cross-examination theme of Christie knowing a young couple in Acton who would look after the baby. The judge interjected and Mr Morris responded, by treating as fact that Christie told Evans that the young couple would collect the baby on Thursday 10th November. But Christie replied: 'No, and I don't know anyone in Acton at all.'

- Morris moved on to the evening of Thursday 10th November.

Commentary – this was the evening the baby was strangled. But if Evans' 'Merthyr 2' statement was true, Evans believed the baby had already been collected by the couple from East Acton.

He asked Christie if he remembered seeing Evans. Christie replied by firstly relating back to the previous evening when Evans came in at about 10:30 p.m. and Ethel offered to put the light on for him. Morris tried to make out that Christie had already said the light was put on for Evans on Thursday 10th and Friday 11th November because 'the hall floor had been up and re-laid'. While Morris aimed to confuse Christie so something might slip, Christie adeptly clarified. His wife put the light on that Wednesday because she expected Beryl and Geraldine to be with Evans. 'She assumed that the three of them would be coming back together as usual.' It was because the light didn't matter to Evans alone that Ethel said, 'but what about Beryl and the baby?' And Evans said, 'I'm by myself; she's gone away for a holiday.'

Morris interpreted Christie as saying the carpenter had started to lift the floor in the hall on Wednesday. Christie was unsure as to whether the carpenter started on the Wednesday or the Thursday.

Commentary - again Mr Morris was interpreting Christie by attributing to him something he never said. Presumably he was trying to discredit the exchange between Evans and Mrs Christie on late Wednesday evening.

• Mr Morris, not having achieved anything over the issue of the late evening meeting between Evans and the Christies, resorted to another accusation against Christie. On the Thursday evening he had Christie saying to Evans, 'the best thing you can do now is to sell your furniture and get out of London somewhere.' Christie denied that, adding, 'On the Thursday he seemed to be in too much of a temper and too angry altogether practically to talk to him at all.

Commentary – yet again, Morris had attributed what Evans said Christie did in 'Merthyr 2' to Christie and Christie, yet again, had rebuffed it with a reasonable reply.

• Mr Morris turned to Evans having sold his furniture in the Portobello Road. Christie digressed, making a remarkable series of statements to the effect that on coming to the court, he had spoken to Evans' brother-in-law, Basil Thorley. The nature of the exchange became confused over what the brother-in-law said and drew questioning from the judge. Mr Morris and Judge Lewis were highly sceptical as to why they would have discussed anything about furniture shops at all. What Christie implied was that the brother-in-law told Evans where he could sell his furniture. The brother-in-law said, 'Evans was a liar.'

Commentary – Evans' statements to the police never mentioned him being advised by Christie or his brother-in-law on how he could dispose of his furniture. Christie, introducing the story, could be seen as trying to cover up the fact that he did indeed tell Evans to sell his furniture to Mr Hookway. In any case, why would Evans have wanted to say anything to his brother-in-law about selling his furniture? It would have got back to Evans' mother, Mrs Probert. She might have gone straight round to see her son to stop that happening as she stood as surety with the hire purchase company. The suspicious disappearance of Beryl and Geraldine might have come out much sooner.

Mr Morris had an opportunity to undermine Christie and link Christie to Evans selling the furniture, if he had been prepared to call the brother-in-law as a defence witness. That, though, would not have fitted the defence strategy of only calling Evans so that Mr Morris would be able to sum up after, not before, the prosecution counsel.

- Mr Morris, again drawing on 'Merthyr 2', suggested to Christie, 'on Thursday evening you advised Evans that if people asked about his wife and child he should say they had gone to Brighton for Christmas, because that would keep people quiet?' Christie replied, 'No.' Morris asked, 'Did you advise him to get out of London?' Again Christie replied, 'No.'

- The cross-examination moved on to events on Friday 11th November. Christie again mentioned that Evans told him his wife and baby had gone to Bristol. He added that he was going to follow at the weekend but he had to dispose of his furniture.

- It moved on again to events on Monday 14th November. Christie stated Evans told him he sold the furniture for £60 and showed him a roll of notes. Morris said £40, but Christie couldn't say whether £60 or £40 based on his seeing the role of notes. Christie was there when the furniture was collected.

- Christie confirmed Evans left some property with him until Evans could collect it or have it sent on. This was stored in the front room and included two suitcases, a pram, a baby chair and some crockery. They were taken away by the police and Evans' mother. Mr Morris made out there were more articles left including some baby clothes, vases, a clock, dishes, saucepans and a bucket. Christie said not; 'pans and stuff and various articles were thrown away in the dustbin.'

- Morris now turned to an earlier visit Mrs Probert and her daughter made to 10 Rillington Place before any police inquiries. Christie claimed only the step-sister [Mrs Westlake] called. She spoke to his wife just as he was returning from having been at the hospital. The step-sister was concerned they had not heard from Beryl. Christie told her that Mrs Evans had gone away on holiday. Mrs Westlake replied, 'I have an idea there must be something wrong, otherwise she would have written.' Christie told her 'you don't want to worry. She will probably ....' Then the judge intervened.

- Christie denied refusing Mrs Westlake permission to go to the Evanses' flat.

- Morris ended going through the events and turned to questioning Christie's character. He said Christie was not in the police force but in the war reserve. He mentioned Christie's four convictions, one in 1929 being for malicious wounding

Commentary – Christie's old convictions being exposed would cost him his job with the Post Office.[10]

- Morris told Christie, 'the accused will say in due course... that you have told him that you procured abortions for a number of young women?' Christie replied, 'That is wrong. That is a lie.'

- Finally, Morris pressed Christie again on him having medical knowledge and having started medical training. Christie again denied that; his knowledge was of first-aid just as laid down in the St John's book.

Commentary – From the transcript of the trial alone, when Morris finished his cross-examination, he achieved nothing that showed Christie and not Evans, was responsible for the murders of Beryl and Geraldine Evans. Christie had adequately answered Morris' questions. As the defence was that Christie killed Beryl and Geraldine, Morris needed to question Christie on why, where, when and how he killed each victim. Morris really needed to be 'in the room' taking Christie through, step by step, what he deemed Christie had done. But he did none of that. In fact, he questioned Christie on nothing to do with the baby's death whatsoever.

There were three chinks in Christie's evidence. Firstly, seeing Mrs Evans outside at lunchtime on Tuesday 8th November through the bay window of the front room when he was supposed to have been confined to his bedroom and doubled up with fibrositis. He did not suffer from fibrositis until Saturday 12th. Was he laying an alibi against the possi-bility of the defence calling Mrs Vincent to give evidence that she had the door to the top flat held against her at lunchtime on the Tuesday? Secondly, his story about Evans' brother-in-law, Basil Thorley, telling Evans to sell his furniture to Hookway in the Portobello Road. Was Christie concerned that Evans had told Hookway that Christie had recommended him? Thirdly, there were some grounds for suggesting Christie did offer an abortion for Beryl. How did Evans, who could not read or write, know Christie had 'medical books', albeit that they were only first aid books? Morris failed to widen those chinks.

Mr Humphreys re-examined:[11]

- Firstly, he referred to the trial Exhibit 8 (Evans' Notting Hill confession). He provided a summary of how and why Evans strangled his wife. He mentioned the body being moved to Kitchener's flat. Humphreys asked Christie, 'was there any reason on that night, the Tuesday night, why your hall was obstructed?' Christie confirmed it was not obstructed.

- Morris objected to the way Humphreys put the question. The reference to Evans' confession was prejudicial.

  Commentary – Humphreys was aiming to put in the jurors' minds that there was no impediment in the hall to Evans taking his wife's body to the wash-house on the night of 8th/9th of November.

- Christie was asked if he appreciated the medical evidence that this woman was 'not killed by abortion, but by strangulation.' Christie replied, 'Yes.'

- Christie was asked if he appreciated that it had been alleged he had strangled Beryl and the baby. Christie replied, 'Yes, I was told that.'

- Humphreys then got Christie to confirm his poor physical condition on the day Beryl Evans died: '…in order to pick up a pin from the floor you had to go down on all fours.'

- Humphreys then moved to rebuild Christie's character. He mentioned his military service in the First World War; that he was gassed and suffered as a result. He pointed out, 'the last time you were in trouble with the police for any offence was in 1933.' He mentioned Christie's war reserve police service during the last war.

  Morris objected to Humphreys asking questions in terms of 'you appreciate this and you appreciate that.' It allowed him to 'make comments during the evidence, before he was entitled to address the jury.'

Commentary - Mr Humphreys had used his short re-examination to cleverly bring the jury's attention back to the key facts that undermined Mr Morris' line of questioning Christie. Beryl had not died in any failed abortion; Christie was physically incapacitated on the day Beryl was killed. It also aimed to neutralise Mr Morris' attempts to undermine Christie's character.

Christie left the witness box. That ended the first of the trial's crucial confrontations.

Commentary –while the words of the cross-examination of Christie by Mr Morris have been recorded, the nuances of the exchange have not. The voice tones, the pauses, the facial expressions, the body language, the reactions of the court, have long since been lost. These nuances, though, would have been evident to the jurors.

Mrs Ethel Christie was the next prosecution witness.[12]
Mr Humphreys examined.

- He opened with a question concerning her being awakened by a bump one night in November. She timed it to the 8th, but was unsure where it came from. Afterwards she 'heard a movement upstairs as if furniture was being moved about.'

Commentary – consistent with her husband's earlier testimony.

- Mrs Christie was asked about seeing Evans next evening. She saw him at 10.30 p.m. when he came in and put the light on in the hall for him. She confirmed Evans was alone and then asked him, 'but what about Beryl and the baby? I always put the light on when they were coming in, so that they would be able to see up the stairs.' Mrs Christie asked, 'Where's Beryl and the baby?' Evans replied. 'they've gone away... to Bristol.' She then said, 'But she never came to tell me she was going away,' and he replied, 'No, and my mother was surprised that she did not go to see her either.'

Commentary - again consistent with her husband's evidence. On the evening of Wednesday 9th November, Beryl Evans was already dead; Geraldine may have been still alive and upstairs.

- Mrs Christie was asked about Evans coming down from his flat on the next day. She said that he knocked on the kitchen door about a quarter to seven. 'He really talked to my husband most,' but she overheard that he had given up his post. He 'was very angry about it.'

Commentary – on the third of the matters raised in the examination, Mrs Christie's evidence was yet again consistent with her husband's.

Mr Morris cross-examined.

- He opened by asking, 'Mrs Christie, your husband is rather interested, is he not, in medical matters?' She replied, 'Well, in first aid.' Morris then asked if Christie was trying to learn more about medicine before the war. Mrs Christie repeated, 'he just keeps to first aid.' Morris put the matter another way, only for Mrs Christie to say yet again his interest was in first aid.

A question on Christie's interest in medicine having been curtailed by an accident 'just before or at the beginning of the last war?' drew a reply from Mrs Christie, 'sorry I do not know what you mean. What accident?' Morris, floundering, 'the difficulty is I do not know what accident it is.' The judge intervened, asking Mrs Christie if there had been any accident, but she couldn't recollect any.

Mr Morris tried another approach, asking Mrs Christie about her husband's medical books. She replied 'Well, he has only one or two first-aid books.' Morris then asked if they contained diagrams of parts of the human body. Mrs Christie replied, 'I do not know. I have never looked at them. I am not interested in medical things.'

Commentary - Mr Morris' line of questioning to get Mrs Christie to support his contention that Christie had shown Evans medical books and could perform abortions, petered out. Mrs Christie's answers were sufficiently different to Christie's to show she was in no way covering up for her husband. Christie, though, did have an accident when he was knocked down in 1924. But that was during the period 1923-33, when he and his wife were separated. So she may well not have known about that accident.

- Mr Morris asked Mrs Christie about her offering to put the light on for Mr Evans in the late evening of Wednesday 9th November. Morris tried to make out that she did so because the floorboards were up. Mrs Christie replied that, 'they were not up on the Wednesday... just Thursday night to Friday.

Commentary – Mrs Christie merely confirmed what she had said to Mr Humphreys. The state of the hall, at least, would not have been an impediment to Evans taking Beryl's body to the wash- house on the night of 8th/9th of November. But Morris did not go on to other matters that could have revealed that Evans could not have taken Beryl's body down that night.

- A bland question followed on when Mrs Christie next saw Evans. She said she had seen him when he called at the kitchen on Thursday and as he went in and out on Friday.

- Mr Morris asked, 'did you ever hear at any time your husband saying anything to him [Evans] about the baby being looked after?' Mrs Christie replied, 'yes, I looked after Geraldine.' The line of questioning had gone wrong. Mrs Christie added that she had last looked after Geraldine on the afternoon of Monday 7th November and she and her husband had not looked after the baby on Wednesday 9th November. Morris attempted to undermine Mrs Christie's recollection. She had given her statement on what happened on the 8th/9th and 10th of November about three weeks afterwards. 'You have not, have you, given the timetable of the days any particular thought before that?' The judge intervened in order to clarify the dates on which she said the events had occurred; the bump in the night was on Tuesday 8th November; being told Beryl and the baby had gone to Bristol was on Wednesday 9th. Mrs Christie confirmed to the judge, 'the last time I saw Beryl and the baby was on Monday.'

- Mr Morris asked if Mrs Christie had 'any particular reason for timing the bump in the night as Tuesday 8th November. Mrs Christie answered, 'I think I remember it because my husband had been up to the doctor that evening, and he always went up on Tuesday evening.'

- Finally, Mr Morris asked Mrs Christie about Evans' visit back to 10 Rillington Place. She did not see him, but she heard his voice. She did not hear him enquiring about Geraldine

Commentary – Mr Morris' cross-examination of Mrs Christie had achieved nothing for the defence. Her testimony did not undermine anything that Christie had said.

But there were a number of issues Morris failed to question her on that could have been helpful to the defence case. For instance:

- Christie's health and how she was looking after him. That might have brought out the fact that Christie was not that ill with enteritis and he did not have fibrositis until Saturday 12th.

- Mrs Vincent's visit. That just may have brought out that her visit was significant.

- Did not Christie go upstairs on the morning after the thud in the night to see what happened? That might have put doubt into Mrs Christie's mind over her husband's behaviour and allowed Morris to ask supplementary questions.

- The workmen and the wash-house. That might have shed light on the impossibility of Evans moving Beryl's body when he said he did and on why the body remained undetected.

- The baby's clothing and equipment being left in the front room after Evans left. Did she not think it odd that such important items for the baby's welfare did not go with the baby?

Mr Humphreys re-examined Mrs Christie:

- Did she ever go into the Evans' flat after she heard the bump in the night? Mrs Christie did not. Nor did Mr Christie.

- Was Mr Christie capability of feeding a baby? 'He knew how to give a baby a bottle.'

- Was he physically capable of going up to the flat at that time and working up there? Mr Morris objected that this was two questions and Mr Humphreys said, 'I will leave it.'

  Commentary - Mr Humphreys was pursuing an interesting line of questioning which could have been helpful to the defence. These were questions Mr Morris should have asked Mrs Christie, yet Morris interfered to stop them.

  If Mrs Christie had confirmed Christie's evidence that he was incapacitated from before 8th November and for some time afterwards, that would not have helped the defence. But what if she had said he was able to go about almost as normal, or something to that effect?

Mrs Violet Lynch, Evans' aunt living in Merthyr Vale, was the next witness.[13] She was examined by Mr Humphreys' junior, Mr Elam:

- Mrs Lynch basically confirmed some uncontroversial evidence.

This included Evans staying at her house in Merthyr Vale from Tuesday 15th November until Wednesday 30th November. He left to go to London on 21st November, returning on the 23rd.

On his return, Evans told Mrs Lynch that 'his wife had walked out of the flat and left the baby in the cot in the bedroom. He did not say why. I asked him what he had done with the baby, and he said he gave it to some people from Newport to look after.'

Commentary – as when Evans would later give his statements to the Merthyr police, he was reluctant to talk about the child. Mrs Lynch had to ask him what had been done with her and DC Evans also had to ask where the baby was.

- Mrs Lynch was then asked about the letter she received from Evans' mother on 30th November. The letter - already considered in chapter 3 of this volume - was read out in evidence. She stated that Evans said his mother was lying.

Commentary - there was the major inconsistency the Lynches would have noticed. Whereas Evans told the Lynches Beryl had walked out and the baby was being cared for by the people from Newport, his mother's letter stated, 'I have not seen Beryl or the baby for a month. Tim came round and told me that Beryl and the baby had gone to Brighton to her father for a holiday.'

- Mrs Lynch concluded her evidence by stating that she and Evans went to Merthyr that same morning.

Mr Morris did not cross-examine.

The next witness called by the prosecution was Detective Constable Gwynfryn Evans of the Merthyr Constabulary.[14] He was examined by Mr Elam:

- DC Evans outlined the circumstances of Evans coming to

Merthyr police station on the afternoon of 30th November 1949. Evans told DC Evans, 'I want to give myself up... I have disposed of my wife... I put her down the drain.' DC Evans cautioned Evans and took a statement from him.

- Evans' first Merthyr statement – set out and discussed in Chapter 3 of this volume – was then read out by the Clerk of the Court.

- Mr Elam questioned DC Evans on the events that followed Evans giving his 'Merthyr 1' statement. DC Evans spoke to the police in London. He went back to speak to Evans at about 9 p.m. to tell him 'the drain which you say you put your wife's body down has been examined and there is nothing there.' Evans couldn't have lifted the drain. Evans told him, 'No, I said that to protect the man named Christie.' DC Evans cautioned Evans before he gave his second statement.

- Evans' second Merthyr statement – set out and discussed in Chapter 3 – was then read out by the Clerk of the Court.

- DC Evans had a further interview with Evans on the morning of 1st December. Evans stated that he knew Mrs Lynch had a letter from his mother, 'but I don't know what was in it.' Evans last saw his wife's body, 'just before Christie took it to Kitchener's flat.' He heard Christie puffing and blowing while taking Beryl's body down and Christie asked him to 'come down and give me a hand.' Evans picked up her legs and they took her to the flat.

- DC Evans added that Evans told him that he 'went back on the Wednesday or Thursday of the week after I came down [to Merthyr]. I wanted to see about my child.' Christie told him, 'she's all right. You can't see her yet. It would be too early.' Evans then returned to Merthyr Tydfil.

- DC Evans also asked Evans how he tore up his wife's clothes and eiderdown and cut up the blankets. Evans claimed he tore up the clothes but DC Evans did not think he could tear up a coat. Evans added he started it with scissors.

- DC Evans mentioned that at the finish of the interview, Evans stated, 'I may have made a few mistakes but as far as Christie is concerned, I have said the truth.'

Mr Morris' cross-examination of DC Evans was only to correct the witness on the date Evans arrived in Merthyr Vale.

Commentary – DC Evans' evidence was largely substantive. It did not address what he had stated elsewhere, in that in making his 'Merthyr 1' statement, Evans was reluctant to talk about the child. DC Evans, himself, had to take the initiative in getting Evans to state who was caring for the baby. This raised the question – why Mr Elam did not draw D C Evans out on Evans' reluctance to talk about the baby?

Detective Chief Inspector George Jennings of F Division, Metropolitan police was the next prosecution witness.[15] He was examined by Mr Humphreys:

- Firstly, DCI Jennings gave evidence of finding the bodies of Beryl and Geraldine Evans in the wash-house at 11.50 a.m. on Friday 2nd December. The bodies were photographed and identified; Dr Teare performed post mortems.

Commentary - Jennings was not questioned on the detail surrounding the discovery of the bodies, e.g. how they were hidden; how the Christies reacted.

- Mr Humphreys questioned the Chief Inspector on the events following Evans being brought back to Notting Hill police station on the evening of 2nd December. Jennings stated that his initial words to Evans were, 'I am Chief Inspector Jennings, in charge of this case. At 11:50 a.m. today I found the dead body of your wife, Beryl Evans concealed in the wash-house at 10 Rillington Place, Notting Hill, also the body of your baby daughter, Geraldine, in the same outbuilding, and this clothing was found with them. Later today I was present at Kensington Mortuary when it was established that the cause of death was strangulation in both cases. I have reason to believe you were responsible for their deaths.' Jennings then said Evans replied, 'Yes' and he was cautioned. Evans then gave the first of his Notting Hill statements which was recorded in DCI Jennings' pocketbook. Evans' statement, 'NH1' - already set out and discussed in Chapter 5 of this volume – was read out by the Clerk of the Court.

- DCI Jennings stated that after Evans made the statement he said 'it's a great relief to get it off my chest. I feel better already. I can tell you the cause that led up to it.' Evans was again cautioned and he gave his second Notting Hill statement. This was written down by DI Black. Evans' statement 'NH2' – already set out and discussed in Chapter 5 of this volume – was read out by the Clerk of the Court.

  Commentary - the advocates of Evans' innocence claimed that Jennings gave Evans the information in his initial exchange that was repeated back to him in the confession. This claim is considered further in Chapter 10 of this volume and under various contexts in volume II.

- Jennings was asked what Evans said when, on 3rd December, he was charged with murdering his wife. Mr Morris objected, as he considered the evidence inadmissible. The judge did not agree.

- Mr Humphreys established that when Evans was charged with the murder of his wife, he said, 'Yes, that is right.' Later on 15th December, when he was charged with murdering his daughter,

Evans made no reply.

Commentary - the examination of DCI Jennings provided the jury with Evans' confession. This was the substance of the prosecution case.

Mr Morris' cross-examination would be crucial:

- Mr Morris wanted to know when Jennings first spoke to Evans having met him coming back from Merthyr at Paddington Station. Jennings replied that he first spoke to him at Notting Hill police station.

- Morris asked, 'did he appear to you to be frightened or nervous?' Jennings answered, 'No.' Pressed by Morris, Jennings said that he became nervous and frightened 'after he had seen the clothing on the floor and I was saying what I had to say to him.'

Commentary – Mr Morris was hoping to build justification for Evans' claim that he confessed because he was afraid the police might take him into the cells and knock him about. Jennings' responses appeared to show that the police behaved properly.

- Mr Morris got Jennings to agree Evans could not read or write. He said to Jennings, 'he is clearly not a very educated man?' But Jennings replied, 'not really educated, but he is quite worldly.'

Commentary – Mr Morris took this line no further. Commentators who later argued that Evans was innocent tended to emphasise Evans' lack of education, deeming him naive as a result. But this was not what Jennings said, and Jennings actually knew Evans.

- Morris tried to get Jennings to agree that the police had informed Evans of what he needed to know to make his confession. Jennings agreed that he had told Evans exactly what he and the Chief Superintendent had found at the wash-house. Morris then indicated that they therefore explained 'how his wife's body was wrapped up in a green tablecloth'. Jennings backtracked: 'Not at this stage – I found them concealed.' Jennings did concede that the tablecloth was with the clothing found on the floor. He also conceded that the blanket and the cord used to tie the body were also on the floor.

- Morris then asked, 'But you said it [Mrs Evans' body] was concealed behind pieces of wood?' Jennings replied, 'No.' Morris disputed, but Jennings still denied mentioning wood or timber.

Commentary – In his confession, Evans provided detail about his wife's body being wrapped that went far beyond what the police stated they told him. 'That night I carried my wife's body downstairs to the kitchen of Mr Kitchener's flat as I knew he was in hospital... I then went downstairs when I knew everything was quiet, to Mr Kitchener's kitchen. I wrapped my wife's body up in a blanket and a green table cloth from off my kitchen table. I then tied it up with a piece of cord from out of my kitchen cupboard.[16]

Advocates for Evans' innocence have argued that the use of the blanket was indicative of Christie as when Christie's later victims were found some of them were wrapped in blankets.

If Evans was involved with Christie in moving Beryl's body to the wash- house, even if he had not killed her, he would have known how her body was wrapped and how it was hidden.

- In response to further questions, Jennings confirmed no rope was found around Mrs Evans' neck but the tie found around the baby was on the floor. He confirmed he said nothing to Evans about the items on the floor.

- Jennings confirmed that he told Evans that, 'I had been present at a post-mortem examination where it was established the cause of death was strangulation in both cases.'

- Mr Morris completed his cross-examination by confirming: that Evans was in employment in the week commencing Sunday 6th

November with the Lancaster Food Products earning £5.10 a week; that Beryl Evans was not in employment; that Evans sold his furniture to a firm on the Portobello Road for £40; that he gave various items of torn clothing to a rag dealer on Sunday 13th November.

Commentary – Morris sought to make out that Jennings told Evans all the facts he needed to make the confession. Jennings conceded there were relevant items on the floor and that he did tell him information about where the bodies where and that both had been strangled. But he denied giving Evans all the detail he needed. But if Evans' 'Merthyr 2' was true, how could he have woven what he saw on the floor and what he was told into the correct context for his confession?

Mr Morris did not ask questions on a number of key issues. For instance, he was silent on how long the confession took, what DCI Jennings and DI Black did to corroborate his confession and the obvious omissions such as a motive for killing the baby. Had he probed deeper, he could have started to unravel the confession - see Chapter 10 of this volume.

Advocates for Evans' innocence. particularly Ludovic Kennedy, were highly critical of the police methods to obtain Evans' confession - see Chapter 14 of volume II.

Detective Inspector Neil Black of F Division, Metropolitan Police, was the final prosecution witness.[17]Mr Humphreys had no questions for DI Black.

Cross-examination from Mr Morris:

- DI Black confirmed that nothing was said to Evans about why he was brought to London.

- Mr Morris asked a series of questions concerning what DCI Jennings had said to Evans before Evans made his Notting Hill statement. DI Black confirmed Jennings' evidence, except for one important point. Morris asked, 'Did he tell him that he had found the body of his baby concealed behind some timber in the outhouse?' Black replied, 'Yes.'

Commentary - Later Black's notes of the interview with Evans would reveal that there was no record of Jennings having told Evans about any timber. [18]

• Finally, Mr Morris wanted to know if Evans was upset when he saw the articles of clothing. Black replied, 'he was slightly upset when he picked up the garments and also the tie, but he was not unduly distressed.'

That ended the case for the prosecution.

Commentary – In his opening remarks to the jury, Mr Humphreys stated that the issue before it was the death of the baby. The Crown argued that Evans killed the baby 'deliberately, as he himself set out not once but twice.' Evans, 'tells another story, which is a terrible accusation if it is true of murder by a man downstairs of his wife.' [19]

At the conclusion of its case, the prosecution rested essentially only on Evans' confession. The defence had made little progress in undermining that confession or showing Christie had been the murderer.

Defence case

Mr Morris opened the case for the defence by calling the accused. The defence would call no other witness.

Evans' examination and cross-examination were crucial. They are set out in full, drawing on Tennyson Jesse's Evans trial transcript (Jesse, pp 60-81). Commentary is added to highlight counsels' objectives, key issues and areas of contention, as appropriate.

Examination of Timothy John Evans

Timothy John Evans sworn. Examined by Mr Malcolm Morris.

Commentary - Mr Morris led Evans through the different statements he had given, most particularly the 'Merthyr 2' statement that Evans claimed was the truth.

Morris - How old are you?

Evans - Twenty-five.

Morris - Did you strangle your baby daughter Geraldine?

Evans - No, sir.

Morris - Were you in any way responsible for her death?

Evans - No, sir.

Morris - When did you first know she was dead?

Evans - The night I came to Notting Hill Police Station and Chief Inspector Jennings told me.

Morris - Did you strangle your wife?

Evans - No, sir.

Morris - Were you in any way responsible for her death?

Evans - No, sir.

Commentary - Mr Morris veered from the line of questioning - he did not ask, 'When did you first know that she [his wife] was dead?' He returned the focus to the baby.

Morris - So far as your daughter is concerned, Geraldine, which is the main matter we are considering today, have you ever harmed her?

Evans - No, sir.

Morris - Were you fond of her?

Evans - Yes, sir.

Morris - We know that on 30th November you went to the police in

Merthyr Tydfil?

Evans - That is right, sir.

Morris - And you said, did you, to the police officer there, Detective Constable Evans, that you wished to see a police officer and tell him something?

Evans - Yes, sir.

Commentary - The first example of Mr Morris giving the evidence and inviting Evans to agree. This technique operated throughout the examination. If counsel is examining his own witness, leading questions - where the answer is effectively in the question itself - should be avoided in English trials. However, Mr Humphreys and Mr Justice Lewis were content to let it pass.

Morris – Did you say to him, as he has said, that you wanted to give yourself up for having disposed of your wife?

Evans – That is right.

Morris – And did you tell him that you had put her down the drain?
Evans – I did, sir.

Commentary – Morris went through events with Evans chronologically from when he went to the Merthyr Police on 30th November. But was it beneficial to emphasise to the jury that there were so many lies in his initial dealings with DC Evans?

Morris – Later, but without saying anything else of importance, did you make a statement, which is the one we have heard read, which mentions your meeting a man in a café?

Evans – That is right, sir.

Morris – So far as the man in the café is concerned, is that true or not true?

Evans – Not true, sir.

Morris – That statement, which is Exhibit No.6 ['Merthyr 1'], also says that your wife was pregnant; is that true?

Evans – Yes, sir.

Morris – And it says at the beginning that she was minded, if she could, to bring about an abortion?

Evans – That is right, sir.

Morris – Is that true?

Evans – That is true, sir.

Morris - I do not want to go into that statement in detail, because apart from that, is the part about the man in the café and your arriving home and finding her dead untrue, or incomplete in this latter case?

Evans - Incomplete.

Morris - You have already told us the part about the man in the café is untrue?

Evans - That is untrue, sir.

Morris - And the part about you arriving home and finding your wife dead is incomplete?

Evans - The part about arriving home and finding my wife dead is true, sir.

Morris - Is it true you found her dead?

Evans - Yes, sir.

Morris - After you had signed that statement, do you remember Detective Constable Evans speaking to you again and asking you about the cover of the manhole?

Evans - Yes, he did mention it.

Morris - Do you remember him saying that he did not think your wife's body had ever been in that drain?

Evans - That is right.

Commentary – before Morris moved on from 'Merthyr 1' he got Evans to confirm parts that were consistent with 'Merthyr 2'. Mrs Evans was pregnant but wanting to get rid of the baby. He came home to find his wife dead.

Morris now moved on to the defence argument that he had already introduced when he cross-examined Christie. Reg Christie murdered Beryl and Geraldine Evans. But the judge, quite correctly, moved it back to the issue of the manhole. Morris realised that he had overlooked allowing Evans to give the jury an explanation as to why he said he disposed of his wife's body down the drain.

Morris – Did you say that you had said it to protect a man named Christie?

Evans – Yes, sir.

Morris – And admit it was not true about the man in the café?

Evans – Yes.

Mr Justice Lewis – Mr Morris, I am not following this. He said something about a manhole to protect a man named Christie; is that what he says?

Morris – Is that what you said, Evans, that you had put your wife's body down a manhole to protect a man named Christie?

Evans – No, sir. I said I put my wife's body down a manhole, sir.

Morris – Was that true or not?

Evans – No, sir.

Morris – You did not put your wife's body down a manhole?

Evans – No, sir.

Morris – Then why did you say you did?

Evans – Well, that is what Mr Christie told me that is what he was going to do with the body.

Morris – After you had said something about protecting a man named Christie – which I think you will agree you said – did you make another statement which mentioned Christie and the part that he played?

Evans – Yes, sir.

Morris - That is in the statement which we know as Exhibit 7 ['Merthyr 2']?

Evans - Yes.

Morris – Is that true?

Evans – Yes, sir.

Morris – Now, I do not want to put it all to you, it is better that you should tell my lord and the jury what happened, but just to start off is it true that one evening when you came home from work Christie said to you that he would like to have a chat with you about your wife taking tablets to bring about an abortion?

Evans – Yes, sir.

Morris – And that he, Christie, knew she was trying to get rid of the baby?

Evans – That is right, sir.

Morris – Did he go on to say anything else to you?

Evans – Well, he turned round and told me if my wife and myself had gone to him in the first place he could have done the job without any trouble at all.

Morris – What did you say to that?

Evans – I told him I was not interested.

Morris – Where were you speaking? Where were you when this conversation took place?

Evans – In his front room.

Morris – His front room?

Evans – Yes.

Morris – Did he say anything to you about his ability to do any such thing?

Evans - Well, he had mentioned it that he had done jobs with other young women before, sir.

Morris – He had done this sort of job for other young women before?

Evans – Yes, sir.

Morris – Did he say whether he had been successful or not?

Evans – Well, he said he had been successful, sir.

Morris – Did he show you anything?

Evans – No, sir.

Morris – Did you ask him anything about his medical knowledge?

Evans – Well, I have seen – he has shown me medical books, sir.

Morris – He has shown you a medical book?

Evans – Yes, sir.

Morris – Can you read?

Evans – No, sir.

Morris – Can you tell my lord and the jury anything about that book which he showed you?

Evans – Well, it had diagrams of men and women's bodies, sir, that is all.

Morris – Of course, you could not understand it because you cannot read; is that right?

Evans – That is right, sir.

Morris – Did he say anything about himself with regard to his medical knowledge?

Evans – Well, he told me he had been training for a doctor before the War, sir, and he had to give it up owing to an accident.

Morris - Did he say what sort of accident?

Evans - No, sir, and I did not ask him.

Commentary - That Christie was injured in a road accident was put forward by the Attorney-General at Christie's own trial in 1953. The Attorney-General put two questions to Inspector Albert Griffin.[20] Was Christie in 1934 knocked down by a motor car, unconscious for an hour, suffering from concussion, and treated at Charing Cross Hospital?' And, 'You do know that he had two operations, one on the knee at Westminster Hospital and one on the right collar-bone at St Thomas Hospital?' To both questions, Inspector Griffin answered, 'I do not know.'

Morris - Did you ask him how he would bring about an abortion?

Evans - I did, sir. He would not tell me.

Morris - Do you remember what his reply was?

Evans – Well, when I asked him how he brought about an abortion, sir, he just said only him and a doctor would know how to do that sort of thing.

Morris – You already told us that you said you were not interested?

Evans – That is right.

Morris – Did you say that at the conclusion of the conversation or earlier?

Evans – Earlier, sir.

Morris – Were you interested?

Evans – No, sir.

Morris – What was the situation when you left Christie?

Evans - I just said goodnight and went upstairs, sir.

Morris – When you went upstairs was your wife there?

Evans - Yes, sir.

Morris - Did you have some conversation with her?

Evans - Well, she asked me if Mr Christie had spoke to me on my way in.

Morris - If Mr Christie had spoken to you?

Evans - Yes, sir, and I answered yes, and she turned and asked me if he had mentioned anything about what he had been speaking to her about, and I told her --

Mr Justice Lewis - Is that what she said to you?

Evans - Well, she asked me if he had mentioned anything about an abortion, so I said he had and I did not want any part of it and she was not to have anything to do with it.

Mr Justice Lewis – You said she was not to have anything to do with it?

Evans – That is right, sir.

Morris – I think what you said was 'I would have no part with it and she was to have nothing to do with it?'

Evans - I told her she was to have nothing to do with it either.

Morris - What did she say to that?

Evans - She told me to mind my own business and she said she trusted Mr Christie, so I did not mention anything else to her about it.

Commentary - Mr Morris had led Evans through the first part of 'Merthyr 2'- Christie, playing on Beryl's desperation and Evans' naivety, pretending he was competent to perform an abortion.

Morris - Now, do you remember the Monday which we know was the 7th November?

Evans - Yes, sir.

Morris – It would be the Monday, a week before your furniture was ultimately removed?

Evans – Yes, sir, that is right.

Morris – Was your wife with you at home then?

Evans – Yes, sir.

Morris – Did you go to work?

Evans – That is right, sir.

Morris – When you came back on the Monday evening was anything said to you or by you of importance in this matter?

Evans – Well, when I went upstairs my wife told me Mr Christie had made all arrangements for first thing Tuesday morning.

Morris – That would be the next day?

Evans – That is right, sir.

Morris – What did you do?

Evans – I did not take any notice of it.

Mr Justice Lewis – Did you believe it?

Evans – No, sir.

Mr Justice Lewis – You did not believe it?

Evans – No, sir.

Mr Justice Lewis – You thought she was lying about Christie having made all arrangements?

Evans – Yes, sir.

Morris - Did anything happen on the Tuesday morning?

Evans - Well, when I got up at six o'clock, sir, to go out to work, my wife got up with me and she told me as I was going downstairs to tell Mr Christie everything was all right. So as I came downstairs, Mr Christie came out and met me and I just turned round and said to him everything was all right and then I went to work.

Morris - So you knew then there must have been some arrangement between Christie and your wife?

Evans – Yes, sir.

Morris - Did you work during that day, Tuesday?

Evans - Yes, sir.

Commentary - Mr Morris continued to lead Evans through the 'Merthyr 2' statement. A crucial point of conflict was reached.

Morris - Did you ultimately return to Rillington Place?

Evans – I did in the evening, sir.

Morris – Had you seen your wife after you left in the early morning of Tuesday?

Evans - No, sir.

Morris - Before you returned?

Evans - No, sir.

Morris -When you returned on Tuesday evening did you go in through the front door in the ordinary way?

Evans – Yes, sir; that is the only way in.

Morris – Did you see anyone?

Evans – Yes, sir. I met Mr Christie.

Commentary - Morris was sticking to the script of 'Merthyr 2'. It would have been interesting if he had asked at what time Evans got home on the Tuesday evening. There was the critical conflict between Evans getting back and being met by Christie or Christie being out visiting Dr Odess.

Morris - What, if anything, did he say?

Evans - He just turned round and told me it was bad news.

Morris - Then what happened?

Evans – Then I went upstairs and he came up behind me.

Morris – Did you go up to your flat on the second floor?

Evans – Yes, sir.

Morris – Did you go in?

Evans – I went into the kitchen and lit the gas.

Morris – What happened then?

Evans – Then he told me about my wife being dead.

Morris – What did he say?

Evans – He turned round and told me that it did not work, and then I asked him where my wife was, and he said she was in the bedroom lying on the bed.

Morris – Did you go into the bedroom?

Evans – Yes, sir, I went into the bedroom and lit the gas.

Morris – Was your wife there?

Evans – Yes, sir, my wife was laying on the bed.

Morris – Did she appear to be alive or dead?

Evans – She appeared to be dead, sir.

Morris – Was there an eiderdown there?

Evans – Yes, sir.

Morris – Where was that?

Evans – On the bed, sir; she was sort of wrapped in it.

Morris – Did you move it?

Evans - No, sir.

Morris - Were you able to see in what condition your wife was?

Evans - Not very well, sir.

Morris – What did you notice about her?

Evans – l knew she was laying on her right side; that is the only thing I did notice, sir.

Morris – Did you see any blood?

Evans – There was blood on the pillowslip, sir.

Commentary – In 'Merthyr 2' Evans stated, 'I pulled the eiderdown back to have a look at her.' There was no mention of a pillowslip. Any pillowslip would presumably have gone to the rag dealer.

Morris – Did you see where that had come from?

Evans – Well, it appeared to come from her mouth and nose, sir

Morris – Anywhere else?

Evans – Well, there were some stains on the eiderdown, sir.

Morris – Whereabouts?

Evans – At the bottom.

Morris – What do you mean by at the bottom? At the bottom or top of her legs?

Evans – Well, I should say it was on the bottom of the eiderdown, sir.

Morris – Yes, but what part of her?

Evans – Well, the top part of her legs, sir.

Mr Justice Lewis. – The eiderdown was not covering her legs?

Evans - Well, not covering all her legs up, sir.

Morris – You noticed blood on that part of her, did you?

Evans - Yes, sir.

Commentary - In his 'Merthyr 2' statement, Evans mentioned that 'she had been bleeding from the bottom part.' The statement made no mention of there being blood on the eiderdown. In his evidence on the post mortem, Dr Teare told the court that there had been no interference with Beryl Evans' pregnancy. Therefore, there would have been no blood around the top of her legs.

Furthermore, in his post mortem, Teare only mentioned swelling to Mrs Evans' right eye and upper lip due to bruising. He did not mention any haemorrhaging from these wounds.

Morris - I think you said she had a black skirt, a checked blouse and a kind of light blue jacket, is that right?

Evans – Yes.

Morris – When you had seen the body of your wife lying there what did you do next?

Evans – I went over to the cot and picked Geraldine up.

Morris – Was she all right?

Evans – My daughter was all right.

Morris – What did you do with her?

Evans – Wrapped her in a blanket and took her into the kitchen, sir.

Morris – Where was Christie?

Evans – Christie was already in the kitchen.

Morris – What happened then?

Evans – I put the kettle on, sir, to feed my daughter.

Morris – To feed the baby?

Evans – Yes, sir.

Morris - Did Christie say he would wait to speak to you after you fed the baby?

Evans - Yes and he went downstairs.

Commentary - In 'Merthyr 2, Evans did not say he went downstairs. He was silent on what Christie did.

Morris – And you fed the baby, did you?

Evans – I fed the baby, and just as I was finishing he came back up.

Commentary – In 'Merthyr 2' Evans mentioned he changed the baby and put her in front of the fire. According to the leading advocate of Evans' innocence, Sir Ludovic Kennedy, during this short interval, Christie behaved amazingly. He went to see his doctor as he needed a certificate to stay off work.[21]

Morris – Did you ask him anything then?

Evans – Well, he just told me to shut the kitchen door and stop in the kitchen.

Mr Justice Lewis – Do what?

Evans – He told me to stop in the kitchen and close the door.

Mr Justice Lewis – Did you say anything to him, you were asked? Did you say anything to him? Evans – No, sir.

Morris – Was anything said about the time when your wife had died?

Evans – He said it had happened in the afternoon time.

Morris – Did he say anything more about her, about the state she was in, so far as you remember?

Evans – He told me if she had been another day late she would have had to have gone to hospital with a septic stomach.

Morris - Now you say that he told you to stop in the kitchen and shut the door?

Evans - Yes, sir.

Morris – Did you stop in the kitchen and shut the door?

Evans – I did, yes.

Morris – We can see from the plan that if you are in the kitchen with the door shut someone can go in and out of the bedroom without being seen by you?

Evans – That is quite right, sir.

Morris - And, indeed, from the bedroom downstairs?

Evans - That is right.

Morris - What was the next thing that happened?

Evans - Well, I opened my kitchen door and I heard Mr Christie puffing and blowing on the staircase.

Commentary - In 'Merthyr 2' Evans stated that Christie came back after a quarter of an hour and told him he had forced the door on Kitchener's flat and put his wife's body there. There was nothing in 'Merthyr 2' about Christie puffing and blowing.

Morris - What time was this?

Evans - I could not say the time, sir.

Morris – Can you say how much later?

Evans – I should say somewhere round about seven o'clock.

Morris – You say you heard Mr Christie puffing and blowing on the stairs?

Evans – Yes sir, and I went down to him.

Morris – What was he doing, or trying to do?

Evans - Well, he was trying to shift my wife's body from my bedroom into Mr Kitchener's place.

Morris - Where was your wife's body then?

Evans - On the staircase.

Morris - Is it a narrow staircase?

Evans - Well, pretty narrow, sir.

Morris – What did you do?

Evans – I helped him to carry my wife's body into the kitchen, sir.
Morris – Would that be the kitchen of Kitchener's flat?

Evans – That is right, sir.

Commentary – the story about Christie puffing and blowing on the stairs and Evans having to help him take his wife's body down to Kitchener's flat was told to DC Evans in an interview on 1st December [22]. Even if the 'puffing and blowing' incident had not occurred on the Tuesday evening, could it have occurred if Christie and Evans together had moved Beryl's body to the wash-house at the week-end, being a prelude to Christie's fibrositis?

Morris – Then what happened?

Commentary – it was at this stage in 'Merthyr2' Christie told Evans, 'I'll dispose of it down one of the drains.' Morris came to that later.

Evans – Then I went back upstairs and he come up behind me and told me to go to bed as usual tonight, and he would do the rest.

Morris – Did you ever see your wife's body again?

Evans – No, sir.

Morris – When you went back upstairs on that Tuesday night was your daughter all right?

Evans - Yes, sir.

Morris - Did he, Christie, say anything about what was to be done with your daughter then, or was it later?

Evans – It was later, sir.

Commentary – In 'Merthyr 2' at this stage, Christie told Evans to go to work as usual and he would see about getting someone to look after the baby.

Morris – When did he say that?

Evans – On the Wednesday, sir.

Morris– What did he tell you?

Evans – He told me that he had made arrangements for my daughter to go over to East Acton, and the people were coming to collect her on Thursday.

Morris – Did he say who the people in East Acton were, or anything about them?

Evans – No, sir. He just said that the young couple could not have any children of their own.

Morris – A young couple who could not have children of their own?

Evans – That is right, sir.

Morris – Did he say what he was going to do with your wife's body?

Evans – He told me he was going to put it down a drain, sir.

Morris – What did you say, if anything, to that?

Evans – Well, I told him he knew what he was doing, sir.

Morris – Did he say anything?

Evans – He never spoke anything about it.

Morris – He never spoke anything else about your wife's body?

Evans - No, sir.

Morris - Now, on Wednesday, did anyone - first of all, did you go out?

Evans – I went to work on Wednesday, sir.

Morris – What time?

Evans – My usual time, sir; half-past six in the morning.

Morris – Was any arrangement made about anyone looking after your baby while you were out?

Evans – Yes, sir; he told me to feed the baby in the morning as usual, and he would slip in through the day and see she was all right.

Morris – Did you feed the baby in the morning as usual on that Wednesday?

Evans – Yes, sir.

Morris – Before you went to work?

Evans – Before I went to work, sir.

Morris – Had you said anything to Christie about wanting to take your baby anywhere else?

Evans – Yes, sir; I told him I wanted to take the baby round to my parents.

Mr Justice Lewis – Where do your parents live?

Evans – No. 11 St. Mark's Road, sir.

Mr Justice Lewis – Where is that?

Evans – North Kensington.

Morris – Did he say anything to you?

Evans – Yes, sir. He told me not to take my daughter round to my parents as that would cause suspicion straightaway.

Commentary – While the order of interactions between Evans and Christie was altered, the examination maintained the timings given in 'Merthyr 2'. Conversations about Christie minding Geraldine took place on the Tuesday evening and the Wednesday morning. The conversation about Evans not taking Geraldine to his parents was on the Tuesday evening. The conversations about getting Geraldine looked after by the young couple in East Acton were on the Wednesday morning and the Wednesday evening.

Morris – Now after working on the Wednesday did you return home?

Evans – Yes, sir.

Morris – At what sort of time?

Evans – Somewhere between half-past five and half-past six, sir.

Morris – Did you go up to your flat?

Evans – Yes, sir.

Morris – Was your baby all right?

Evans – My baby was all right, sir.

Morris – Did you do anything?

Evans – I done the usual thing; lit the gas, made the feed for the baby and lit the fire and I stopped in all night with her.

Commentary – if he stopped in all night, he couldn't have been coming in at 10.30 p.m. when Mrs Christie put the light on for him and inquired about Beryl.

Morris – Did you see Christie on the Wednesday night?

Evans – Yes, sir.

Morris – Did he come into your flat then?

Evans – He come up to my flat.

Morris – What, if anything, did he say?

Evans – He told me he had made arrangements for the people to come and collect my baby on the Thursday.

Mr Justice Lewis - This is the Wednesday evening?

Evans - Yes, sir.

Morris - I think you told my lord and the jury he had already said that before?

Commentary - Evans had. Earlier in the examination when Morris was questioning him on the events of Tuesday evening, Evans corrected his counsel regarding the young couple from East Acton taking the child. Christie first told him about them on Wednesday morning. On Wednesday evening Christie informed Evans on what needed to be done ahead of the young couple collecting Geraldine (on the Thursday). This issue, though, would lead to a hostile interruption by the judge and the evidence becoming distorted. Nevertheless, in the exchange with the judge, Evans remained consistent with 'Merthyr 2'.

Evans - Yes, sir.

Morris - Had he?

Evans - Yes, sir.

Mr Justice Lewis - When?

Evans - I think it was on either Tuesday - the Tuesday, I think, sir; either the Monday or Tuesday.

Mr Justice Lewis - When you were asked about it before you did not agree with your counsel he said it on Tuesday, because you said Christie said late on Wednesday what was to be done, namely to make arrangements with the people at East Acton to fetch your daughter on Thursday. What is right?

Evans - What I mean is on Wednesday he told me he made all the arrangements.

Mr Justice Lewis - Had he mentioned it before?

Evans - Yes, sir; he had mentioned it.

Mr Justice Lewis - Then why did you tell me when you were asked by your counsel whether on the Tuesday night he said something about arrangements being made with Acton, you said Christie said that later on Wednesday night arrangements had been made? Which is right? Did he say it twice?

Evans - Yes, sir.

Mr Justice Lewis - Then I have to correct that statement of yours. What was the first time he mentioned it?

Evans - On the Tuesday, sir.

Commentary - according to 'Merthyr 2', the first mention of the young couple from East Acton was on the morning of Wednesday 9th. 'He also told me in the morning that he knew a young couple over in East Acton who would look after the baby, and he'd go over and see them.' [23]

Morris - When he said that did he tell you what you had got to do with regard to Thursday morning?

Evans – Yes.

Morris – What did he say?

Evans – He told me I had to get up, feed my baby as usual, dress her and leave her in the cot and the people would call later in the day for her.

Mr Justice Lewis – Leave her in the cot, do you say?

Evans - Yes, sir.

Mr Justice Lewis – That is the third time he told you?

Evans – Yes, sir.

Morris – Did he say if he had made any arrangement about these people from Acton getting into the house?

Evans – Yes.

Morris – What did he say?

Evans – He told me he had told them to knock three knocks and he would let them in while I was at work.

Morris - Now we come to the next day, which is Thursday, the 10th. On that morning did you do what he told you to do?

Evans - Yes, sir.

Morris - Did you go out?

Evans - Well, I went to work at half-past six.

Morris – When did you come back?

Evans – Between half-past five and six.

Morris – Did you see Christie?

Evans – Yes, sir.

Morris– When?

Evans – I went up to my flat, and I had been up there about three minutes and he walked in.

Morris – What, if anything, did he say then?

Evans – I asked him where the baby had gone, and he told me the people from East Acton had collected her.

Morris – Did you ask him anything about your wife's body?

Evans – No, sir.

Morris – Then what else did he say, if anything, to you?

Evans – Then he suggested l should sell my furniture.

Morris – Sell your furniture, yes, and what?

Evans – Get out of London.

Morris – What did you say to that?

Evans – I agreed to, sir.

Commentary – the next question had to be, 'Why did you agree? Morris never asked it.

Morris -Where were you going to sell your furniture?

Evans - Well, I do not know off hand, but the man who I sold it to, Mr Christie recommended me to - told me about.

Commentary - the man, Mr Hookway, was a long standing acquaintance of Christie.

Morris – And where was his shop, or whatever it was?

Evans – In Portobello Road.

Morris – Did Christie give you any advice as to what you were to say if you were questioned about your wife and child?

Evans – Yes, told me to tell people that they had gone away on a holiday.

Morris – I do not think there is any dispute about this: on the Friday did you make some inquiries from this firm in Portobello Road about selling your furniture?

Evans – Yes, sir.

Morris – And did they tell you they would pick it up on the following Monday?

Evans – No, sir; he told me he would come down and look at the furniture first, sir.

Morris – When did they come down to look at the furniture?

Evans – On the Friday afternoon, sir.

Morris – Was a price agreed then?

Evans – Yes, sir.

Morris – What was the price?

Evans – £40, sir.

Morris – When was it arranged that the furniture should be collected?

Evans - Monday.

Morris - Then on the Sunday did you do anything in particular, do you remember?

Evans - Well, I got in touch with this rag dealer, sir.

Morris - What is his name?

Evans – Albert Rollings.

Morris – What did you do with him?

Evans – I told him if he would come down to my flat on Monday he could have two or three sacks of rags.

Morris – Did you prepare some material for him to collect?

Evans – Well, I did not offhand, sir; I went to the pictures in the afternoon.

Morris – But later on did you?

Evans – Later in the day.

Morris – And on the Monday did he come and collect?

Evans – Yes, sir.

Morris – Various items, some of which you had cut up and some of which you had torn up?

Evans – That is right, sir.

Morris – Did you get anything for them?

Evans – No, sir.

Morris – Did the van come and take away the furniture?

Evans – In the afternoon, sir.

Morris – Did it take away the furniture?

Evans – Yes, sir.

Morris – Were you paid?

Evans – Yes, sir.

Morris – How much?

Evans – £40, sir.

Morris – How?

Evans – In £1 notes.

Morris – Did you tell Christie about that?

Evans – I mentioned to him I had had the money, sir.

Morris – Did you say how much?

Evans – No.

Mr Justice Lewis – Did you show him a roll of notes?

Evans – I showed him the roll.

Morris – Were there certain articles left which did not go either to the rag and bone man or away with the furniture?

Evans – Yes, sir.

Morris – I want to take them in two parts. Was there the pram and your baby's chair and her clothes?

Evans – Yes, sir.

Morris – What happened to those?

Evans – They were left in the bedroom, sir.

Morris – With any instructions of any sort?

Evans – Yes, sir.

Morris – To whom?

Evans – Mr Christie. He told me to leave them there and he would get them sent off to East Acton to where my daughter was.

Morris - Were there also left over, but in a different category, some vases, a clock, some dishes, saucepans and a bucket?

Evans - Yes, sir.

Morris - What happened to them?

Evans - As far as I know Mr Christie had them.

Commentary – in 'Merthyr 2' Evans only stated Christie had the stuff left in the house. If the baby stuff was left in the second-floor bedroom, why would Christie have bothered to take them to his front room where they were found by the police? He was suffering from severe back pain/fibrositis before Evans went away.

Morris – What did you do on the Monday, that would be the 14th, after your furniture had been removed?

Evans – Well, I left the house with my suitcase and took it to Paddington Station.

Morris – At what time?

Evans – I should say four o'clock, sir.

Morris – Then what?

Evans – Then I went to the pictures in the afternoon, sir, and I come out of the pictures and I went to the public house.

Morris – We know that in the end you went to Wales to stay with your aunt, Mrs Lynch?

Evans – Yes.

Mr Justice Lewis – When did you go?

Evans – I caught the five to one train on Tuesday morning.

Mr Justice Lewis – Midday?

Evans – No, a.m. sir; in the morning.

Commentary - some advocates of Evans' innocence pointed out that the timings on Evans' 'Notting Hill' statements were in numbers and included the abbreviations 'p.m.' which would have been beyond Evans' comprehension. Clearly the answer above showed Evans knew what a.m. and p.m. were.

Mr Justice Lewis - Five to one in the early morning?

Evans – Yes, sir.

Morris – A sort of milk train, is it?

Evans – I believe so.

Morris – Where did that go to?

Evans – It went to Newport and Cardiff, sir.

Morris – Then did you stay with your aunt, Mrs Lynch?

Evans – Yes, sir.

Morris – At that time, so far as you knew, was your baby alive and well?

Mr Justice Lewis – Do you say this is a milk train and it starts at five to one?

Evans – So far as I know.

Morris – I suggested it, my lord.

Mr Justice Lewis – Do you agree with that?

Evans – I do not know whether it is a milk train, sir.

Morris – I am afraid I suggested it is a milk train.

Mr Justice Lewis – A train from Paddington to South Wales which goes at five minutes to one in the early morning?

Evans – Yes, sir.

Commentary – 'Merthyr 2' ended with Evans arriving at his aunt and uncle's house in Merthyr Vale around twenty to seven on the morning of Tuesday 15th November 1949.

Morris - Now, after staying with your aunt for some time did you come back to London?

Evans - Yes, sir.

Morris – Was that on or about 23rd November?

Evans – Yes, sir.

Morris – Why did you come back?

Evans – I come back to see Mr Christie.

Morris – What about?

Evans – About my daughter.

Morris – So far as you knew was your daughter by that time perfectly all right?

Evans – Yes, sir.

Morris – In East Acton?

Evans – Yes, sir.

Morris – Did you see Mr Christie?

Evans – Yes, sir.

Morris – What did you or either of you say?

Evans – He asked me what I was doing back in London, and I told him I had come up to find out about my daughter; and he told me my daughter was perfectly all right.

Morris – Anything more?

Evans – I asked him when I could see her, and he said in about two or three weeks' time.

Morris - Did he say why he suggested you should wait for two or three weeks to pass before you saw her?

Evans - Yes, he said to give her time to get settled in.

Morris - Time to get settled in?

Evans - Yes, sir.

Morris – What did you do then when you heard that?

Evans - Well, I walked up Cambridge Gardens with him, sir; and got on a No.7 bus and went back to Paddington Station.

Morris – And did you later return to Wales?

Evans – Yes, sir.

Morris – Is that all you did in London then?

Evans – Yes, sir.

Morris – Was there any point in your journey to London other than to find out how your baby was?

Evans – That was the only reason I come to London, sir.

Commentary – Evans left Merthyr Vale on Monday 21st November. He did not get back until Thursday 24th November. If it was just to see Christie, what did he do in London on Tuesday 22nd and earlier on Wednesday 23rd?

Morris – While you were staying with your aunt, on or about the 30th November, did a letter arrive from your mother?

Evans – Yes, sir.

Morris – Which mentioned you had been away from the flat?

Evans – Yes, sir.

Morris – And that she had not seen your wife or child?

Evans – Yes, sir.

Morris - Later that day did you go to the police station, as you have told us?

Evans - I did, sir.

Morris - When you told Detective Constable Evans that you had disposed of your wife's body by putting it down a drain, why did you say that?

Evans – Well, I was given to believe that was what Mr Christie had done with my wife's body.

Morris – Did you think then your wife's body was down the drain at Rillington Place?

Evans – Yes sir.

Mr Justice Lewis - But why did you say you had disposed of it?

Evans – Well, I said that to protect Mr Christie.

Mr Justice Lewis - To protect Mr Christie?

Evans – Yes, sir.

Morris – And was it for the same reason that you made up this same story about the man in the cafe?

Evans – Yes, sir.

Commentary – Morris needed to ask why Evans was protecting Mr Christie. He did not.

Morris – And you then made this statement which has been referred to?

Evans – Yes, sir.

Morris – At that time, after making both those statements, had you any reason to believe that any harm had come to your daughter?

Evans – No, sir.

Morris – On the 2nd of December in the afternoon, did Mr Black bring you up from Wales to Paddington?

Evans - Yes, sir.

Morris - When you arrived at Paddington, were you met by Chief Inspector Jennings, as you know him?

Evans - Yes, sir.

Morris – Did you go to Notting Hill Police Station?

Evans – Yes, sir.

Morris – What happened when you got there?

Evans – He told me about my wife and baby being dead, sir.

Morris – Now you will speak up; this is most important, and it is most important that you should speak without any unnecessary questions being asked. Just tell your own story. He told you that your wife and baby….?

Evans – Had been found dead, sir.

Morris – Did he say where?

Evans – Yes, sir, No. 10 Rillington Place in the wash-house, and he said he had good reason to believe that I knew something about it.

Morris – Did he say how it appeared they had died?

Evans – Yes, sir, by strangulation.

Morris – Did he say with what?

Evans – Well a rope, sir, my wife, and my daughter had been strangled with a neck tie.

Morris – Was anything shown to you at the same time?

Evans – Yes, sir, the clothing of my wife and my daughter.

Morris – Was there also a green tablecloth and blanket?

Evans – Yes, sir.

Morris – And a length of rope?

Evans – Yes, sir.

Morris – I do not want to ask the same question twice, but before he told you had you any idea that anything had happened to your daughter?

Evans – No, sir; no idea at all.

Morris – Did he tell you, when he said the bodies had been found in the wash-house, whether they had been concealed or not?

Evans – Yes, sir, he told me they had been concealed by timber.

Commentary – Jennings had denied mentioning the bodies were hidden by timber. Black confirmed Jennings had told hm they were, though later he would backtrack on that.

Morris – Having told you that and shown you those garments and said that he had reason to believe you knew about their death, did he say he had reason to believe you were responsible for causing their deaths?

Evans – Yes, sir.

Morris – What did you say?

Evans – I just replied, 'Yes, sir.'

Morris – Why?

Evans – Well, when I found out about my daughter being dead I was upset and I did not care what happened to me then.

Morris – Were you very fond of her?

Evans – Yes, sir.

Morris – Did you then make the statement which the Chief Inspector took down in his notebook?

Evans - Yes, sir.

Morris - Before we go to that, was there any other reason why you said yes, as well as the fact that you gave up everything when you heard that your daughter was dead?

Evans - Well, sir, I was frightened at the time.

Morris – Why were you frightened, or what were you frightened of?

Evans - Well, I thought if I did not make a statement the police would take me downstairs and start kicking me about.

Commentary - at this point Morris should have asked something along the lines of what was happening with the way DCI Jennings was conducting the interview that made him feel threatened.

Morris – You really believed that, did you?

Evans – Yes, sir.

Morris – Did you then make this statement saying that your wife was incurring one debt after another, 'I could not stand it any longer so I strangled her with a piece of rope?'

Evans – Yes, sir.

Morris – And later that you had strangled the baby on the Thursday evening with your tie?

Evans - Yes, sir.

Morris - Had you in fact got any rope in your flat?

Evans - No, sir.

Morris - Is it your tie which is Exhibit 3 in this case?

Evans - No, sir.

Morris - Had you ever seen it before you were shown it by the Chief Inspector?

Evans - No, sir.

Commentary - Evans had to deny having any rope and owning the tie otherwise his whole defence would have crumbled there and then. In his evidence, Christie did not identify the tie as belonging to Evans, though he did say that he had seen Evans wearing striped ties.

If the tie wasn't Evans', it had to belong to Christie. If it was Christie's, then Ethel Christie would have recognised it and would undoubtedly have suspected that her husband could well have killed the child. There was no indication of this in the documentation of the case or Mrs Christie's behaviour. There was, though a third possibility, albeit unlikely. The tie could have belonged to Mr Kitchener. Christie and/or Evans had supposedly accessed his flat on the Tuesday evening, two days before the baby was strangled. Murdering the baby using Kitchener's tie would have implied a degree of cunning that would surely have been beyond Evans but not Christie. Mr Kitchener was not asked if he could shed any light on who owned the tie.

Evans is seen wearing a striped tie in this photograph of himself, his half-sister Maureen, baby Geraldine and his wife Beryl.

Morris – Is it true that your wife was incurring debts?

Evans - Yes, sir.

Morris - But untrue that you strangled her?

Evans - It is untrue that I strangled her.

Morris - Did you then sometime after ten o'clock make this statement, Exhibit 9 ['Notting Hill 2']?

Evans – Yes, sir.

Morris – Mr Black took it down?

Evans– Yes.

Morris – In that statement at the beginning you speak about the way in which your wife was incurring debts, do not you?

Evans– Yes.

Morris – How you had to borrow £20 from your 'guv'nor' and how you lost an earlier job?

Evans – Yes, sir.

Morris – Is that part of it true?

Evans – Yes, sir.

Morris – Is it true that she had not paid the money you had given her to pay hire purchase instalments on the furniture?

Evans– Yes.

Morris – And is it true that she said she was going to pack up and go down to her father at Brighton?

Evans – Yes, sir.

Morris – Now, unfortunately, as you cannot read I cannot put a statement in front of you, but perhaps you can tell my lord and the jury this: did you ask her if she was going with the baby, and did she say she was going to take the baby down to Brighton with her, and did you say that would be a good job and a load of worry off your mind?

Evans - Yes, sir.

Morris - Was that all about Monday, the 7th November?

Evans - Yes, sir.

Morris – When you came home that Monday night did you say, 'I thought you were going to Brighton,' and did she say, 'What for? For you to have a good time,' or something like that?

Evans – That is right.

Morris – And then you say, 'I took no notice of her. I went down-stairs and fetched the push chair up. I came upstairs; she started an argument again. I told her if she did not pack it up I'd slap her face.' Is that true?

Evans – Yes, sir.

Morris – With that she picked up a milk bottle to throw at me. Is that right?

Evans – Yes sir.

Morris – This is the Monday night. 'I grabbed the bottle out of her hand. I pushed her; she fell in a chair in the kitchen, so I washed and changed and went out.' That is true, is it?

Evans – Yes, sir, that is true.

Morris – I went to the pub and had a few drinks?

Evans – Yes, sir.

Morris – That would be the Kensington Park Hotel?

Evans -Yes.

Morris – Which you referred to as the 'KPH'?

Evans - Yes.

Morris - 'I got home about 10.30 p.m. I walked in; she started to row again and I went straight to bed?'

Evans - Yes, sir.

Morris - Now we come to the Tuesday morning, the 8th November.

'I got up Tuesday morning and went straight to work'?

Evans – Yes, sir.

Mr Justice Lewis – 6.30 as usual, was it?

Evans – I went out at 6.30, yes.

Morris – 'I came home at night about 6.30 p.m.'?

Evans – Yes.

Morris – Then you say: 'My wife started to argue again, so I hit her across the face with my flat hand'?

Evans – Yes, sir.

Commentary - In his post mortem report, Dr Teare referred to considerable swelling to Beryl Evans' right eye and upper lip. He considered it was most likely from a single blow from the back of the assailant's hand. Dr Teare pointed out that Mrs Evans must have lived for some time after being hit for the bruising to have formed. Evidence of this injury to Mrs Evans' face was not given at any of Evans' appearances at the magistrates' court. But what Evans stated in his confession and in this part of his examination was supported by post mortem evidence.

Morris – Now, which is true? Was she alive then or not when you got back?

Commentary - Morris realised he was taking Evans on to dangerous ground. He was starting to repeat his confession to the jury! Morris altered his style of questioning to steer Evans away from doing that.

Evans - No, sir.

Morris - Why did you say that 'In a fit of temper I grabbed a piece of rope from a chair which I had brought home off my van and strangled her with it?

Evans - As I said before, I was upset and I do not think I knew what I was saying.

Morris – You do not think you knew what you were saying?

Evans – No, sir.

Morris – Did you bring a piece of rope home off your van?

Evans – No, I had no rope on my van.

Morris – You made that up?

Evans – I made that up.

Morris – I need not go through that in detail, but later you say that on the Thursday you went home, picked up your baby from her cot in the bedroom, picked up your tie and strangled her with it. You now say that is untrue too?

Evans – That is untrue too.

Morris – And made up for the same reason?

Evans –Yes, sir.

Mr Justice Lewis – The reason being you did not know what you were saying?

Evans –Yes, sir.

Morris – Not only did you not know what you were saying, but you have given us two other reasons?

Evans – Yes, sir, I was upset and I was afraid the police would take me downstairs.

Morris - Is that why you told a lie to them?

Evans - Yes, sir.

Morris - You said two things then, 'I was upset and I was afraid the police would take me downstairs. 'When you said you were afraid the police would take you downstairs, did you mean to beat you up?

Evans - Yes, sir.

Morris – When you say you were upset, how much were you upset?

Evans – I was upset pretty bad, sir; I had been believing my daughter was still alive.

Morris – Had you anything left to live for when she was dead?

Evans – No, sir.

There the examination ended.

Commentary – Mr Morris' examination of Evans was largely in two parts. Firstly, he 'spoon fed' Evans through his 'Merthyr 2' statement. The dialogue between Morris and Evans would have been more dramatic for the jury than the bland reading of the statement they had heard during DC Evans' evidence. Secondly, Morris got Evans to deny the killings he had described in 'Notting Hill 2'. But a string of 'No, sirs' and the 'nothing to live for' and 'being afraid of being beaten up' justifications were less than convincing.

The whole examination was remarkable in that, despite leading questions, an uneducated man, who could not read or write, was able to recall so accurately what he had said some six weeks prior.

Having not really been able to undermine Christie's evidence was a blow given that the defence case was that Christie did it. That meant it was critical for Morris to put questions to Evans that would have, at the very least, planted doubt about Christie in the jurors' minds. For instance:

- *How incapacitated was Christie around 7th -14th November?*
- *How could the baby's crying not have been heard by Mrs Christie or the workmen on Wednesday 8th while he was at work, if Christie had not been looking after her?*
- *Did your brother-in law, Mr Thorley, advise you on who you could sell your furniture to?*
- *When Christie sent you round to see Mr Hookway to sell your furniture, did Hookway say how he knew Christie?*
- *Did you know Christie had criminal convictions, including one for malicious wounding?*

Furthermore, having failed to show that Evans' confession was part nonsense when he cross-examined DCI Jennings and DI Black, Morris could have examined Evans to show that his confession contained nonsense, thereby undermining the backbone of the prosecution case. For instance:
- *How could you have carried your 7½ stone wife, doubled up and wrapped in an awkward bundle, down from Kitchener's flat to the*

wash-house and not make such a noise as to draw the Christies from their bedroom? All this being done in the dark!

- *How did you know how the door to the wash-house worked? Did you know where the lever was kept?*

- *How did you know that Beryl's body could be fitted in under the sink and that you would need to double it up and wrap it to make it fit?*

- *If you killed your wife at around 7 p.m., how did you double up your wife's body later that evening when rigor mortis would have set in?*

- *From where did you find the timbers to pile up in front of the sink?*

- *Why was Geraldine's body not wrapped like her mother's?*

- *Why did you put Geraldine's body in a different part of the wash-house to her mother?*

- *From where did you find the timbers to cover the baby's body?*

- *You must have realised that the bodies could not stay in the wash-house; they would be discovered by the Christies. So why did you leave 10 Rillington Place, thereby losing control of the bodies?*

- *Why did you not sell the baby's equipment?*

The more Evans floundered with his answers, the better.

Cross-examination

The cross-examination was conducted by Mr Humphreys.

Commentary – Mr Humphreys aimed to show that Evans had confessed on a number of occasions, that he lied repeatedly to cover his tracks and that there was no substance to his accusations against Christie.

Humphreys – Is it true that on five different occasions and to different persons you have confessed to the murder of your wife, and to the murder of your wife and child?

Commentary – Evans had confessed, fully or partially, on only three occasions. To DCI Jennings and DI Black in his Notting Hill confession, to Sergeant Trevallian on the morning after and to Dr Matheson when he was remanded to Brixton Prison. Humphreys got away with a gross exaggeration.

Evans - I have confessed it, sir, but it is not true.

Humphreys – Is it right you have confessed it five times in different places and to different persons?

Evans – Yes, it is.

Humphreys – Are you saying on each of those occasions you were upset?

Evans – The biggest part of them, sir. Well, I was not upset on the five, but the last one I was.

Humphreys – If you were not upset on the five, why did you sometimes confess to wilful murder if you were not upset – unless it was true?

Evans - Well, I knew my wife was dead; but I did not know my daughter was dead.

Humphreys - What had that got to do with it?

Humphreys – Is that a reason for pleading guilty to murder, because you are upset because your daughter is dead by some other person's hand?

Evans – Yes.

Humphreys – Is it?

Evans – Yes.

Humphreys – Let us just look at those occasions. It is you who voluntarily go to the police on the 30th November after having read to you a letter from your mother to your aunt?

Evans – That is right.

Humphreys – It was because in the letter your previous lies were exposed that you decided to go to the police, was it?

Evans – It was not because of the lies.

Humphreys – Why then did you suddenly go to the police?

Evans – Well, I was getting worried about my daughter.

Humphreys – Are you saying that seriously to the jury, that you go to the police and confess to murder because you are worried about the whereabouts of your daughter?

Morris – With great respect, there is no confession of murder. He said, 'I have disposed of my wife; I have put her down the drain.'

Mr Justice Lewis – It sounds very like murder.

Morris – All he said was he had put her, it might well be her body, down the drain and it is quite clear that is his evidence today.

Humphreys - I will amend my question. Because you are upset about your daughter, who so far as you knew was perfectly well, you go to the police and confess to the disposition of your wife's body, is that right?

Evans – Yes, sir.

Commentary – Humphreys' first incidence of a confession was shown to be false by Mr Morris. Evans never confessed to killing Beryl or the baby at Merthyr Tydfil. However, the judge's intervention was clearly unfair.

Humphreys – You then on a later occasion are spoken to by Chief Inspector Jennings, who makes a little speech to you about what has been found, being your wife's body and your daughter's body, and then he says, 'Later to-day I was present at the mortuary when it was established that the cause of death was strangulation in both cases. I have reason to believe you were responsible for causing their deaths,' and you said, 'Yes'?

Evans – I did say Yes.

Humphreys – Why?

Evans – As I said before, I was upset when he told me about my daughter's death.

Humphreys – You were upset, and therefore you pleaded guilty to their murder?

Evans – I plead not guilty to the murder, sir.

Humphreys – You were then saying you were responsible for causing their deaths?

Evans – I did say it, yes.

Mr Justice Lewis - What did you mean by that, what did you think the police officer meant by saying he thought you were responsible for causing their deaths?

Commentary - another biased and unnecessary intervention by the judge.

Evans - In other words, in my opinion, good enough to say as I had done it, sir.

Humphreys - Yes; you were saying you had done it, were not you?
Evans – I did say I had done it, yes.

Humphreys – Later you signed a written statement in some greater detail, did you not, exhibit 8 ['NH1'], saying of your wife she was incurring one debt after another. 'I could not stand it any longer, so I strangled her with a piece of rope and took her down to the flat below the same night whilst the old man was in hospital, waited till the Christies downstairs had gone to bed, and then I took her to the wash-house after midnight. This was on Tuesday, the 8th

November.' Did you say that?

Commentary – 'NH1' was not in 'some greater detail.' What Humphrey's quoted, though, was from 'NH1'.

Evans – I did say that.

Humphreys – Then you go on to say: 'On Thursday evening after I came home from work, I strangled my baby in our bedroom with my tie and later that night I took her down into the wash-house after the Christies had gone to bed.' Did you say that?

Commentary – Humphreys' questions were unfair. Not 'did you do that?' which would have allowed Evans to deny he did. But 'did you say that?' trapping Evans into incriminating himself.

Evans – Yes.

Humphreys – Why?

Evans – Well, as I said before, sir, I was upset and I did not know what I was saying.

Humphreys - Still upset?

Evans - Yes, sir.

Humphreys - Hour after hour, day after day?

Evans – I did not know my daughter was dead till Detective Inspector Jennings told me about it.

Humphreys – I see; that is your defence, that you pleaded guilty, that is what it comes to, and confessed to the murder of your wife and child because you were upset on learning that your daughter was dead?

Evans - Yes, sir; because I had nothing else to live for.

Humphreys – Have you anything more to live for now?

Evans – Yes, sir, I have a lot of things to live for.

Humphreys - And therefore you make an allegation in terms through your counsel against a perfectly innocent man that he caused the murder.

Commentary – Mr Humphreys was way out of order in the sarcastic way he effectively dismissed Evans' replies and in referring to Christie as an 'innocent man'.

Morris – Well, my lord, is that the proper way of asking the question with the greatest respect?

Mr Justice Lewis - Presumably it was done on his instructions, Mr Morris.

Morris – Yes, certainly, my lord; this witness now says that he was not responsible for the murder of his wife and his child, and my learned friend says, 'Therefore you make an allegation against a perfectly innocent man.' My learned friend has no right to say that.

Mr Justice Lewis – He wishes to know whether or not it was owing to his being upset he was making an allegation against an innocent man.

Commentary - Mr Humphreys was making no such inference.

Morris - My lord, it was nothing of the kind.

Mr Justice Lewis – Well, the jury can judge as to that. They have listened to your cross-examination of Mr Christie, and if they think that is not a suggestion that Mr Christie murdered the wife and the daughter I do not know what is.

Morris – Of course, it is, and I hope I never shirk any issue of that sort; but for my learned friend to say now, 'You make an allegation against a perfectly innocent man,' can only be a question which is based on the assumption that his witness is innocent and my witness is not. My friend has no right to incorporate that into a statement. He can say, 'And now you make an allegation that Mr Christie has done it,' but he cannot describe Mr Christie as a perfectly innocent man.

Mr Justice Lewis – Why not?

Morris – Well, it can only be done for the purpose of prejudice, in my submission.

Humphreys – I crave leave not to have to believe that everything the accused says is true.

Commentary – again the judge was biased. The judge was supporting Humphreys when Humphreys was blatantly wrong. There was no causal link between Evans being upset and him accusing Christie. Evans had already accused Christie when he gave his 'Merthyr 2' statement and that was two days before he became upset by finding out his daughter was dead.

Humphreys – Now will you look at your next statement, Exhibit 9 ['NH2']. I will not trouble you to look at it if you cannot read it. You agree that there in a very long statement – very long; it must have taken some time – you set out in the greatest detail in your own words how and why you murdered your wife and child. Is that right?

Evans – Well, I did make the statement, sir.

Humphreys – In which you set out in the greatest detail how and why you murdered your wife and child?

Evans – I did say it, yes.

Humphreys – Are you also saying that during the whole of that statement, which must have taken you a long time, you were still upset?

Evans – I was not upset when that statement was made.

Humphreys – That is a clear and deliberate statement of fact?

Evans – Yes.

Humphreys – Is it true or untrue?

Evans – It is untrue.

Humphreys – Why did you make it?

Evans – As I said before, I was trying to protect Mr Christie.

Humphreys – At the risk of a charge of murder being made against you?

Evans – I was not looking at a charge of murder.

Humphreys – In the certainty of a charge of murder being made against you, was not it?

Evans – I was charged with murder, yes.

Humphreys – If you go to the police and describe to them in detail how you have murdered your wife and child, and their bodies are found strangled in the way you have described, you would expect a charge of murder to be made against you, would not you?

Evans – Yes.

Humphreys – And you were asking for that charge of murder to be made against you in order to protect a man whom you say is the murderer; is that right?

Evans – Yes.

Humphreys – Why? No answer.

Mr Justice Lewis – This was done in order to protect Mr Christie, Exhibit 9 ['Notting Hill 2'], the last statement you made?

Evans – No, sir, not the last statement I made.

Mr Justice Lewis – That is what you are being asked about, Exhibit 9. You see, there is Exhibit 7 ['Merthyr 2'], Mr Humphreys, where he describes how Mr Christie was apparently going to perform some operation, and then Christie meets him and says 'Go upstairs,

I will tell you. It is bad news; it did not work.'

Commentary – This exchange went wrong when Humphreys and Evans came to cross purposes over which statement was being asked about. While Humphreys clearly signalled he was asking about 'Notting Hill 2', Evans drifted to answering in terms of 'Merthyr 1'. 'Merthyr 1' was made to protect Christie. In his Notting Hill confession, Evans took all the blame unto himself because he was upset, did not care what happened to him and was scared of being beaten up. Protecting Christie did not come into it.

Humphreys - I was coming round to those statements. So far I have only put to him the various alleged confessions and asked him why he made them.

Commentary - Humphreys had put only two of the supposed five incidents of Evans confessing. One was blatantly false and the other - at Notting Hill - was true. He never returned to the other three supposed confessions in the rest of the cross-examination.

Humphreys - Now we will come back to the series of statements, and I am putting to you the general proposition that you are a man who is prepared to lie, if necessary upon oath, for your own convenience?

Evans – Not for my own convenience.

Humphreys – As and when it suits you?

Evans – Not even when it suits me either.

Humphreys – All right; we will have to consider this. You made a statement to the police, and this is the first you made, Exhibit 6 ['Merthyr 1'], in which you talk about meeting a man in a café and how your wife took these pills and died of them, and you found her dead. Do you remember that statement?

Evans –Yes, I remember that statement.

Humphreys –That is untrue?

Evans – That is untrue, yes.

Humphreys – You then make a statement ['Merthyr 2'] in which you set out in some detail how Mr Christie gave your wife something which would cause an abortion and how she died of that. Do you remember that one?

Evans – Yes, I remember that one too.

Humphreys – Is that true or untrue?

Evans – It is true.

Commentary – Evans never said Christie gave his wife something to cause an abortion. He said Christie wouldn't tell him how he did it. Whatever he did failed. Beryl's 'stomach was septic poisoned.'

Humphreys – Then you made a statement ['NH1'] which is a short statement, in which you confess to murdering your wife and your child, is that true or untrue?

Evans – I was told of my daughter's death before I made that

Humphreys – True or untrue?

Evans – It is true I made the statement.

Humphreys - Is that statement true or untrue?

Evans - Untrue.

Humphreys - So that is the second statement you made to the police in some detail which is untrue?

Evans - Yes.

Humphreys - Then you make a fourth statement, which is Exhibit 9 ['NH2'], which is a long written one with the detailed confession of the murder of your wife and child. Is that true or untrue?

Evans - Untrue.

Humphreys - So that three of the statements you made to the police - one, three and four are untrue?

Evans - Yes.

Humphreys - And No. 2 is true?

Evans - Yes.

Humphreys - Would it not be right to say you are a person who is prepared to lie or tell the truth at your own convenience?

Evans - Why would I tell lies? My life is at stake here.

Humphreys - My learned friend reminds me that after you made Exhibit 8 ['NH1'], which is the short statement of confession, you said to the police, 'it is a great relief to get it off my chest. I feel better already. I can tell you the cause that led up to it,' and you then made a long statement?

Evans - Yes.

Humphreys - Did you say that?

Evans - Yes.

Humphreys - was not it a relief to you to tell the truth at last to the police which was a confession of murder?

Evans – It was not the truth; it was a load of lies.

Humphreys – It was a relief to you then to get off your chest a lot of lies?

Evans – As I said before, I was upset.

Mr Justice Lewis – Do answer the question. Was it a relief to you to tell a lot more lies?

Commentary – the judge acting as prosecuting council. Humphreys had twisted things to guide Evans into a nonsense position. His question was surely rhetorical.

Evans – No, it was no relief to me at all.

Humphreys – Now you are going back to the second of your four statements and accusing Mr Christie; is that right?

Evans – Yes sir.

Humphreys – Mr Christie is a person who commits an abortion on your wife that she dies of it; is that right?

Evans – Yes, sir.

Humphreys – Knowing that he is responsible for her death, he organises the disposition of her body and the removal of your child to some other place, is that right?

Evans – Yes, sir.

Humphreys – And then comes along and commits foul perjury against you, against your life; that is what you say Mr Christie is?

Evans – Yes.

Humphreys – Let us look a little further at what I suggest is your habit of lying to suit your convenience. You lied to the Christies, did not you, that your wife was away, and all the rest of it, did not you?

Evans – I lied to Mrs Christie, yes.

Humphreys – All right, you lied to Mrs Christie. You lied to your aunt down in Wales, Mrs Lynch, did not you?

Evans – Yes, sir.

Humphreys – When it suited your convenience you lied to her. You then told half a dozen separate, distinct, deliberate lies to the police, inventing any story that came into your head, is not that right?

Evans – Not any story that came into my head.

Humphreys – Well, you began by lying about putting your wife's body down the drain, that is untrue, is it not?

Evans – That is untrue, yes.

Humphreys – You lied to them about the rags, did not you? You never tore up those clothes?

Evans – If I did not who done it then?

Humphreys – I am not asking who did it. You never tore them up, did you?

Evans – Yes.

Humphreys – You practically confessed to the police when they challenged you that you could not tear a coat with your hands?

Evans – Well, I started them with the scissors, yes.

Humphreys – You practically dropped that story to them, did you not, when the officers said to you, 'You say you tore all your wife's clothes and the eiderdown and cut up the blanket?' How did you do it? You said, 'I cut the blanket with the scissors and I tore the rest with my hands.' The officer said, 'Do you mean to tell me that you can rip a coat down with your hands?' and you said, 'Well, I may have started it with the scissors.' Then the offer said, 'I don't think you are saying the truth,' and you replied, I may have made a few mistakes, but as far as Christie is concerned, I have said the truth. Was not what you were saying there just another set of lies?

Evans – No; I was telling the truth.

Humphreys – Then about the letter: do you remember Mr Evans, the police officer from Wales, when he asked you after you had made one of your statements, I think the second, after another telephone call from London, 'You know that your aunt, Mrs Lynch, has had a letter from your mother?' And you said promptly, 'Yes, but I do not know what is in it.' That was a lie, was not it, because it had been read to you?

Evans – It had been read, but I had not taken any notice what was in it.

Humphreys – Oh, I see, it had been read but you did not know what was in it. You lied about helping Mr Christie to carry your wife's body down to that flat did not you?

Evans – No, I did not.

Humphreys – Do you not realise from what you have heard in Court today that he was physically incapable of doing that, or even of carrying the baby?

Evans – I heard what was said to-day, but I still say I helped carry my wife's body.

Commentary – at this point Evans should have said there was nothing physically wrong with him. Ask the workmen; ask Mrs Christie.

Humphreys – Between you, you helped carry the body of a woman?

Evans – Yes.

Humphreys – I suggest that is just another lie. You lied to the 'guv'nor' at your employment, did not you? He asked you what you wanted your wages for, and you said you wanted to post some off to your wife first thing in the morning?

Evans – Yes, that is right.

Humphreys – That was another lie?

Evans – Yes, it was a lie.

Humphreys – So you lied to Mrs Christie, your aunt, the police and to your boss?

Evans – Yes; I did it all on the advice of Mr Christie.

Humphreys – All on the advice of Mr Christie. That is a new one, is it…

Morris – He has already said it on oath today.

Humphreys – Has he ever said Mr Christie told him to lie to his aunt in Wales or to his boss?

Evans – Mr Christie told me if anybody asked me any questions about my wife and daughter I was to say they had gone on holiday.

Humphreys – Now, you are the person who alleges that Mr Christie is the murderer in this case; can you suggest why he should have strangled your wife?

Evans – Well, he was home all day.

Humphreys – Can you suggest why he should have strangled your wife?

Evans – No.

Humphreys – Can you suggest why he should have strangled your daughter two days later?

Evans – No. Humphreys sat down.

Morris – My Lord, that is the case for the defence.

Commentary – perhaps Humphreys decided not to go back to the other three supposed cases where Evans confessed, as he had scored so heavily in exposing Evans' catalogue of lies. Still, it meant that the prosecution case for the killing of the baby rested only on Evans' confession. And Evans was vague on that, never providing any motive.

After the 'mauling' Evans got from Humphreys, he must have presented a forlorn demeanour to the jury. But, from the standpoint of 'Merthyr 2' being what really happened, Evans' answers to Humphreys were true.

Closing speech for the prosecution[24]

Mr Humphreys' closing speech was remarkably short:

- The man being tried claimed that the principal prosecution witness was the murderer. He was also an abortionist and perjurer.

- The jury will look at Mr Christie, against whom the allegations were made. He fought in the First World War and was wounded and badly gassed. He got into trouble with the police, but the last time was 17 years ago. He served in the police with distinction in the last war.

- On 7th-9th November he was physically incapacitated. He had to get down on his hands and knees to pick something off the floor. He could not have taken a fully-grown woman to the outhouse.

- The issue is the attack on Christie against the case for the prosecution. But do you believe there is a word of truth in the allegations against Christie. If there is any doubt the jury must acquit.

- Why would Christie have wanted to strangle Evans' wife and child?

- Mrs Evans was strangled. She did not die of anything else.

- The jury are concerned with the murder of the child, and of the wife only because the judge held the facts of the two murders marched together.

- The fact that Christie strangled her because he tried to help her commit an abortion does not make sense. 'It is bosh'.

- Even if Christie was responsible for the woman's death, why should he strangle the innocent baby of 14 months unknown to 'this man'? 'Even this fluent liar, who will lie as and when he pleases, cannot invent an answer for that question.'

Commentary – Mr Humphreys effectively reduced the trial to the question of who the jury believed, Evans or Christie. He bolstered Christie's character and depicted Evans as a fluent liar. He claimed Christie could not have done it as he was too weak physically at the time. But that was only because Christie said so. [In 1953 it came out that Christie did not have the fibrositis he claimed at the time of the murders of Beryl and Geraldine.]

But Humphreys did not give the jury the crucial facts of when, how and why Evans killed the baby. He did not even mention the confession – the only of evidence against Evans. [And that confession was in part nonsense.]

Closing speech for the defence[25]

Mr Morris did not expect to have to make his closing speech until Day 3 of the trial. He was taken unawares by Mr Humphreys' closing speech being so short and the judge not then adjourning the court, despite it being late in the day for it to remain in session.

Mr Morris addressed the jury:

- He expressed his anxiety. 'It is indeed an anxious task, when one is defending someone on a capital charge, to make certain that you have said on his behalf everything that is humanly possible to say.'

- He immediately disputed Mr Humphreys' contention that it was not the jury's duty to say, 'Is it Evans or is it Christie?' The only point was, 'is it proved – beyond any doubt – that Evans killed his little daughter? That is all. If you say that it is not proved... you are not saying, and beginning to say, Christie is guilty.'

- Morris mentioned the jury being sent out on the previous day and, when they returned, they heard the whole of the evidence, including, 'all the circumstances and all the conflicting evidence that is available attendant upon the death of Mrs Evans... You must be extremely careful... even if you were satisfied that Evans murdered his wife, you would not necessarily be satisfied that he murdered his child... You have to consider every possibility that there is. If for some reason you think that a different hand might have murdered the child from the one that murdered the wife, you must say so... It might be that you would decide that you could not believe either Christie or Evans, which is a possibility, and it might be that that woman herself murdered her child before she was killed.'

- Mr Morris then provided a scenario of Christie being an abortionist, the abortion on Beryl failing, Beryl killing the child and Evans killing Beryl. It was not impossible. He came back to remind the jury of the only issue. 'Did that man murder his little girl?'

- Morris acknowledged that in the case of killing the grown woman there could be provocation. In this case, killing the child, there could be none.

- When he cross-examined Christie on his past, he laid Evans open to cross-examination on his. But there were no questions of violence in Evans' past. 'This man is a perfectly peaceful man.'

- Mr Morris then drew the jurors' attention to a 'most extraordinary element' of the case that must worry them. 'He goes round to the police, and he says he has disposed of his wife.' Not as the prosecution counsel unfairly claimed, 'an admission of guilt to murdering his wife.' Then he makes a part untrue statement and after questioning, 'he makes another statement, which he says is true, implicating Christie.' He says, 'his little daughter Geraldine is alive and being well looked after, and no suggestion she is dead until after her body is found.' If Evans is going to the police and telling them a story about what he has done with his wife's body he must surely know 'that in due course the bodies of his wife and his baby, killed in the same way, will be found in the same place at the same time.' What is the point of him not saying Christie murdered my child? But he does not say Christie killed them both. Evans cannot read or write; he is not intelligent. DCI Jennings said he is a fairly worldly man. There are limits to anyone's imagination. 'You should take with you that statement, which is the second statement he made, Exhibit 7 ['Merthyr 2'], ... You find there something which is very, very difficult to believe as being made up.'

- Evans made his statement on the evening of 30th November. Yet six weeks later, and he cannot read or write, 'he told you almost word for word what he said in that statement. In a man who is put forward by the prosecution as a liar, and who on his own confession is a liar, it is a most remarkable thing – that he can, without any notebook to refresh his memory like a police officer, by just thinking in his mind, remember, if they are lies, exactly the same lies he told to Police Constable Evans on the evening of 30th November.'

- Mr Morris then read to the jury that part of 'Merthyr 2' relating to Evans talking to Christie about his wife taking pills. Christie offered the abortion and Christie feigned medical knowledge. 'He started shortly showing me books and things on medicine.' Which Evans could not understand. Morris asked, 'do you think that the whole of this was made up?'

- Mr Morris referred to a question that he asked Christie in cross-examination but which was deemed improper. 'Christie said he had never shown that book [the St John's Ambulance Handbook] to Evans.' I asked him, 'can you think of any way in which he could have known it was there?' He did not answer. 'But can you think of any way in which he could have known it was there?' He would never have picked up a book in someone else's flat as it would have been no use to him, being unable to read or write. He must have been shown it. He 'may be telling the truth about that interview with Christie; Christie may be an abortionist; and if that is so, something may have happened to Mrs Evans at Christie's hands on the afternoon of Tuesday the 8th November... There was no point in my cross-examining Christie as to the various hypotheses, the ways in which he might have killed that woman, because he says he did not; and so we are entitled, you and I, to consider what the possibilities are.'

- Mr Morris put forward a scenario where perhaps some sort of instrument is inserted into the private parts of a woman. There may be such a shock, without causing serious damage, that temporarily she loses consciousness. Christie, doing this in trying to carry out an abortion, found himself with a seemingly dead body on his hands. 'That woman, alive but unconscious at the hands of Christie, was in a condition which he did not understand and it frightened him...he would have been frantic... that he might have strangled her.' But given all the difficulties over debt between Evans and his wife it looks 'as if Evans is responsible for that woman's death; because the abortionist, if abortionist he is, has no reason, no reason at all, to strangle. That in my submission is a possibility.'

- Christie had four convictions for dishonesty and served six months' imprisonment for a malicious wounding. It gave Morris 'no pleasure when he is beginning to live down that past to raise it up, but another man's life is at stake.' So, 'the one witness for the prosecution who matters comes before you as someone who is not a man of good character, and the man in the dock comes before you as a man who is... You will not, of course, fly in the face of the evidence... but if you think that there might be a shadow of doubt... you can use it as a wedge to break open the door which will set the prisoner free.'

- 'Knowing what you know now you would not convict Evans, you would not dream of it, if it were not for the last two statements that he is alleged to have made; and, indeed, it might well be that the prosecution would not have proceeded at all.'

- Christie's service in the First World War, in which he was gassed, and in the last war as a Special Constable has 'nothing to do with the case, nothing at all.'

- Morris reminded the jury how he objected when the prosecution counsel called Christie 'a perfectly innocent man.' He warned, 'so do be careful – I know you will – do be careful about Christie.'

- When Thursday 2nd December dawned, only the murderer knew Geraldine Evans was dead. Evans 'never said one word to lead anyone to think, to imagine for a moment, that anything untoward happened to the little girl... He loved her, he was her father.' Evans was in custody, frightened and suddenly he is brought up from Wales to Paddington. He is illiterate and small while Inspector Black, other officers and the Chief Inspector who met him are larger than he is. 'He does not know then what in the world is going to happen to him.' If what he said in his last statement, in which he brings in Christie, is true, 'he knows his wife is dead and he thinks that Christie put her body down the drain. He does not know that this child is dead; he thinks she is being looked after by a young couple in East Acton... Just think... what are the chances of this sort of man having made up a story like that? The little touch about [the couple] not being able to have children of their own; is not that put in because it is true? Is he likely to have been able to make it up?'

- Mr Morris then devised a scene for what happened in the charge room at Notting Hill Police Station. Morris exaggerated what DCI Jennings said to Evans concerning the condition of Beryl's and Geraldine's clothing, which was in the room. He had it bloodstained when it was not.

- He stated, 'on the assumption which I have asked you to make for the moment, that the statement Exhibit 8 ['NH1'] is true, cannot you see that the man had nothing left to live for? His wife was dead, and he had run away because he was frightened ... and then he is told that his little daughter, who he thought was alive, is dead too.' Not only had he nothing to live for, but he feared getting 'beaten up by these police officers if I don't confess, because they've told me they have reason to believe I am responsible for the deaths of my wife and child... I would not suggest for one moment and you would not imagine that people like Jennings and Black would beat him up. But that is not the point: the point is, what did he think?' Morris ran through again the traumatic experiences Evans had been through earlier in the day of 2nd December. He stated why Evans confessed. He did not want to be beaten up and he had nothing left to live for so, 'I'll say I did it.' His wife was driving him mad because she would spend his money improperly.

- Morris then mentioned Evans 'expands that statement into a longer one ['NH2']. He protects Christie incidentally – 'heaven knows why he should.' The shock of hearing that his daughter is dead 'is enough, temporarily perhaps, almost to turn his brain... He may have thought that that was half true, that in a way he did and in the way he did not.'

- Morris mentioned his lordship would be summing up tomorrow. He would explain the law and he would review the evidence. His lordship would refer in detail to exhibits 8 and 9 [the Notting Hill statements]. The circumstantial detail – it was difficult to believe it was made up. Morris said, 'you should have exhibit 7 ['Merthyr 2'] with you when you go out to consider your verdict as well, because when you look at that, and look at it carefully, you will find there the same little pieces of circumstantial detail, which are not the sort of thing that is made up...What I ask you to say in this case is that you do not know which is true. It may be that you think Exhibit 9 ['Notting Hill 2'] is probably true, but that is not enough – not enough to mean a conviction in a case of any sort.'

- Morris reminded the jury of its duty. He summed up his plea on Evans' behalf. 'Well, the case is black against him, but – I hope I'm not blinking anything in this case – but we are not absolutely happy, we are not absolutely certain in this case that the witness, the main witness who matters for the prosecution, Christie, was telling the truth; and if he is not, then it may be that Evans in his second statement ['Merthyr 2'] was telling the truth: we just don't know... Look into your hearts...I hope you will try to forget it [the case]; of course you will if you come to the right verdict, if you are absolutely certain; but if you are not you will not forget it...When you think about it tomorrow bring every effort that you conceivably can to bear, ... and when you have done that, and have been as careful and as fair as I know you will be, Evans will be satisfied, and I, as his advocate, cannot ask for anything more.'

Commentary – there can be no doubt Mr Morris made a powerful closing speech. He warned the jury, more than once, to be careful about Christie and drew its attention again to Christie's criminal past. He brought out passages in 'Merthyr 2' which rang true and could not have been made up by Evans – thereby implying Christie was the murderer.

He painted the scenario in which Evans was frightened by what was happening to him and then he had the shock of learning his daughter was dead. His world had fallen in, he had nothing left to live for and he was frightened the police would beat him up. Evans gave a false confession. But in this regard, Morris never mentioned the police feeding him the information he needed, even though he had suggested it in his cross-examinations of DCI Jennings and DI Black.

If Morris raised doubts in the jury's mind, maybe it was too late in the day. He had failed to undermine Christie and, more especially, Evans' confession – see next chapter.

Judge's charge to the jury[26]

The third day of the trial opened with Mr Justice Lewis giving his charge to the jury. The judge outlined the law pertaining to murder and then he reminded the jury of the evidence they had heard.

Mr Justice Lewis' summing up was severely biased against Evans and he always portrayed Christie in a favourable light. He continually strove to undermine Mr Morris' argument that Christie's evidence was untrustworthy.

There is no need to go through all the evidence again, but it is necessary to set out passages that highlighted the bias the judge put into his charge to the jury:

- 'Do not be frightened by the suggestion which was made to you by the learned counsel for the defence of the bogey of sleepless nights if by any chance you should afterwards think you had given a wrong verdict, if your verdict be one of guilty. Members of the jury you do your duty, bearing in mind – and I will repeat it – bearing in mind that before you can find this man guilty you have to be satisfied beyond reasonable doubt that he is guilty. Bearing that in mind you will act according to your conscience and in accordance with the evidence you have heard.'

Commentary – Mr Morris never used the expression, 'the bogey of sleepless nights.' What Morris said was, 'if you say that it is not proved, if you say that you will not sleep happily afterwards because of a doubt in your minds, then you are not saying, and not beginning to say, Christie is guilty.' The judge completely belittled what Mr Morris said, and, in any case, his interpretation was entirely detached from its context.

- As regards Christie's evidence, the judge pointed out, Mrs Christie corroborates Christie in a certain amount of those particulars. He covered Mrs Christie mentioning that the floorboards were up on the Thursday night and Friday but only in the context of them not being up on the Wednesday when Mrs Christie spoke to Mr Evans about his wife being away

Commentary - Mrs Christie's evidence did not so much corroborate her husband's, rather it was consistent with it. She was asked a different set of questions. With regard to the floorboards being up, the judge ignored a crucial exchange between Morris and Mrs Christie that was particularly pertinent to the circumstances of the baby's death and, therefore, should have been highlighted to the jury. In response to Mr Morris asking if the floorboards in the hall were up on Wednesday 9th November, Mrs Christie replied that they were not. Then Mr Morris asked, 'when were they up?' Mrs Christie replied, 'They were up on Thursday night and Friday.'[27] The fact that the floorboards were up on the night Evans supposedly took the baby's body to the wash-house had to have been an important consideration for the jury. How could Evans, in the dark, have carried the baby's body over such a dangerous passageway without making such noise that would have brought Christie out to see what was going on?

- Mr Justice Lewis told the jury Christie's account of Evans' visit to 10 Rillington Place on Wednesday 23rd November 1949.

  Commentary – but he only provided Christie's version of what was supposedly said. He did not give Evans' contrary version of him being concerned about his child and wanting to see her.

  - The jury's attention was repeatedly drawn to instances where Evans lied, individually or collectively. These were:

  - to Mrs Christie over the whereabouts of Beryl and Geraldine;

  - to Mrs Lynch on a number of occasions when he was in Wales, including the whereabouts of Beryl and Geraldine and the denial of what Mrs Probert stated in her letter;

  - to DC Evans when he said he put his wife's body down the drain;

  - to DC Evans in his 'Merthyr 1' statement;

  - to DCI Jennings and DI Black when he confessed at Notting Hill.

- Prior to reading out Evans' longer Notting Hill statement, the judge stated that the reason he made that statement was, 'he felt that he had nothing more to live for and might as well make a confession that he had murdered the baby.'

  Commentary – but the judge should have also mentioned, in this context, the other reasons Evans gave – that he was upset and that he was frightened he would be taken downstairs to the cells and knocked about.

- The judge stated, 'now, it is on that ['NH2'] that the prosecution base their case, and they ask you to say that there is evidence before you which should satisfy any jury that this man is the man who strangled the small child.'

Commentary – the judge just could not leave the point at that. What 'NH2' included concerning the killing of the child was very flimsy. Evans was vague about how the baby's body was disposed of – he never mentioned it was behind the door. Worse still, he never provided the all-important motive. Furthermore, there was no mention of the police doing anything to corroborate the veracity of the confession.

- 'Counsels do not invent defences for their clients; they take their client's instructions, and do not let it be thought I or anybody else is suggesting that this defence was the fertile imagination of Mr Malcolm Morris.' That was then coupled with a statement pointing out that the doctor found 'no evidence whatsoever on the woman's body that an abortion had been attempted.'

Commentary – this linking was not in context and clearly prejudicial to Evans.

- The jury was told that Evans stated ['Merthyr 2'] that Christie showed him medical books and told him, 'that the stuff that he used one in every 10 would die with it.' The judge claimed that this, 'was ambiguous.'

Commentary – he did not mention what Morris said – a man of Evans' intellect could not have made that up; and how could he have known Christie had medical books?

- In a different context, reference was made to Mr Morris' point that Evans had provided descriptions in his statements, particularly 'Merthyr 2' that he could not have made up. But the judge attacked that by saying, 'he has invented three stories which are entirely untrue. Remember that.'

Commentary – the judge was making an unfair comparison. The issue was whether the descriptions were made up or not. The judge needed to expand on the issue he raised, but he did not. He just made an out of context prejudicial remark.

- According to Mr Justice Lewis, 'He [Christie] did serve in the First World War and he has told you, and it is not contradicted, that he was blinded for three-and-a-half years owing to gas.'

Commentary – Christie did not say he was blinded for 3½ years. When being re-examined by Mr Humphreys he said he was gassed twice, he was blinded for three months and never spoke for 3½ years.[28] In actual fact, there was no record of him ever being blinded. He did have throat and respiratory problems following the gassing but he was discharged three months after the gas attack. He may have had a relapse in the spring of 1919.[29]

- A significant amount of the judge's charge to jury focused on the veracity and character of Christie. He whitewashed Christie. He played down Christie's criminal past. Four of his five convictions were for dishonesty and the one for unlawful wounding was 17 years ago. 'Since then he has no stain on his character whatever. He is apparently happily married and he is living with his wife in this ground floor flat and is employed as a ledger clerk. It would be a terrible thing if a person who has been in trouble with the police and has had a term of imprisonment passed upon him, but has for years lived straight after that, should have it said of him because seventeen years ago he was in trouble with the police that he cannot be believed on his oath and he is a practiced abortioner and a murderer.'

Commentary – but Christie covered up his prosecutions, even to get into the police and into the job that he had at the time. Mr Humphreys should have brought those prosecutions to the jury's attention in his examination and not left it to Mr Morris to do so. But in a trial in which another man's life was at stake, the judge had to balance his praise for Christie going straight by pointing out that he was covering up his past.

- 'Mr Christie has given the lie, the direct lie to a very large number of statements which had been made against him.'

Commentary – Christie only denied the allegations made against him. It was for the jury to decide which of those statements against Christie were lies and which were not. It wasn't for the judge to direct them as lies. Ironically, the statement from the judge implied that some of the statements made against Christie were true!

- Christie was praised for his first aid work. 'You may think it possible that a person who is a War Reserve policeman, or any other constable, is sometimes careful to acquaint himself with some of the remedies to be applied in cases of firstly aid; and that man told you that he has a certificate from St John's of Jerusalem and from the Red Cross.'

- The judge then stated, 'I am saying this – it is a matter for you, you know, you have got to decide this, not me, but you may think Evans' performance, if I may use that expression, from the beginning of November until today has been one tissue of lies from start to finish.'

Commentary – that remark was completely out of order. In any case, it actually implied that the confession, upon which the prosecution case rested, was part of the tissue of lies as well.

- Evans' lies were raised yet again. The judge stated, 'the accused man says that throughout all this business he was acting under the domination of Christie; that Christie told me not to take the baby to my mother's otherwise it would create suspicion; Christie told me to say if I was asked that my wife and baby had gone to Bristol. …. But I am bound to tell you this: that man had lied and lied and lied again.'

Commentary – Evans never said he was acting under the domination of Christie. Evans only mentioned Christie in his 'Merthyr 2' statement. Certainly Christie was providing guidance to Evans, but that guidance was always for a purpose. Certainly Evans lied, but the whole prosecution case was based on the premise that the Notting Hill statements were not lies, but true. Yet the judge only had it that 'that man had lied and lied and lied again.'

- The judge continued his attack on Evans, asking, 'why did he go back and, apparently, in his third and fourth statements [Notting Hill statements] again try to protect Christie?… Why if he did not strangle the little girl, which he only discovered on the 2nd December when he came to London and was told of it, the little girl who was the apple of his eye – if he had not strangled her himself what was there then to protect Christie for?'

Commentary – neither Evans nor Mr Morris said anything about the Notting Hill confession being to protect Christie. They only stated that the confession was because Evans was upset, had nothing left to live for and was frightened the police were going to beat him up if he did not give them what they wanted.

- Mr Justice Lewis poured scorn on the suggestion that Evans was driven to confess by fear of being beaten up. He had Mr Morris having properly told the jury that he [Mr Morris] 'knew that nothing of that sort could happen.'

Commentary – but the judge could not leave it at that. Morris went on to say, 'but that is not the point; the point is, what did he [Evans] think, having been, as I say whisked up from Wales on this evening, met at Paddington in the car, taken off to the police station and shown the clothing that had been stripped only that day from the bodies of his wife and child?' [30]

- More scorn followed. 'Do you really believe that having confessed first of all in his short statement and then in his long statement, the last one, most of which I have read to you – do you believe that that man would admit to the murder of the child whom he loved unless he had done it?... I was so heartbroken at hearing of the death of my child, the apple of my eye, that I had nothing left to live for... Very dramatic and very tragic, but do you accept that?'

Commentary – Geraldine being the apple of her father's eye was the judge's own terminology, not Evans'. In this occasion the judge did give part of the defence's argument, but he did so with his own dismissive comment.

- The screw was turned yet again against Evans. Mr Justice Lewis read from 'Notting Hill 2', 'on Thursday evening after I came home from work I strangled my baby in our bedroom with my tie and later that night I took her down to the wash-house.' The judge then added, 'It may be a small matter, but when you are considering the truth of this case (and, after all, you are only here to find out the truth) you may think that that points possibly to the prisoner knowing more about the strangulation of the baby than he says he does.'

Commentary – That was very wrong. It has never been that a jury should be asked to think about what was never given in evidence.

- Finally, the judge condemned Evans for not asking Christie if he had disposed of Mrs Evans' body when he revisited London and for lying to Mrs Lynch about his furniture not being removed from his flat.

Commentary – To conclude on these two matters was purely prejudicial as they had no bearing on the real issue of the trial.

That Mr Justice Lewis's speech was prejudicial against Evans was undeniable.

The jury was sent out. It returned after 20 minutes and delivered a verdict of guilty - the verdict of them all. Evans was duly sentenced to death. He made no comment. Christie was heard sobbing in court as the trial concluded.

Appeal

There was an appeal lodged against Evans' conviction by Mr Morris. Judgement was delivered in the Court of Criminal Appeal on Monday 20th February 1950.[31]

Mr Morris had appealed on two main grounds. Firstly, evidence pertaining to the death of Mrs Beryl Evans should not have been admitted by the judge. Secondly, Mr Humphreys established the credit of Christie before the defence had questioned it and, furthermore, Mr Humphreys declared Christie an innocent man.

The Court effectively reduced the appeal to whether or not evidence with regard to the death of Mrs Evans should have been admitted. The judgement proceeded through the outline of the case and then delivered the following conclusion. 'In our opinion, the learned judge was perfectly right in admitting the evidence, because it was relevant and not on any grounds that it would be very inconvenient, as it would have been, to try to disentangle the sentences which dealt with the daughter and not the mother. It was one and the same story he told. In our opinion, that evidence was clearly relevant.'

The appeal failed. 'In our opinion the prisoner was properly convicted and there are no grounds for interfering with the conviction, and the appeal is dismissed.'

Commentary – Mr Morris did not appeal on the grounds that the judge's charge to the jury was biased and unfair.

Between the dismissal of his appeal and his execution on 9th March 1950, Evans maintained he was innocent. Near the end, Evans made a final confession to Father Joseph Francis. Father Francis did not disclose what Evans said, remaining steadfast on the sanctity of the confessional.

References Chapter 9

1. Evans' trial a dreary case, not worth reporting – Procter, p173

2. Biographies of lawyers – Wikipedia

3. Defence of insanity for Evans ruled out – Brabin, p114

4. Morris took instruction based on 'Merthyr 2' – Brabin, pp 114-5: Kennedy 10RP, pp 138-9

5. Admissibility of evidence on Mrs Evans' death – Trial of Evans, Jesse, pp 3-8

6. Mr Humphreys' opening speech – Trial of Evans, Jesse, pp 8-13

7. Dr Teare's evidence – Trial of Evans, Jesse, pp 14-5

8. Examination of Christie – Trial of Evans, Jesse, pp 16-21

9. Cross-examination of Christie – Trial of Evans, Jesse, pp 22-39

10. Christie lost his job at the Post Office because his convictions were revealed – Oates, p93

11. Re-examination of Christie – Trial of Evans, Jesse, pp 39-40

12. Evidence of Mrs Ethel Christie – Trial of Evans, Jesse, pp 41-5

13. Evidence of Mrs Violet Lynch – Trial of Evans, Jesse, pp 45-6

14. Evidence of Detective Constable Evans – Trial of Evans, Jesse, pp 46-53

15. Evidence of Detective Chief Inspector George Jennings – Trial of Evans, Jesse, pp 53-9

16. Evans' remarks in 'Notting Hill 2' about wrapping his wife's body – Trial of Evans, Jesse, pp 55-6

17. Evidence of Detective Inspector Neil Black – Trial of Evans, Jesse, pp 59-60

18. DI Black's notebook had no mention of DCI Jennings telling Evans about the bodies being hidden behind timber – Scott Henderson Supplementary Report, Jesse, p369

19. Quote comparing the prosecution and defence cases drawn from Mr Humphreys' opening speech – Trial of Evans, Jesse, p13

20. Attorney-General's questions on Christie's road accident – Trial of Christie, Jesse, p153

21. Christie's dash to see his doctor just after telling Evans his wife had died in his failed abortion – Kennedy, 10RP, pp 67-8

22. Evans tells DC Evans about Christie puffing and blowing on the stairs moving Mrs Evans' body – Trial of Evans, Jesse, p52

23. First mention of the young couple in East Acton in 'Merthyr 2' – Trial of Evans, Jesse, p51

24. Closing speech for the prosecution – Trial of Evans, Jesse, pp 81-2

25. Closing speech for the defence – Trial of Evans, Jesse, pp 82-91

26. Mr Justice Lewis' charge to the jury – Trial of Evans, Jesse, pp 92-117

27. Mrs Christie's evidence concerning the floorboards being up – Trial of Evans, Jesse, p43

28. Christie's evidence of his First World War wounds – Trial of Evans, Jesse, p49

29. Christie's possible relapse from gassing – Oates, p9

30. Mr Morris' justification for Evans being frightened the police would beat him up – Trial of Evans, Jesse, p89

31. Evans' Appeal Judgement (20th February 1950) – Appendix 1, Jesse, pp 297-301.

Mr Morris and Evans' Trial

The question arises – could Morris have made a stronger defence for Evans? There are two strands to this. Firstly, was there an alternative and better defence that could have been made not dependent on Evans' 'Merthyr 2' statement being the truth? Secondly, could Morris, while working from 'Merthyr 2', still have done more to discredit the confession upon which the prosecution case was built?

Alternative Defence

The alternative defences that could have been available to Morris would have been based on conceding that Evans was a murderer. If that was conceded, then the defence could have considered mitigating circumstances. These include:

- provocation
- self defence
- mental impairment
- intoxication
- diminished responsibility.

Provocation and self-defence would have been out of the question with the killing of a baby. Mental impairment or intoxication or diminished responsibility would have been desperately difficult to justify.

Perhaps Mr Morris had no alternative but to base the defence on Evans' 'Merthyr 2' statement. That Christie did it was the truth. There was one other possibility – that Beryl killed the baby and that provoked Evans to kill Beryl in response. Dr Teare's report did not actually state how long each of the bodies had been dead, but the defence would need solid proof before a jury would accept that a wife could strangle her child with a neck tie. There was no such solid proof.

Actual Defence

Mr Morris' defence, as instructed by Evans, was that the 'Merthyr 2' statement was true. Thus the real killer was Christie.

Morris' tactics had two strands. To try to discredit Christie; to make him appear a disreputable man – an abortionist, a liar, a killer. To try and establish 'Merthyr 2' as the truth in his examination of Evans, or at least plant sufficient doubt in the jurors' minds that they could not be sure whether to believe Christie or Evans. If there was doubt, the jury had to acquit.

Morris' vital cross-examination of Christie did not undermine Christie. One wonders why Morris did not open by raising Christie's criminal past, especially his 1929 conviction for malicious wounding. That would have unsettled Christie right away.

Furthermore, Morris did not always correct Mr Humphreys when he was over-reaching in building the case for the prosecution. Most seriously, early in the trial, he failed to challenge Humphreys for attributing motives for Evans murdering his wife and the baby that were blatantly untrue. In his opening speech for the prosecution, Humphreys stated, 'The case for the Crown is that this man and his wife got on badly, that he got depressed because he lost his job, that he got more depressed, and that then, as he himself said, he killed his wife, and then killed the child.'[1] Even supposing Evans' confession was true, the wife was killed before Evans lost his job and he stated he killed her 'in a fit of temper.'[2] In his confession, he never stated why he supposedly killed the baby.

Morris' defence could well have been more effective if he had added another dimension? Why did he not aim to show the jury that Evans' confession was false?

We cannot tell why Mr Morris decided not to open up the dimension of discrediting the confession. Had he not seen for himself the crime scene at 10 Rillington Place? When Rupert Furneaux visited 10 Rillington Place in 1953, he described it as a 'dolls house'.[3] How could he not realise Evans could not have disposed of the bodies in the way he stated in his confession?

The defence opportunity missed

Morris could have pressed to show that the confession was false in his cross-examinations of DCI Jennings and DI Black. They were present when Evans made the confession. Both men could have been subjected to similar questions, perhaps along the following lines.

Q. Both Evans' statements to DC Evans at Merthyr Tydfil concerned Mrs Evans wanting to abort the child she was carrying. That she was taking steps to do so was confirmed by Mr and Mrs Christie. Yet there is no mention at all in Evans' Notting Hill statements about an abortion. You will agree with me that that does not make sense?

Mr Humphreys would have objected to the question on the grounds that it was asking the witness to give an opinion. The judge would have supported him. No matter. Morris would have got the point across to the jury.

Q. In his supposed confession to you, Evans stated, 'I had a letter from Mr Broderick's telling me I was behind in my payments for my furniture on hire purchase.' Did you follow up on how Evans knew what the letter said considering Evans cannot read or write?

A work colleague could have read the letter to Evans. But the police should have established that.

Q. On Tuesday 8th November after work, Evans stated, 'I came home at night about 6:30 p.m., my wife started to argue again, so I hit her across the face with the flat of my hand. She then hit me back with her hand. In a fit of temper I grabbed a piece of rope from the chair which I had brought home off my van and strangled her with it.' You will agree with me, will you not, that Evans described striking his wife and strangling her as a continuous transaction?

Forces a reply of: Yes.

Q. Dr Teare has stated there was at least a 20-minute delay between Mrs Evans being struck in the face and her being strangled, that allowed the bruising and swelling to form. Did you follow up on this inconsistency?

We have no record of the police having followed up on this inconsistency. Jennings/Black would have been forced to answer: No.

Q. In your experience, if someone was strangling someone else in a fit of temper, you would expect, would you not, that they would do so with their bare hands and not with a length of rope conveniently brought home?

Mr Humphreys would have objected to such a question as it is, of course, asking the witness to give an opinion. But Mr Morris would not have minded. He would have brought to the jurors' attention an obvious flaw in Evans' confession.

Q. In his supposed confession to you, Evans stated, 'I then took her into the bedroom and laid her on the bed with the rope still tied round her neck.' Yet when her body was found in the wash-house there was no rope around her neck. Did you ask Evans when he removed the rope?

Forces a reply of: No.

Q. What did he do with the rope once he had removed it?

We have no record of the police having followed up on this. Jennings/ Black would have been forced to answer: I don't know.

Q. In his supposed confession to you, Evans is supposed to have doubled up his wife's body. He then wrapped it in a blanket and tablecloth and tied the bundle with a length of cord. Did you ask Evans why he doubled up and wrapped the body?

We have no record of the police having followed up on this. Jennings/ Black would have been forced to answer: No.

Q. Did you ask Evans if he knew that the body needed to be doubled up to hide it under the sink?

We have no record of the police having followed up on this. Jennings/ Black would have been forced to answer: No.

Q. So, according to Evans' supposed confession, at dead of night, he carries his wife's body, doubled up in a clumsy bundle, down the stairs, along the passageway and out into the yard. Then he fumbles with the lock, carries her body in and forces it under the sink. He then goes round the yard picking up pieces of wood to pile up in front of the sink. Did you ascertain whether Evans did all this in pitch dark?

We have no record of the police having followed up on this. Jennings/ Black would have been forced to answer: No.

Q. Now Evans is a slim man. According to Dr Teare, Mrs Evans' body weighed about 7½ stone. Did you check the feasibility of Evans being able to carry such a heavy, awkward load from Mr Kitchener's flat, down a flight of stairs, along the passageway beside the Christies' bedroom, out into the yard beside the Christies' bedroom, to the wash-house – and all without making any noise so that the Christies would not come out of their bedroom to see what was going on?

We have no record of the police having followed up on this. Jennings/ Black would have been forced to answer: No.

Q. The wash-house door requires a special device for opening it. Did you check with Evans that he actually knew what needed to be done to open the wash-house door?

We have no record of the police having followed up on this. Jennings/ Black would have been forced to answer: No.

Q. In his supposed confession to you, Evans was supposed to have covered up his wife's body under the sink with pieces of wood. Did you ascertain from Evans from where he had obtained those pieces of wood?

We have no record of the police having followed up on where Evans sourced the wood. Jennings/Black would have been forced to answer: No.

Q. In his supposed confession to you, Evans supposedly fed the baby before midnight on Tuesday 8th November and put her to bed. When he went to work on the morning of Wednesday 9th November the baby was still asleep. Evans supposedly did not return until 5:30 p.m. So the baby was unattended and had not been fed or changed in some 10–11 hours. Did you follow up with Evans whether he came back during the day to tend to the baby?

We have no record of the police having followed up on this. Jennings/
Black would have been forced to answer: No.

Q. Did you ask Evans why he didn't arrange for someone else, say Mrs Christie, to look after Geraldine during the day - as his wife had gone away?

We have no record of the police having followed up on this. Jennings/
Black would have been forced to answer said: No.

Q. In his supposed confession to you, Evans stated that on the Thursday, he again supposedly left the baby unattended all day. On coming home after having lost his job he supposedly strangled the baby with his tie. But the statement is glaringly silent on his supposed motive. What was Evans' motive in killing the baby?

Jennings/Black could have fallen back on what Evans was reported
to have told Sgt Trevallian in the cells on the morning after he had
made his confession. Evans was said to have told Trevallian that the
baby was killed because it wouldn't stop crying. Mr Morris could
have rammed home the absurdity in supplementary questions. Evans
had been at work all day and he supposedly strangled the baby just
after he came home. The baby's crying would not have come into
it. Alternatively, Jennings/Black would have had to own up to the
serious omission of the motive for strangling the baby.

Q. With supposedly two bodies hidden in the wash-house did you follow up with Evans why he felt it necessary to abandon such incriminating evidence by selling his furniture and departing 10 Rillington Place?

We have no record of the police having followed up on this. Jennings/
Black would have been forced to answer: No.

By going through the above questions with DCI Jennings and

secondly with DI Black, Mr Morris could have twice exposed that the police had done next to nothing to test whether or not Evans' confession was feasible. This should have been enough to put doubt in the jurors' minds over whether this main pillar of the prosecution case could be relied upon.

But there was one other 'bombshell' question Mr Morris could have asked.

Q. Is it really that you did nothing to check out whether or not Evans' confession was true?

This was the question that could have blown the confession apart. The police would have had to reply that they had taken steps to check Evan's confession. They had interviewed the workmen. They had taken statements from the workmen who had been carrying out repair work on the outbuildings and ground floor of 10 Rillington Place right through the period when the bodies were supposedly placed in the wash-house. Those statements (and timesheets) that had been withheld from the defence by the Prosecution Service, would now have had to be released to the defence.

The court would have had to be adjourned. The statements (and timesheets) would have had to be given to the defence. The workmen's original statements would have been exposed. On reading them, Mr Morris would have recognised straightaway that they contradicted Evans' confession.

The first statements of Mr Willis, the Plasterer, and Mr Jones, the Builder's Labourer, were taken by Detective Sergeant Fensome and witnessed by Detective Sergeant Corfield. The second statements were taken by DCI Jennings, written down by DI Black.

Mr Morris could have played the resumption of the court in one of two ways. He could have called the workmen as defence witnesses and examined them in court. This would have lost him the right to make his closing speech to the jury after the prosecution's speech. Alternatively, he could have questioned DCI Jennings and DI Black on the workmen's statements, keeping his right to close after Mr Humphreys.

After Morris had obtained the workmen's statements and studied them, suppose that Mr Morris still considered it vital to address the jury after the prosecution, so he decided to address the workmen's statements through the cross-examination of the police officers. He would have resumed the cross-examination of the police officers when the court resumed.

Mr Morris could have had the workmen's statements admitted into court as trial exhibits.

The exchanges between Mr Morris and DCI Jennings/DI Black could have continued along the following lines:

Q. In his first statement of 7th December, Mr Willis stated that he completed plastering the ceiling of the wash-house about the middle of the morning of Wednesday 9th November. The workmen kept their tools there until they left the job at about 3 p.m. on Friday 11th November. Mr Willis said the only things he saw in the wash-house were about four timber shores and these were cleared during the morning of Friday 11th. The workmen left the place completely bare.[4] Is that not so?

Forces the answer: Yes.

Q. That does not fit with Evans' confession, does it not?

Forces answer: No.

Q. You took a second statement from Mr Willis on 8th December in which he stated, 'I feel now that it would have been quite possible for anything to have been under the sink in the corner with timber in front of the sink, as we left some old wood flooring behind for the tenants to use as firewood.'[5] Is that not so?

Again forces the answer: Yes.

Q. If Mr Willis did not know if there was anything under the sink or not, how could he possibly have mentioned anything about timber being in front of the sink?

Jennings/Black could have 'tripped up' and admitted that they suggested to Mr Willis that there had been timber in front of the sink. Alternatively, they could have replied that Willis would have seen the wood and not bothered about anything behind it.

Q. You agree with me, do you not, that Mr Willis' second statement was therefore directed by the police because his first statement seriously contradicted Evans' confession?

Jennings/Black would have denied that. If they said more, then Morris may well have had an opportunity for damming supplementary questions.

Q. Turning now to the statement of Mr Jones, the builder's labourer. In his first statement of 7th December,[6] he stated that the shores were removed from the washhouse on 9th November, supposedly after Evans had put his wife's body in the wash-house. Is that not so?

Forces the answer: Yes.

Q. And Mr Jones said the tools were kept in the wash-house until the afternoon of Friday 11th November. Is that not so?

Again forces the answer: Yes.

Q. And in that first statement Mr Jones says, 'all the time we were there I saw nothing at all in the wash-house other than the materials we were using and our tools.' Is that not so?

Again forces the answer: Yes.

Q. Further, Mr Jones stated that, 'After completing the work on Friday afternoon, the 11th November 1949, I personally swept out the wash-house and also cleaned the copper which was in it. There was definitely nothing whatever in the wash-house or the copper.' Is that not so?

Yet again forces the answer: Yes.

Q. Then, as with Mr Willis, Mr Jones was required to make a further statement because his first statement seriously contradicted Evans' confession. Is that not so?

Forces the answer: Yes.

Q. And in his second statement of 8th December,[7] Mr Jones has the shores being removed a day earlier on Tuesday 8th November. Is that not so?

Forces the answer: Yes.

Q. You will agree with me, will you not, that the plasterer's and the labourer's accounts are in conflict after the second statements, whereas they were not in conflict after their first statements?

Forces the answer: Yes.

Q. What steps did you take to reconcile the discrepancies in the plasterer's and the labourer's second statements?

There is no record that the police attempted to reconcile the key differences. Jennings/Black may well have had to admit they did nothing.

Q. So, even after they amended their statements to try to make them more compliant with Evans' confession, the plasterer was still plastering the ceiling on Wednesday 9th after Evans supposedly put his wife's body under the sink. The plasterer has the wash-house left completely bare on Friday 11th, though there could have been a body under the sink and a body behind the door. The labourer says he personally swept out the wash-house and cleaned the copper on the Friday and then, amazingly, forgets he did all that and states he only went into the wash-house on the Friday to collect the tools. You will agree with me, will you not, that the statements of Larters' men, even as amended, don't add up?

Jennings/Black would have to agree. If they answered otherwise they would lay themselves open to even more damning supplementary questions from Mr Morris.

Q. So you will agree with me, will you not, that Mrs Evans body was not put in the wash-house over the night of the 8th/9th November and so Evans' confession is false?

That would be an almost impossible question for Jennings/Black to answer.

Q. And if Mrs Evans' body was not put in the wash-house on the 8th/9th November, you will agree with me, will you not, that the baby's body was not put in behind the wash-house door over the 9th/10th November, before the workmen had swept it out and left nothing there? When Mr Jones swept it out he could not have missed the body behind the door?

Again an almost impossible question for Jennings/Black to answer.

Before each police officer was excused, Mr Morris could have finished with a flourish, by asking:

Q. You would agree with me, would you not, that the supposed confession falls apart under scrutiny?

There was nothing that could be said in reply.

Mr Morris would have undermined Evans' confession and undermined the only pillar of the prosecution case. Having exposed the falsity in the confession in cross-examining the police officers, Mr Morris could have driven the point home in his closing speech to the jury, perhaps adding something along the following lines:

'It is not your duty to decide whether Evans was more likely to have murdered Geraldine Evans than Christie. The question you have to address is – has the prosecution proved beyond doubt that Evans murdered the baby? The pillar of the prosecution's case against Evans is Evans' so-called Notting Hill confession. But my cross-examinations of Detective Chief Inspector Jennings and Detective Inspector Black have laid bare that the confession is riddled with incidents that could not possibly have happened.

'It is nonsense that Evans could have taken his wife's body to the wash-house, in the dark, on the night of 8th November. The Christies' would have heard the racket of Evans moving such a heavy and awkward bundle right past their bedroom door. It is nonsense that Evans could have left his 14-month-old child all alone in the flat for some 10-11 hours on the Wednesday and the Thursday without the Christies or the workmen hearing her crying. It is nonsense that Evans could have taken the baby's body to the wash-house, in the dark, with the floorboards treacherously up, on the night of 10th November. Again the Christies would have been woken up. It is nonsense that he would put his wife's body under the sink, but did not put his baby's body alongside her mother's. And worse still, the workmen, in their first and far more believable statements, have stated that the wash-house was empty when they left it on Friday 11th November.

And to cap it all, there was absolutely no motive for killing the baby. In his opening speech my learned friend suggested Evans killed his wife and child because he was depressed because he lost his job. He had not lost his job at the time Mrs Evans died and the prosecution have not put forward a scrap of evidence to show Evans was depressed at that time.

Furthermore, if Evans had any knowledge at all that the baby was dead before he left 10 Rillington Place on 14th November, why on earth would he have left the baby's clothes and equipment behind with the Christies? And if it wasn't to find out about the welfare of his daughter, Geraldine, what was the point of him coming back to 10 Rillington Place to see Christie on 23rd November?

By the time Evans went to the police at Merthyr Tydfil on 30th November, he would have had time to compose his first statement – the one about the man in Colchester giving him pills and him putting his wife's body down the drain. But when the police exposed that as nonsense, Evans – a man who could not read or write and was not well educated – would have had no alternative but to fall back on the truth for his second Merthyr statement. That was that Mrs Evans died in the failed abortion and Christie had arranged for Geraldine to be fostered by the young couple in East Acton. Could that man have made that up right out of the blue? Think, members of the jury, about Evans knowing about Christie's medical books.

Evans told you when he found out his daughter was dead that he was upset and that he had nothing left to live for. He believed that if he did not give the police what they wanted he would be taken down to the cells and beaten up. Chief Inspector Jennings told him that he believed he had done it. Evans was disorientated, frightened and cornered. He concocted a confession based on what the police told him and what he could see in front of him. But he was spinning a yarn. The scrutiny of the confession, that I have carried out in my cross-examinations of Chief Inspector Jennings and Inspector Black has shown that the confession – to quote my learned friend – 'is bosh'.

If the confession had only been shown to have been fabricated, even in part, the pillar of the prosecution case would have been knocked away. It would have been an absolute travesty to have found Evans guilty.

Other authors

Later, key authors on the Evans/Christie case referred to the discrepancies in Evans' confession with regard to the workmen. Mr

Scott Henderson in his 1953 report wrote, 'At least one of them [the workmen] is now satisfied that no bodies could have been in the wash-house between the 8th and the 11th and that there was no timber in the wash-house (as was found by the police on the 2nd December 1949) when they cleared up on Friday, the 11th November 1949. As no work was done in the wash-house after 8th

November 1949, I do not think that workmen would have paid any attention to pieces of timber put against the sink after that date, and in any case, it is not certain that the bodies were put there before 11th November.' [7]

Rupert Furneaux in his 1961 book, *The Two Stranglers of Rillington Place*, referred to an exchange between Mrs Ashby, Evans' sister and Mr Morris following Evans' appeal being dismissed on 20th February 1950. Mrs Ashby 'says that she asked Mr Morris why he hadn't called the workmen and Mrs Vincent (who had gone to see Beryl at lunchtime on 8th November) as witnesses?' Mr Morris replied that he never heard of them, nor had he received any statements they had made.'[8] Whether Mr Morris followed up on what to him would have been crucial new evidence does not appear to be recorded.

Ludovic Kennedy in his 2002 book, *Thirty-Six Murders & Two Immoral Earnings*, stated, 'Evans' counsel at his trial, Malcolm Morris, put up a brilliant defence, but not even he could wipe from the jury's mind the ever-present stain of the two confessions.' Kennedy considered that those confessions were false in detail and contradictory as to duration. 'Mr Morris might have had more success had he analysed the two confessions, as I have done,[9] showing them to be false in detail.'

Sir Daniel Brabin's 1966 report devoted a chapter to 'the activities of the workmen employed at 10 Rillington Place at the time of the deaths of Beryl and Geraldine Evans.' On considering the workmen's statements, the manner in which they were made to amend them and their worksheets, Sir Daniel Brabin wrote, 'I do not think there were any bodies in it [the wash-house] at the time [midday Friday 11th November].'[10]

What if?

What would have happened had Mr Morris been able to undermine Evans' confession and Evans had been acquitted? The Home Office would have demanded that the police should get to the bottom of what did happen to Beryl and Geraldine Evans. The Prosecution Service could not simply have considered a further prosecution of Evans for the murder of his wife. This would have been problematic. Again the prosecution would have had to rely on the confession, which was already tainted. The police would have had to reopen the whole case, this time with the best detectives from Scotland Yard. They would have had to go through the evidence painstakingly.

Certainly, they would have had to treat Christie as a prime suspect and look into every aspect of his life in depth. One possible line of inquiry would have been missing female persons in the West London area in the last, say, ten years. This may well have brought to light the disappearances of Ruth Fuerst and Muriel Eady. Certainly, Christie was associated with Eady and, perhaps, inquiries could have brought to light a Fuerst-Christie association. Further questioning of Christie and Mrs Christie may have provided the police with a lead sufficient to make them search 10 Rillington Place and the garden more thoroughly. Fuerst and Eady's bodies may have come to light in 1950 rather than in 1953. Four lives could have been saved.

But could Christie have given the new police inquiry evidence that showed Evans did kill his wife and daughter?

References Chapter 10

1. Humphreys invents false motives for Evans killing his wife and child – Trial of Evans, Jesse, pp 8-9

2. In 'NH2', Evans claimed he strangled his wife in a fit of temper – Trial of Evans, Jesse, p55

3. 10 Rillington Place a 'doll's house' – Furneaux, p16

4. First statement of the Plasterer, Mr Willis – J Eddowes, pp 196-7

5. Second statement of Mr Willis – J Eddowes, p198

6. First statement of the Builder's Labourer, Mr Jones – J Eddowes, pp 198-200

7. Scott Henderson Report raised doubts over when the bodies were put in the wash-house - Scott Henderson Report, Appendix II, Jesse, p315

8. Mrs Ashby confronts Mr Morris concerning the workmen and Mrs Vincent – Furneaux, p99

9. Ludovic Kennedy suggested Mr Morris should have analysed the confessions – Kennedy, 36 Murders, p33

10. Sir Daniel Brabin did not believe the bodies were in the wash-house until after midday Friday 11th November – Brabin, pp 135-136.

Conclusion – Volume One

Volume One has covered the people and events that brought about the murders of Beryl and Geraldine Evans and outlined the possible scenarios for how the murders could have occurred. The conflicting evidence has been set out, taking note of fresh information that arose once Christie's definite murders came to light in 1953. It was not just the 'what' happened; consideration has been given, as far as possible, to the 'how' and 'why'.

Volume One then set out what happened after Timothy Evans went to the police at Merthyr Tydfil on 30th November 1949 and told them he had disposed of his wife's body down a drain. The conflicting statements Evans then gave have been set out with commentary. An account of Evans' trial has been given, again with commentary.

The case against Evans murdering his daughter rested on his Notting Hill confession, yet that contained obvious falsehoods. Unfortunately, the defence counsel did not expose those false-hoods in the trial. The prosecution counsel lost sight of his ethical responsibility to ensure fairness to the accused, and the judge was totally biased against Evans.

The conclusion at the end of Part One is that Evans should not have been found guilty of murdering his daughter in January 1950. But that still leaves open the questions of who did kill Beryl Evans and who did kill Geraldine Evans? As Mr Morris stated in his closing speech to the jurors, 'if you say that you will not sleep happily afterwards because of a doubt in your minds, then you are not saying, and not beginning to say Christie is guilty, and it would be a most appalling thing if you thought you were. All that you are saying is, we are not absolutely satisfied that that man is guilty.'

INDEX

Volume One

Westlake, Mrs Maureen, 42, 170

Willis, Mr, plasterer, 140, 267, 268, 269

Wood, Robert, vii

BV - #0115 - 220426 - C3 - 229/152/18 - PB - 9781861515834 - Gloss Lamination